T0315141

"Effectively adapting to the dramatic pace of change brought by the internet is now a necessary condition for survival and future business success, but the best strategic judgment will need to draw also on experience. In an intensively competitive and challenging environment, business decision-takers cannot afford to disregard the lessons of the past, including mistakes that have been made before. This book *Strategy for the Corporate Level*, based on research into business experience over 25 years, gives authoritative guidance on how strategic decision-taking processes can be value-additive but also value-destructive. It is a rich quarry and 'must read' for those involved in the formation of strategy at both business unit and corporate level."
Sir David Walker, Chairman, Barclays

"One of the most influential books I read as head of strategy for Clorox in 1994 was *Corporate-Level Strategy: Creating Value in the Multibusiness Company*. The entire concept of Parenting Advantage was a simple yet very compelling way to think about how the center adds value. With twenty more years of experience under my belt, I still have not found anything better – until this updated version."
Dan Simpson, Chief Strategy Officer (retired), The Clorox Company

"As one who followed the authors' corporate strategy journey over the past 30 years I found in this book, which is sure to become a classic, the most comprehensive, practical and balanced approach to corporate-level strategy. By combining added value logic with business logic and capital markets logic, the authors offer concrete and tested guidance for those corporate and business managers willing to invest time in clarifying the main sources of added value and building them into their decisions and focus."
Philippe Haspeslagh, Dean Vlerick Business School

"Too many companies still hang on to businesses they should sell to better owners. Too many companies still diversify unwisely in the name of growth, and make themselves unmanageable in the process. The authors have a deep understanding of these issues, and their book provides help and advice."
Martin Taylor, Vice Chairman RTL Group, Member Bank of England Financial Policy Committee, previously Adviser to Goldman Sachs International and CEO, Barclays

"Campbell and Goold's *Corporate Level Strategy* introduced us to Parenting Advantage, one of the most useful business insights of recent years. Parenting Advantage is still one of the most important and least understood areas of strategy. In this excellent update they not only bring new examples and explanations on how corporate parents can add ... and subtract ... value but also they integrate Parenting Advantage with the better understood sources of value from business unit strategy and capital markets strategy. I highly recommend this book."
Robin Buchanan, Chairman, Michael Page, previously Dean of London Business School and Senior Partner of Bain & Company

"Goold, Campbell and Alexander have been the thought leaders on *Corporate-Level Strategy* since they introduced the concept of 'parenting advantage' in 1994. We have used their recommendations and tools extensively and successfully over the years. The ideas helped us make important portfolio decisions and changed the way we manage the group. Now, with Whitehead, they have not only developed their work on parenting advantage, but have integrated this thinking with the more traditional concepts of business attractiveness and capital markets valuations. The new framework is a further step forward. I am sure it will impact our thinking and practice as much as their original ground breaking work."
Paulo Azevedo, CEO, Sonae

"Corporate strategy is a subject often misunderstood by Boards around the world. While there is a plethora of books on business level strategy there are in my opinion very few that address the fundamentals of corporate-level strategy. Campbell and his co-authors are leading thinkers in this field and explain the concepts in a clear and practical way in this book – how the centre can really add value and also (importantly) how to avoid it destroying value! We derived immense benefit from applying these principles to our businesses in Africa."
Dr Graham Edwards, Chief Executive, AECI (retired 2013)

"The authors have been pioneers in the field of corporate level strategy. With this book they share with us their rich experience gained in countless projects over more than two decades, and they give us new tools, which can help to conceptualize corporate-level work. This book is important reading not only for the top management team, but also for strategy officers and leaders of corporate functions."
Prof. Dr Guenter Mueller-Stewens, IFB Institute of Management, University of St. Gallen

"*Strategy for the Corporate Level* is a particularly useful book for the many Asian companies that are now moving from an incoherent portfolio of unrelated businesses to creating an effective corporate strategy."
George S. Yip, Professor of Strategy and Co-Director, Centre on China Innovation, China Europe International Business School

"*Strategy for the Corporate Level* highlights the challenge managers face when responsible for multiple activities. Strategy is as relevant for those in government as for those in business. In both areas, strategy can make things worse – subtract value, or make things better – add value. If you aspire to add value, please buy and read this book."
William Dartmouth (The Earl of Dartmouth), Member of the European Parliament

"This book is concerned with a key issue in most developed economies; how best to manage large multi business businesses. It is based, not only on the authors' scholarly understanding of the field, but also the experience they have gained in working over three decades with executives in large corporations. The authors pose questions and challenges fundamental to corporate-level strategy and provide invaluable guidance to those who have to deal with such challenges. As such it is a book that all managers charged with managing multiple businesses, or those who aspire to do so, should read. The ground they cover is, however, significant not just to the executives who run such businesses but to all who work in them, invest in them or analyze and study them."
Gerry Johnson, Emeritus Professor of Strategic Management, Lancaster University Management School and co-author of *Exploring Strategy*

"This work, the latest contribution to business strategy from the Ashridge Strategic Management Centre, distils the knowledge and insights from more than 20 years of research. It addresses two key questions – what businesses should a company invest in and how should they be managed. It is particularly relevant to managers of multi-divisional businesses, but it has much to offer for students of management and, indeed, all those who have to deal with questions of organisation design – in the public as well as the private sector. Reading this could save many thousands of pounds in consultants' fees."
Philip Sadler CBE, Tomorrow's Company

Strategy for the Corporate Level

The Corporate Level

Where to Invest, What to Cut Back and How to Grow Organisations with Multiple Divisions

Andrew Campbell
With Jo Whitehead,
Marcus Alexander, and Michael Goold

JB JOSSEY-BASS™
A Wiley Brand

This edition first published 2014
© 2014 by John Wiley & Sons, Ltd

First edition published 1994 under the title *Corporate-Level Strategy*.

Under the Jossey-Bass imprint, Jossey-Bass, 989 Market Street, San Francisco CA 94103-1741, USA
www.josseybass.com

Registered office
John Wiley & Sons Ltd, The Atrium, Southern Gate, Chichester, West Sussex, PO19 8SQ, United Kingdom

For details of our global editorial offices, for customer services and for information about how to apply for permission to reuse the copyright material in this book, please see our website at www.wiley.com.

Wiley publishes in a variety of print and electronic formats and by print-on-demand. Some material included with standard print versions of this book may not be included in e-books or in print-on-demand. If this book refers to media such as a CD or DVD that is not included in the version you purchased, you may download this material at http://booksupport.wiley.com. For more information about Wiley products, visit www.wiley.com.

Designations used by companies to distinguish their products are often claimed as trademarks. All brand names and product names used in this book are trade names, service marks, trademarks or registered trademarks of their respective owners. The publisher is not associated with any product or vendor mentioned in this book. This publication is designed to provide accurate and authoritative information in regard to the subject matter covered. It is sold on the understanding that the publisher is not engaged in rendering professional services. If professional advice or other expert assistance is required, the services of a competent professional should be sought.

Library of Congress Cataloging-in-Publication Data
Campbell, Andrew,
    Strategy for the corporate level : where to invest, what to cut back and how to grow organisations with multiple divisions / Andrew Campbell, with Jo Whitehead, Marcus Alexander, and Michael Goold.
        pages cm
    Includes index.
    ISBN 978-1-118-81837-4 (cloth)
    1. Multiproduct firms—Management.   2. Diversification in industry.   3. Strategic planning.
I. Title.
    HD2756.C347 2014
    658.4'012—dc23
                                    2013050104

A catalogue record for this book is available from the British Library.

ISBN 978-1-118-81837-4 (hardback) ISBN 978-1-118-81836-7 (ebk)
ISBN 978-1-118-81835-0 (ebk)

Cover design: Dan Jubb

Set in 11/15pt ITCGaramondStd-Bk by Toppan Best-set Premedia Limited, Hong Kong
Printed in Great Britain by TJ International Ltd, Padstow, Cornwall, UK

Contents

Preface

This book is the end of a long journey – one that started in 1983, when Michael Goold joined London Business School (LBS) from the Boston Consulting Group. As a member of the LBS faculty, Michael started research work on decision making in hierarchies. In 1984, Andrew Campbell joined Michael from McKinsey. At the time, the Centre for Business Strategy was led by Professor John Stopford and contained such modern-day luminaries as Gary Hamel and Rob Grant. It was a stimulating place to work.

Michael was trying to understand "strategic management" in multi-business companies: how do strategically managed companies make decisions and how different are companies that are not strategically managed? The work resulted in a book, *Strategies and Styles*, published in 1987, that categorised companies into strategically driven (Strategic Planning Style), financially driven (Financial Control Style) and somewhere in between (Strategic Control Style).

More important, looking back, was the discovery that the involvement of top managers can be positive, leading to better decisions, or negative, leading to worse decisions. Their influence, the research exposed, was significant and rarely neutral. Of course, in academic circles, it can take some years to discover something that every manager knows well: "your boss is influential, and his or her influence is not always positive"!

The research also resulted in a new contingency theory. The influence of top managers was more likely to be beneficial if the style matched the challenge facing the business. If the business was long term, like oil or pharmaceuticals, a Strategic Planning Style seemed to be more successful. If the business was short term, like bricks or rubber belting, a Financial Control Style seemed to be more successful.

However, it was the observation that top management's influence could be and frequently was negative that spurred further work. At the time, in the late 1980s, a new phenomenon was occurring. Conglomerates were failing, and some large companies, like ICI and Courtaulds in the UK, were voluntarily getting smaller and breaking themselves up. What is more, this was creating value. The negative impact of some corporate groups was being fully exposed for the first time.

Michael and Andrew, by then joined by Marcus Alexander, and installed at Ashridge Business School, dug deeper into the conditions that caused added value and the conditions that caused subtracted value. We looked globally for the best managed corporate groups and uncovered a much finer grained contingency theory: corporate groups add value when the activities and influences from headquarters address the specific needs of each business division. They subtract value in pretty much all other circumstances.

This research made another significant contribution: the idea of "parenting advantage". Corporate groups are competing with each other for the right to own businesses. They, therefore, need to add more value (or subtract less value) than rival parent companies to be sure of winning the competition. In other words, a parent company needs to have advantage over its rivals in just the same way that a business division needs to have advantage over its competitors.

The parenting advantage concept, published in *Corporate Level Strategy* in 1994, felt like the end of the journey. Michael, Andrew and Marcus began to turn their attention to related topics – how to create synergies between business divisions, the size of corporate centres, organisation design, growth into new businesses, international strategy, the role of headquarters functions, collaborating with business partners, and why capable people sometimes make stupid decisions.

At the same time, however, we continued to teach corporate-level strategy and to do consulting projects with companies all over the world. Nearly 20 years on, we now realise that 1994 was not the end of the journey. Our own thinking had moved forward without us fully realising it.

In 1994, we were reacting against Boston Consulting Group's matrix. We wanted to replace it with our "Ashridge Portfolio Display". But over the years, we have realised that the two ideas are not in conflict. Corporate groups need good businesses and an ability to add value. Both are important. Both should be part of corporate-level strategy.

Jo Whitehead joined Ashridge more recently, bringing a different perspective partly from his 20 years in management consulting and partly from research he led on why companies appear to give less attention to "parenting advantage" thinking than seems appropriate. He noted that there are other legitimate drivers of corporate-level decisions. In addition to a desire to own "good businesses", managers are also affected by the state of the capital markets. Seemingly sound strategies can become impossible to execute because capital markets are overvaluing or undervaluing some businesses. New strategies open up because certain types of businesses are available at good prices. Of course, capital market influences were always evident in our consulting work, but we had not previously tried to formalise this element into the way we developed corporate-level strategies.

This book, therefore, contains the current state of our collective thinking. It feels less like a call to arms and more like a description of the sensible path all companies need to follow. For sure, it will not be the end of the journey, but it feels like the journey will be smoother in the future than it has been in the past.

One part of the journey still to be completed is the synthesis of corporate-level strategy and international strategy. Many of the issues are the same, but the tools and language used are different. In the appendix, we (mainly Marcus) have made a stab at linking the two, with a particular desire to show where one discipline may be able to help the other. We have made a start but more work is needed.

We have enjoyed our journey and believe that we are now much closer to understanding how to help companies with multiple business divisions be more successful. We hope you will find our conclusions helpful.

Andrew, Jo, Marcus, Michael

Acknowledgements

This book is derived from 30 years of research, teaching and discussion. Along the way many, many people have contributed their stories and comments – far too many to list or even to remember!

We have, however, had particular support with case studies for this book, which we would like to acknowledge. Unfortunately, a few of the people who have helped us have chosen to be anonymous or their companies preferred not to be named, making it hard for us to thank them publicly. However, we can mention Henry Elkington, Chris Floyd, Paul Marsh, Phil Renshaw, Ian Weston and Sven Kunisch.

We would also like to acknowledge the support of our fellow directors at the Ashridge Strategic Management Centre – Felix Barber, Stephen Bungay, Anthony Freeling and Neil Monnery – and the contributions made over the years by the heads of strategy of the Centre's member companies. We also recognise the broader support provided by Ashridge Business School, led by Kai Peters.

But this book has more unacknowledged contributors than acknowledged. So we dedicate it to all those who have, over the years, provided their insights and anecdotes, in the belief that their contributions would help future generations. We might particularly mention Sir Christopher Hogg, Sir David Walker and Philip Sadler, who were instrumental in helping launch the Ashridge Strategic Management Centre in 1987. We hope this book justifies the faith they showed in us.

PART I

INTRODUCTION AND HISTORY

CHAPTER ONE

STRATEGY FOR THE CORPORATE LEVEL: SUMMARY OF THE MAIN MESSAGES

Almost all companies need a strategy at the corporate level that is in addition to the strategies for products or markets or business divisions. So this book is for any manager with responsibilities for multiple business divisions. It is also for any student, adviser or more junior manager who wants to understand the challenges that corporate managers face and how they make decisions. The book will help answer two important questions that can only be addressed at the corporate level:

1. What businesses or markets should a company invest in, including decisions about diversifying into adjacent activities, about selling businesses, about entering new geographies or markets and about how much money to commit to each area of business?
2. How should the group of businesses be managed, including how to structure the organisation into divisions or units or subsidiaries, how to guide each division, how to manage the links and synergies between divisions, what activities to

centralise or decentralise and how to select and guide the managers of these divisions?

We will refer to the first as "business" or "portfolio" strategy and the second as "management" or "parenting" strategy. The combination of these two types of strategy makes up corporate-level strategy.

Terms like business division, corporate headquarters or corporate-level strategy may suggest that this book is only relevant to managers running old-fashioned conglomerates. Far from it. This book is just as relevant for focused companies like Apple or Google. It is also relevant for public sector organisations, although much of the language used is commercial.

Blacklock[1]

In 2010, Blacklock Inc., a US engineering company, was being threatened with hostile takeover approaches from two companies: Vantex, another US engineering company, and Molsand, a Scandanavian company skilled at turnarounds and business improvement. Blacklock had two business divisions: Carlsen, a company manufacturing pumps, water equipment and air conditioners, and CIW, a company supplying wire, wire equipment and related consumables (see Figure 1.1).

The Carlsen division was itself organised into business divisions. Some of the business divisions were focused on products, such as a type of equipment or conditioner. Some were focused on market segments, such as the utilities sector. Some were focused on regions, such as AsiaPac or Europe. All business divisions contained both manufacturing and sales. Linking the business divisions together were processes for sharing technology, manufacturing and purchasing as well as typical group functions, such as finance, HR and IT.

Some of Carlsen's business divisions also contained business units. For example, Danlogan, a division focused on con-

Figure 1.1: Blacklock organisation structure (simplified)

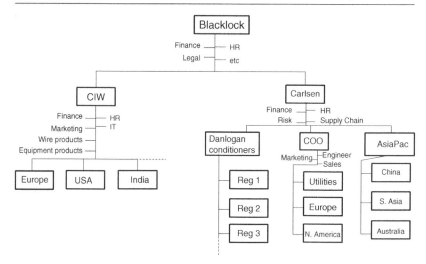

ditioners and acquired in 2005, was divided into seven geographic regions. Also, the AsiaPac division included business units in Australia, China and South Asia.

CIW (originally Commercial & Industrial Wire) was also organised into business divisions. CIW's business divisions were geographic: Europe, North America, South America, China, India, etc. Each division had its own manufacturing and sales, but technology and product development were centralised at the CIW level, along with group marketing. Also at the CIW level were typical group functions covering finance, HR, IT, Safety and Lean.

At the Blacklock level, there were a handful of managers covering legal and financial issues.

For a company like Blacklock, this book is about the following questions. Should Blacklock own both Carlsen and CIW? What other business divisions should Blacklock seek to develop or acquire, if any? Should Blacklock resist the acquisition approaches by Molsand and Vantex? If not, which company should they seek to align with? What should be the main focus of the management team at the Blacklock level? Which activities should be centralised at the Blacklock level? How should Blacklock appoint, interact with and guide the management teams running Carlsen and CIW? How much collaboration should Blacklock encourage between Carlsen and CIW?

Blacklock is a parent company and this book is helpful to managers at this level in the organisation. But this book is just as relevant for managers at the Carlsen and CIW levels. The management teams of Carlsen and CIW are both running organisations with multiple business divisions. For Carlsen, this book will help with the following questions. Why does it make sense for Carlsen to own businesses involved in both pumps and conditioners? What other products should Carlsen seek to develop or acquire, if any? Does it make sense for Carlsen to be involved in bespoke equipment for the water industry as well as off-the-shelf equipment for general industrial uses? Is it necessary for Carlsen to have a global footprint? How should Carlsen group its business units into business divisions: by geography, by market sector, by product or by a combination of all of these? How should Carlsen manage the links and overlaps among divisions? Which activities should be centralised at the Carlsen level? How should Carlsen's top managers appoint, interact with and guide the managers running its business divisions?

Even within Carlsen, this book will help the management team running the Danlogan division or the Asia division. Why does it make sense for Danlogan to be a global company rather than focused in just one region? What other countries should Danlogan enter? How should Danlogan control or guide the links among its country-based business units? Which activities should be centralised at the Danlogan level? How should Danlogan appoint, interact with and guide the managers running its business units?

For CIW, this book helps answer similar questions. Should CIW own businesses in India and South America? What other geographies should CIW seek to expand into? Should CIW produce both wire products and wire equipment? What other products, if any, should CIW produce? Which activities should be centralised at the CIW level? Should CIW be organised into regional business units or should it be a global functional structure? How should CIW's top managers select, interact with and guide the management teams running its regional units?

Hence, it is important that readers do not presume that this book is only relevant for management teams at the parent company level of diversified companies. It is equally relevant for, and potentially has more to offer to, management teams trying to integrate closely linked businesses and for management teams running divisions that themselves contain sub-businesses.

Molsand was the winning bidder and acquired Blacklock. A similar set of questions then needed to be asked at the Molsand level. Why will Molsand benefit from paying a significant premium over the quoted market price for the Blacklock businesses? Why did it make sense for Molsand to outbid Vantex? Having acquired Blacklock, should Molsand retain the Blacklock level of management? Should Molsand keep both business divisions or should it sell either Carlsen or CIW or parts of these companies? Should Molsand retain Carlsen and CIW in their current shape or should Carlsen be divided, for example, into two companies each reporting directly to Molsand: conditioners and water equipment? What other companies should Molsand seek to acquire? What should be centralised at the Molsand level? (At the time of writing, Molsand had fewer than 20 people in its corporate centre.) How should Molsand appoint, interact with and guide the managers of Blacklock, Carlsen and CIW once they are under full ownership?

So, this book is for a wide range of managers and covers a wide range of decisions. Even a single hotel can be considered to have multiple businesses or profit centres – accommodation, business conferences, restaurant and spa – and hence needs a corporate-level strategy. Ashridge Business School, a charity, with revenues in 2012 of about £40 million, needs a corporate-level strategy. Ashridge has profit centres for open programmes, tailored programmes, conferences, hotel and facilities, qualification programmes, consulting and research centres. It needs a strategy that explains why these different activities are part of one organisation and how the leadership team is going to manage the organisation. So, this book is about more than diversified conglomerates, it is about the strategic thinking that is required to run any complex organisation.

Portfolio strategy

How should managers make decisions about which businesses, markets or geographies to invest in and which to avoid, harvest or sell? There are three logics that guide these decisions:

1. **Business logic** concerns the sector or market each business competes in and the strength of its competitive position. Is the market attractive or unattractive and does the business have a competitive advantage or competitive disadvantage?
2. **Added value logic** concerns the ability of corporate-level managers to add value to a business. Is this business one that corporate-level managers feel able to improve or create synergy with other businesses, or is it one that corporate-level managers may misjudge and damage?
3. **Capital markets logic** concerns the state of the capital markets. Are prices for businesses of this kind inflated and hence likely to be higher than the net present value of future

cash flows, or depressed and hence likely to sell at less than net present value?

These three logics are each important for making good portfolio decisions. If a business is likely to sell for more than it is worth (capital markets logic), there is little reason to buy and good reason to sell. You would only buy if you felt that the business would perform much better under your ownership (added value logic). If you are already in the business, you might consider selling now or doubling your investment with a view to selling soon (capital markets logic).

If a business is in a low margin industry and has a significant competitive disadvantage (business logic), you are likely to want to sell it or close it, unless you can help the business overcome its disadvantage or improve the margins in its industry (added value logic) or unless you believe that owning the business adds value to your other businesses (added value logic), or unless the price you can sell it for is less than the value of continuing to own it (capital markets logic).

If a business is in a high growth market and is earning high margins (business logic), you are likely to want to invest in it, unless you believe that you are a bad owner of the business (added value logic) or you could sell it for significantly more than it is worth to you (capital markets logic).

If a business is one you are able to significantly improve or one that will add value to your existing businesses (added value logic), you are likely to want to invest in it or acquire it. Even if it is likely to sell at a price that is higher than the value of cash flows it generates (capital markets logic), you are still likely to want to retain the business.

Business logic

Business logic looks at the market the business is competing in and the position the business has in that market. The core thought is that a company should aim to own businesses in attractive markets and that have significant competitive advantage. These businesses are highly profitable. This analysis – market attractiveness and competitive advantage – is part of the normal work done for business-level strategy. Hence, business logic is the main area of overlap between business-level strategy and corporate-level strategy: it is a tool used by both disciplines.

The attractiveness of a market can be assessed by calculating the average profitability of the competitors in the market. If average profitability is significantly above the cost of capital, the market is attractive. If average profitability is significantly below the cost of capital, the market is unattractive. Michael Porter, the Harvard Business School strategy guru, developed a framework – the 5-Forces framework – that summarises the factors that drive average profitability. He identified competitive rivalry, the power of customers, the threat of substitutes, the power of suppliers and the threat of new entrants as the five forces that influence the average profitability of a sector.

Of course, the attractiveness of a market to a particular company may be influenced by factors other than average profitability. Growth is typically an important factor to most management teams. Size of the market is typically another factor. Individual companies may want to develop their own measures of market attractiveness.

The other dimension, competitive advantage, can be assessed using relative profitability: the profitability of your business versus the average competitor in the market. If your business is more profitable than the average, it is likely to have a competitive advantage. If your business is less profitable than the average, it is likely to have a competitive disadvantage. Competitive advantage may be created by many factors, such as technology or customer relationships or scale economies. Relative profitability captures the result of all these factors.

Figure 1.2: Business Attractiveness matrix

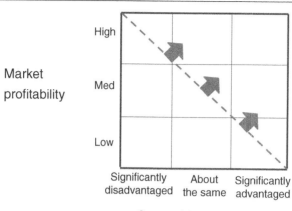

These two measures – the average profitability of the competitors in the market and the relative profitability of your business versus the average – are good surrogates for market attractiveness and competitive position. They can be combined into a matrix – the Business Attractiveness matrix (see Figure 1.2). This matrix is similar to the McKinsey/GE matrix described in most textbooks. Business units that plot in the top right corner of the matrix are most attractive and those in the bottom left are least attractive. In broad terms, companies should look to hold onto or acquire businesses that are to the right of the central diagonal, and exit or restructure businesses that are to the left of the central diagonal.

Business logic steers companies towards investing in attractive businesses: those in markets where most competitors make good profits and where the business has higher profits than the average. **Mexican Foods**[2] owned a portfolio of foods businesses with a bias towards private-label products. These are products that sell under a retailer's brand rather than a manufacturer's brand. The management team predicted that margins on private-label businesses were likely to be squeezed in the future. The problem was the power of the major retailers, as well as the large number of small low cost competitors. Profitability for the average competitor was already low and would be likely to fall.

Branded products, in contrast, would be likely to provide good margins. There were fewer competitors in the branded sector, and, because the brand communicated directly with consumers, branded companies could resist the power of retailers. Mexican Foods owned one or two strong brands, which were well positioned in their product categories.

As a result of this assessment of the relative attractiveness of the two markets, senior managers decided to focus their investment on their strongest brands and look for bolt-on brands to acquire. Over time they decided to shift their portfolio towards brands and away from private label products.

Added value logic

Added value (or parenting) logic looks at the additional value that is created or destroyed as a result of the relationship between the business and the rest of the company. There are two kinds of added value. Added value can come from the relationship between the business and its parent company – hence the term "parenting". But value is also created or destroyed as a result of the relationship between the sister businesses. The first type we can think of as vertical added value and the second type as horizontal added value. Together they make up added value.

In commercial companies, added value is measured by looking at the impact on future cash flows. If the discounted value of future cash flows increases as a result of some headquarters initiative, value has been added. In public sector organisations or charities, added value is measured by a ratio such as cost per unit of benefit. If a headquarters initiative can lower costs for the same benefits or increase benefits for the same cost, the ability of the organisation to serve its beneficiaries has been increased: value has been added.

Value can be added or subtracted. Added value can come from wise guidance from headquarters managers or from a broad range of other sources, such as a parent company brand, the technical know-how of a central technology unit, relationships with important stakeholders, financial strength, etc. Subtracted value happens when headquarters provides less wise guidance, such as the setting of inappropriate targets or inappropriate strategies, or from a broad range of other sources, such as time wasting, inefficient central services, delayed decision making, inappropriate standardisation and poor people decisions.

The potential for added value and the risk of subtracted value can be combined to form a matrix – the Heartland matrix (see Figure 1.3). The issue at stake is the balance between the two types of value.

Figure 1.3: The Heartland matrix

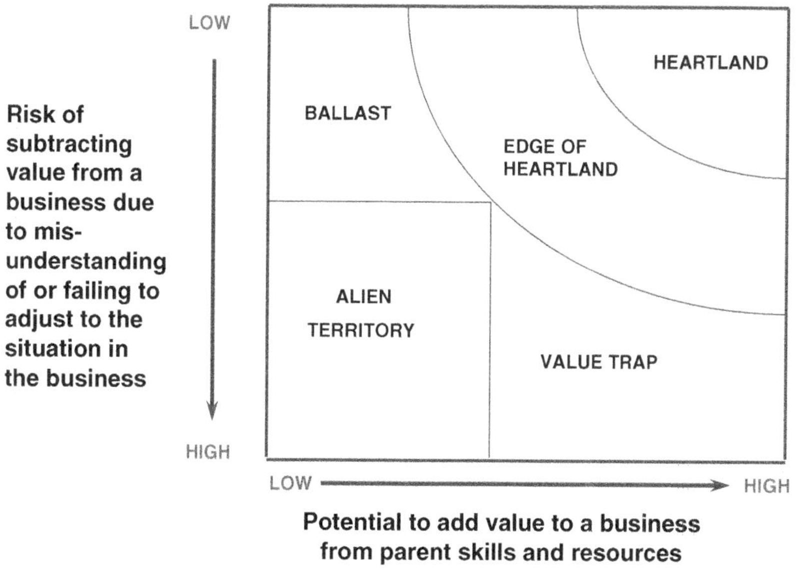

Risk of subtracting value from a business due to mis-understanding of or failing to adjust to the situation in the business

LOW

HIGH

HEARTLAND

BALLAST

EDGE OF HEARTLAND

ALIEN TERRITORY

VALUE TRAP

LOW ⟶ HIGH

Potential to add value to a business from parent skills and resources

Each business unit is plotted on the matrix. Where the potential for the company to add value to the business unit is high and the risk that the company will subtract value from the business is low, it is plotted in the "heartland". In other words there is a good fit between the business and the company.

If the risk of subtracted value is high and the potential for added value is low, the business is in "alien territory". The fit is bad, and the company should almost certainly sell or close this business.

If the risk of subtracted value is low and the potential for added value is low, the business is "ballast". The danger here is that the business will consume the scarce time of headquarters managers without resulting in any extra value. Unless headquarters managers can find ways to add value, these businesses are candidates for selling; but can easily be retained until an opportune moment arrives.

If the risk of subtracted value is high and the potential for added value is high, the business is a "value trap": the subtracted value may well outweigh the added value. It is normally best to exit these businesses unless managers at the group level can find ways to reduce the risks of subtracted value, and hence raise the business into "edge of heartland".

Added value logic steers companies towards investing in businesses that will benefit significantly from being part of the company or that will contribute significantly to the success of other businesses in the company.

Danaher, a diversified US company with a portfolio of businesses that mainly manufacture equipment, is an example of a company driven by added value logic. Danaher delivered over 25% annual share price growth from its founding in 1985 up to the economic crisis in 2008. The largest divisions focused on electronic test equipment, environmental test equipment and medical technologies.

Danaher acquired companies and improved them: more than 50 in the five years before 2008. The driving force was the Danaher Business System, an approach to continuous improvement based on the principles of lean manufacturing. As Larry Culp, CEO from 2001, explained, "The bedrock of our company is the Danaher Business System (DBS). DBS tools give all of our operating executives the means with which to strive for world-class quality, delivery and cost benchmarks, and deliver superior customer satisfaction and profitable growth."[3]

Following acquisition, the new business would feel the influence of Danaher immediately. Within one month, the management team would have an Executive Champion Orientation. This involved getting the top 50 managers in the business to map out the processes in the business and come up with targets for improvement. The improvement targets typically ranged from 20 to 100%.

The next influence came from redoing the business's strategic plan. Particular attention would be given to gains in market share and to understanding why some customers buy from competitors. Typically, the new plan involved doubling the business's organic growth ambitions.

At the same time Danaher would demand a review of people. Most businesses tolerate some managers who are capable at their jobs but not drivers of change and improvement. Danaher would provide replacements from other businesses in the group.

The final influence would come from the Danaher system for ensuring that plans are executed – Policy Deployment. Each manager would be given a set of metrics that linked directly to the plan. The metrics would be pinned to his or her door (or displayed in the work area) and updated monthly. This accelerated the pace of change.

One further source of added value came from bolt-on acquisitions. Danaher liked to acquire businesses that could create a platform for bolt-on acquisitions. A large portion of the back office costs in these bolt-on acquisitions could be saved. There were also often savings in sales and distribution costs as well as opportunities to consolidate manufacturing sites.

Apple is a more integrated company than Danaher. The added value of corporate headquarters, while Steve Jobs was leading Apple, was considerable. Headquarters led the product development process, controlling the heart of Apple's success. Headquarters looked after the brand. Headquarters also ensured that different products shared sales channels and supporting services, such as the retail stores, and online applications and services, such as the Apps Store.

With this degree of centralisation, Apple needed to have a set of product lines, each of which could benefit from its added value. At the time of writing, Apple was expected to enter a new business – television. Added value logic would require Tim Cook, the new CEO, to ask whether television products would be likely to gain as much advantage as phones and tablets from Apple's product development skills, brand, distribution channels and online services. He would also need to ask whether the business model in television is significantly different from that of phones or computers, and, hence, whether there is a significant risk of subtracted value. Is television heartland, edge of heartland or value trap for Apple?

Apple is a particularly interesting example, which we will come back to in Chapter 12. The involvement of headquarters at Apple was so great that it would be reasonable to think of Apple as a single business rather than as a corporate group. However, we will show how corporate-level strategy analysis is as helpful in a company like Apple as it is in a more division-alised company like Danaher.

Capital markets logic

Capital markets logic looks at the market for buying and selling businesses. At certain times, businesses are given low values by the capital markets: there are few buyers and many sellers. This was true for oil refineries during the 1990s, due to excess capacity, and for regional food brands from the late 1980s, because the major food companies were focusing on international brands. At other times, businesses have high values: there are many buyers and few sellers. This was true for dot.com businesses and for mobile telephone licences in the 1990s.

As a result of these market trends, businesses can have market values that differ from the discounted value of expected future cash flows. A difference between market value and discounted value happens partly because some buyers or sellers are not knowledgeable about likely cash flows or appropriate discount rates, and partly because cash flows are not the only factor influencing decisions to buy or sell. Managers can have "strategic" reasons for buying or selling that cause them to pay a price or accept a price that is above or below the discounted cash flow value (net present value).

Figure 1.4 plots the market value against the net present value (NPV) of owning the business. If the two values diverge outside of a corridor where market value and NPV are approximately equal, there are important consequences for portfolio

Figure 1.4: Fair Value matrix

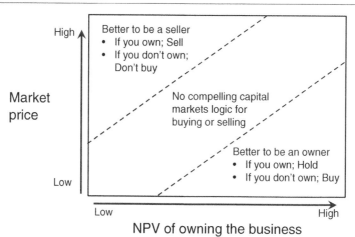

NPV of owning the business

decisions. When the market value is significantly above the NPV, companies should avoid buying and consider selling. When the market value is significantly below NPV, companies should consider buying and avoid selling.

Capital markets logic steers companies towards buying businesses that are cheap and selling businesses that are expensive. It is probably most influential in affecting the timing of portfolio decisions, rather than in being a prime determinant of the composition of the portfolio. However, **Associated British Foods** (ABF), a UK-based conglomerate, is an example of a company that made a number of significant decisions primarily driven by capital markets logic.

ABF started as a bakery in Canada in the 1890s.[4] It grew first as a worldwide bakery group and then, in the 1960s, diversified more widely. In the financial crisis of the 1970s, the company split into two and the UK arm became ABF. Gary Weston, the CEO and a member of the founding Weston family, then built ABF through a series of well-timed acquisitions and disposals.

He sold Premier Milling in South Africa before the apartheid regime resulted in negative sentiment for South African businesses. He sold Fine Fare, a grocery retailer, before the race between Sainsbury's and Tesco to build out-of-town stores reduced the prices of high street retailers. He bought Beresford, the owner of British Sugar, at a point when its stock price was low. Conglomerates such as Beresford were out of favour and the profits from sugar were temporarily depressed. A few years later, the annual profit from British Sugar, a division of Beresford, was nearly the same as the price he had paid for the whole company. As one manager explained, "The basic logic of this portfolio is that they were businesses that were cheap."

In the last 10 years, ABF has expanded its branded grocery business acquiring brands from companies like Unilever. ABF spotted that major companies, like Unilever and P&G, were increasingly focusing on their large international brands. This caused them to sell regional brands and smaller international brands. But, there were not many buyers for these brands, enabling ABF to acquire them at attractive prices.

The three logics – business logic, added value logic and capital markets logic – are best used in combination. Mexican Foods, for example, was driven by business logic, when deciding to focus on brands. But managers needed to consider the other logics as well. Using added value logic, managers recognised that branded businesses were a potential value trap because most of the senior managers had cut their teeth on private-label businesses. So they considered what they would need to do at the group level in order to reduce the risk of subtracted value. They also wanted to increase the amount of value they could add to branded businesses, so they decided to strengthen and centralise brand marketing.

Using capital markets logic, managers asked whether now would be a good time to buy branded businesses or sell private-label businesses. They decided not to sell the private-label businesses. Prices were too low: there were very few buyers. For the reverse reason, it proved hard to buy branded businesses at reasonable prices. Other food companies had done similar analyses about the prospects for branded businesses. As a result, the strategy to focus on brands became an organic growth strategy based on existing brands, and on creating new brands using competences from the private-label businesses.

Danaher also used the three logics to guide its acquisition decisions. While managers were interested in acquiring businesses that would respond to the DBS, business logic caused them to look particularly in markets that would allow high margins and for businesses that had strong competitive positions. As Larry Culp explained, Danaher looked to acquire the number one or two in large markets, or to acquire companies with significant market shares and high margins in fragmented markets. In these situations, their "lean" medicine proved to be particularly effective: they were good at tuning up sound businesses.

Danaher managers also used capital markets logic to guide their decisions. They avoided sectors such as communications equipment, because they were considered hot opportunities by other acquirers. They also made more acquisitions when stock markets were low, such as 2001–2005, than in the boom markets of 2006 and 2007.

ABF was also influenced by all three logics. While the main strategy was about buying cheap, ABF also focused on business logic. In the early 1980s, Gary Weston sold "any part of the business that was not generating cash", and kept businesses, like Primark, that appeared to have a significant competitive advantage.

ABF also exploited added value logic. By bringing in new managers to British Sugar and raising performance targets, ABF more than doubled profits. By adding bolt-on brands to its Grocery Division, ABF exploited its international presence and back office platform. The bolt-on brands could be integrated without adding significant overheads.

Management (or parenting) strategy

Once portfolio decisions have been made (which businesses to invest in and how much to invest in each), managers at the corporate level need to decide how to manage the resulting portfolio. They need to decide how to structure the organisation into business divisions, what functions and decisions to centralise at the corporate level, who to appoint to the top jobs in the divisions and what guidance to give these managers in the form of strategic targets and controls.

The main logic that guides all of these decisions is the logic of **added value**. All these decisions should be guided by the objective of maximising the additional value created from owning multiple business divisions and minimising the negative aspects of creating layers of management above the level of the divisions.

In other words, decisions or activities should be centralised at the corporate level, if centralisation will improve overall performance. Targets should be set for divisions by corporate-level managers, if the targets will help division managers achieve more than they would have achieved without the targets. Decisions delegated to divisions should be influenced by corporate-level managers, if the influence can help improve the decisions or the motivation of the managers in the divisions.

Of course there is also a **governance and compliance** logic that determines the existence of some activities, like financial controls and tax management. These activities must be carried out at the corporate level in any responsible company. Headquarters managers must interact with the owners and with certain stakeholders, such as governments. The corporate level must ensure that financial controls are in place, that there is sufficient money available, that taxes are paid and that employees are acting within the law. Corporate-level managers must develop some business plan and share it with the board. Finally, the CEO and the board must appoint the heads of the businesses under their control.

In some industries, such as financial services, that are highly regulated, these governance and compliance activities can be significant, involving hundreds of central staff. However, in most companies these "required activities" are not the main role of headquarters managers. They are part of the management strategy at the corporate level, but they typically occupy only a small percentage of the managers at headquarters. The remainder of the people have jobs at the corporate level that are about adding value.

Typically, a corporate group will have three to seven **major sources of corporate added value**. This list will then guide all of the difficult decisions about what to centralise, how to organise, who to appoint and how to design group-level processes. For example, if the main sources of added value are

- investing in a company-wide brand,
- creating a company-wide commitment to lean manufacturing and
- helping business divisions grow in China,

there are implications for centralisation, organisation and processes.

First, the corporate level is likely to appoint some marketing people to look after the brand. These people will set policies for how the brand can be used and may require that decisions relating to the brand pass through their department. Their department is likely to be a central function so that it can gain authority from proximity to the CEO. But, this is not the only arrangement possible. Virgin's brand is managed by a separate company that licenses it to Virgin's businesses. In some companies, product brands that are used in more than one division are controlled by the lead division.

Second, the company will need a team of experts in lean manufacturing to drive the lean initiative. The lean effort will probably be supported by an information system that records the progress each business is making with its implementation of lean methods. It may also require some attention from headquarters managers in setting targets and encouraging commitment. The lean department is likely to be located in headquarters, but many of those who work on lean projects may come from all around the organisation.

Third, the company will benefit from having some headquarters managers with years of experience in China, and who have good relationships with Chinese companies and dignitaries. To support the China effort, the company may need an organisation structure that has all businesses in China reporting to one head of China. It may need a reporting process that provides detailed information on the performance of units in China.

Fourth, if these are the only sources of added value, other functions, such as finance and human resources, will probably be decentralised with only small teams at group headquarters, focused mainly on governance and compliance. This is because the contributions of these functions to these three major sources of added value are small.

Danaher's main sources of added value were the DBS, the pool of 2000 internal executives Danaher could draw on and the synergies from bolt-on acquisitions. To deliver this added value, Danaher's headquarters was an unassuming office six blocks from the White House in Washington DC. Danaher's name was not even on the building. Inside, around 50 executives populated functions such as finance, legal, HR, accounting, tax and M&A. While a significant portion of the time of these people was devoted to governance and compliance, they could all be involved in significant acquisitions either in a due diligence role or in helping with integration issues.

Headquarters managers were also all trained in the DBS tools. The DBS office was led by an ex-division president, but all of the DBS staff were located in business divisions rather than in Washington. Following an acquisition or when a business needed help, the DBS office would assemble a team to support the project.

The head of HR was an ex-division president rather than an HR professional. His main role was to help assess people and to maintain records on 2000 internal managers so that he could help fill vacancies with capable managers.

Management or parenting strategy is, therefore, mainly about governance and major sources of added value. However, there are often a large number of other activities where small

gains in performance can be achieved by some limited centralisation or standardisation or other form of central influence.
Proposals to centralise payroll, to improve working capital or
to help an individual business with its market entry in the USA
are typical examples.

These **minor sources of added value** should be included
in the management strategy with reluctance. The main focus of
the management strategy should be the major sources of added
value. Danaher is a good example. With only 50 managers in
headquarters there was little opportunity to become distracted
with minor sources of added value.

The problem is that activities that distract attention from
the major sources can easily generate opportunity costs that
are greater than the benefits. Moreover, subtracted value, the
negative side of headquarters activity, is an ever-present threat.
The more activities that are centralised, the more initiatives that
are led by headquarters managers and the more headquarters
managers "interfere", the higher the risk of subtracted value. As
a result, it is important to challenge all minor sources of added
value, and only include them in the management strategy if the
risk of value destruction, whether from opportunity costs or
other sources, is low.

Headquarters functions are normally looking for additional
ways to improve overall corporate performance and to expand
the remit of their functions. Despite good intentions, their
enthusiasm for additional activity can run ahead of their ability
to genuinely add value. Over time, headquarters functions can
gradually smother both initiative and efficiency at the business
level. There are plenty of examples of business divisions spun
out of larger groups that have performed better as independent
companies. For these divisions, the net impact of the good
intentions of their corporate parents was negative. Released
from this "parenting", the business-level managers were able to
focus on what was important to the success of their business,
instead of considering what their corporate masters wanted.

One way to keep a check on the build-up of bureaucracy at corporate levels is to challenge all new corporate-level initiatives against three hurdles:

1. Is the initiative a necessary part of governance or compliance?
2. If not, is the initiative a necessary part of some major source of corporate added value?
3. If not, does the initiative clearly add some value *and* have low risk of negative side effects?

If the initiative fails all three hurdles, it should be rejected.

So, the management strategy is built from an understanding of the compliance and governance requirements, the major sources of added value and a number of minor sources of added value that have low risk of negatives. These three reasons for activity at headquarters guide decisions about:

- the overall organisation structure (how and whether the business units are grouped into divisions),
- the functions at the corporate level or at the division level,
- the central policies,
- the skills, capabilities and focus of senior corporate managers,
- the design of company-wide processes such as planning and budgeting,
- the degree of centralisation or decentralisation and
- the ways in which managers at the corporate level interact with managers lower down.

Having a management strategy that adds a significant amount of value is a central aim of any company ambitious to own multiple business units. Unfortunately, many companies fail this test. They own business units that are performing less well because of the attentions of their parent company or they create costs at the corporate level that are greater than the value added. This state of affairs is clearly unsatisfactory and immediate action is needed.

However, being a positive parent is not enough. The management strategy should aim higher. Companies should aim to have a **parenting advantage**: they should aim to add more value than other parent companies can. They should aim to be the best owner of each of the businesses in their portfolio. If they are the best owner, there is no opportunity for a different management team to acquire the whole company and make changes that would improve overall value.

We use the phrase parent company to emphasise the fact that corporations are not only competing with other corporations for the ownership of business units. They are also competing with governments, private equity firms, family holding companies, national wealth funds, investment firms like Berkshire Hathaway, and others for the ownership of businesses.

Of course, companies are rarely the best owners of all of their business units all of the time. Sometimes the portfolio strategy has taken the company into some new sector because of its future growth potential. For a period the company many not be the best owner of this fledgling business. But, over time, it should be ambitious to become a good owner. At other times, an opportunity to expand the portfolio has come unexpectedly due to some imperfection in the capital markets. Again, for a period, the company may not be the best owner of this new business. At other times, managers at the parent level retire and need to be replaced. It is not always possible to find replacements with all the required skills. So, for a period while the new managers learn and develop, the company many not be the best parent of all of its businesses.

Nevertheless, despite many situations where the current parent company is not the best possible owner of a particular business unit, it is important that the management strategy is guided by the medium-term aim of being the "best owner". This means that management strategy should include an analysis of **rival parents**. Without a good understanding of the management strategies of other companies, it is hard to make judgements against the best owner metric.

Summary

Corporate-level strategy involves making decisions about which businesses to own and invest in (portfolio strategy) and how to manage or parent the businesses (management/parenting strategy). Part II of this book addresses portfolio strategy and Part IV addresses parenting strategy.

Added value logic is a common guiding thought in both portfolio strategy and parenting strategy. Hence, it is a central pillar of corporate-level strategy: companies should aim to be the best parents of the business units they own. As a result, Part III of this book is dedicated to exploring added value in more detail. We describe different sources of added value. We comment on sources of subtracted value. We also provide some tools to help managers identify the best sources of added value in their companies.

Added value is also a driving logic in international strategy. In the Appendix, we look at the links and overlaps between corporate-level strategy and international strategy. Since most companies in multiple businesses are also in multiple countries, it is important to understand how corporate-level strategy and international strategy fit together.

Added value logic is, however, not the only driver of corporate-level strategy. Companies need to consider the attractiveness of the markets they choose to enter and the strength of their competitive position within these markets (business logic). They also need to consider the state of the capital markets for buying and selling businesses (capital markets logic). Both of these two additional logics can provide reasons to buy or sell or invest or disinvest that are in contradiction to the added value logic.

As a result, good corporate-level strategy work involves balancing the influence of these three logics over time. Sometimes, added value logic will be the primary driver. For example, managers at Danaher between 2000 and 2010 worked hard to improve their ability to add value to their portfolio of engineering businesses and only added business units to the portfolio that were similar to the ones they already had.

At other times, business logic is the driving force. For example, managers at Mexican Foods concluded that they needed to change the balance of their business units, reducing the emphasis on private label and increasing the emphasis on brands. This change involved significant adjustments to both portfolio and parenting.

At still other times, investment logic may be the driving force. For example, ABF expanded in the bakery business at a time when flour milling and bread manufacturing were out of favour and undervalued. ABF was also able to improve these businesses both with stronger management and with economies of scale. But, as the markets changed, ABF sold many of its bakeries earning a premium on the price it had paid.

Corporate-level strategy is therefore a balancing act, where different ideas may be driving activity at different times. The remainder of this book explains in more detail how to be good at developing corporate-level strategy, what analyses are helpful and how to retain a balanced perspective. However, before we dive into the details of corporate-strategy analysis, we should start by looking back at the history of thinking in this field. We need to ground our concepts in the academic literature and the lessons of experience.

Notes

[1] Blacklock is a real company that the authors have advised. It has been disguised at the request of management. Names, dates and locations have been changed.

[2] This is another company where the management team asked us to use a disguise.

[3] Harvard Business School case "Danaher Corporation", Case No. N9-708-445, January 2008.

[4] Harvard Business School case "Associated British Foods", Case No. N9-708-402, November 2011.

CHAPTER TWO

SOME HISTORY: FROM BOSTON BOX TO THREE LOGICS THAT DRIVE CORPORATE ACTION

Corporate-level strategy seeks to answer two questions: How is a portfolio of businesses assembled, and how are these businesses managed for maximum performance? Over the last 50 years, there appear to have been four broad schools of thought. In this chapter we review these four schools, showing how they provide the foundations for the three logics, presented in Chapter 1.

The "professional management" school proposes that it makes sense to have multiple businesses in one company when the leaders of the company have superior professional management skills. These managers know the latest techniques of good business management, like planning, performance management, financial control, financial structuring and decision making. This makes it possible for these managers to expand into new areas and acquire businesses where the managers are less skilled at these management techniques. Corporate-level strategy, according to this school, is about ensuring that the top team has the latest management techniques. Using these techniques, the company can then expand into attractive sectors or acquire businesses that are less well managed.

The "portfolio planning" school proposes that it makes sense to develop portfolios that deliver a combination of growth, profitability and cash flow. To achieve this, a mix of businesses may be required – for example, some large, profitable but mature businesses, which can throw off the cash required to fund the expansion of smaller, growing businesses with good long-term profit potential. Thus, attractive businesses are not all identical – they can have different blends of different qualities. Corporate strategy is therefore about buying and selling businesses to maintain an optimal, attractive mix. It also involves directing resources towards those businesses, which are, or are on their way to being, the most attractive.

The "synergy" school proposes that it makes sense to have multiple businesses in one company when the businesses can be linked together to create extra performance through "synergies". Classically referred to as economies of scale or scope, synergies can come from combining activities where there are economies of scale, or from transferring knowledge across businesses which share some similar scope. Corporate strategy is therefore about identifying businesses where there are opportunities for synergy and developing skills at making the linkages between the businesses work.

The "capital markets" school proposes that it makes sense to buy businesses which are underpriced and sell them when they are overpriced. Capital markets do not always price businesses on the basis of their true underlying value, creating arbitrage opportunities. Corporate strategy is therefore about buying and selling businesses, or stakes in businesses, at the right time.

Each of these schools is described in this chapter, highlighting the insights, tools and frameworks they provide and the issues they present.[1]

The professional management school

An important and enduring justification for the multi-business company, dating back to at least the middle of the twentieth century, is the argument that the managers of successful companies possess better management skills. This enables them to deliver better performance and justifies their owning a range of businesses. Kenneth Andrews, a leading management thinker at the time, argued that there had been a steady development of executive talent in America. The establishment of business schools in the early twentieth century created the basis for the education of professional managers, and the advancement of the science of management. These managers had superior management techniques that made it possible for them to improve business performance. These techniques also enabled managers to operate divisionalised structures and so expand into more and more sectors.[2]

General management skills

During the 1950s and 1960s, much scholarly attention focused on identifying basic principles of management, useful to all managers and applicable to all kinds of enterprises. Peter Drucker, the management guru, argued that intuitive management was no longer sufficient. He encouraged managers to study the principles of management and to acquire knowledge and to analyse their performance systematically.[3]

It was not a great leap to conclude that, if all managers face similar problems, professional managers might be able to use their skills across a range of different businesses. Simple observation, as well as theory, supported this idea. Robert Katz, an expert in management skills, noted that, "We are all familiar with those 'professional managers' who are becoming the prototypes of our modern executive world. These men shift with great ease, and with no apparent loss in effectiveness, from one industry to another. Their human and conceptual skills seem to make up for their unfamiliarity with the new job's technical aspects."[4]

During the 1960s, the growth of conglomerates, with their numerous acquisitions of unrelated businesses across different industries, provided almost laboratory conditions in which to test out the idea that professional managers could apply their skills to many different businesses. Conglomerates such as Textron, ITT and Litton not only grew rapidly, but also profitably, and top managers of these companies perceived themselves as breaking new ground. For example, David Judleson of Gulf & Western claimed, "Without the high degree of sophistication, skills, and effectiveness that management has developed only in the last two decades, the conglomerate could not exist. These management techniques provide the necessary unity and compatibility among a diversity of operations and acquisitions."[5]

Harold Geneen used a system of detailed budgets, tight financial controls and face-to-face meetings among his general managers to build ITT.[6] In 1967, Royal Little, who masterminded Textron's broad diversification, explained that the company succeeded because, "we are adding that intangible called business judgement."[7] Textron had common financial controls, budgetary systems and capital allocation procedures across its many businesses. It provided few central services and had only a very small corporate office. The group vice presidents, who were each responsible for a number of divisions, were appointed from outside the company. They acted as overseers and consultants to the divisions, helping them improve their "business judgement".

For more than 20 years, a belief that some managers had better general management skills than others seemed to justify a kind of virtuous circle of corporate growth and diversification. Andrews summarised that basic premise, arguing that, "successful diversification – because it always means successful sur-mounting of formidable administrative problems – develops know-how which further diversification will capitalise and extend".[8]

The high stock prices of conglomerates in the 1960s reflected the growing belief that this new way of managing – professional managers acquiring and improving a diverse range of businesses in a divisionalised structure – was the future. But economic worries at the end of the 1960s brought the dream to an end. The stock market in 1969 fell by 10% and the prices of conglomerates by as much as 50%.[9]

The financial crisis of the mid-1970s followed, causing many conglomerates to run out of cash. Some, like Ling-Temco-Vaught in the USA and Slater Walker in the UK, failed completely. Others, ITT and Textron, just survived. All of them had to slim down their portfolios to raise cash. Belief that professional managers could make any business perform had been lost, and faith in conglomerates as the way forward never recovered.

The concept of strategy

The 1970s financial crisis and the struggles of conglomerates coincided with the rise of a new management technique – strategic planning. Senior managers, this new technique proposed, should focus their attention on the "strategies" of their companies. Strategy was more than long-range planning or objective setting; it was a way of deciding the basic direction of the company and preparing it to meet future challenges.[10]

C. Roland Christensen, one of the creators of the business policy course at Harvard Business School during the 1960s, argued that the concept of strategy made it possible to simplify the complex tasks of managers.[11] A focus on strategy prevented senior executives from doing harm by meddling in operating details and day-to-day issues that they did not understand.

These should be left to more junior managers with knowledge of the local circumstances. It allowed corporate executives to concentrate on the most important issues facing their companies – and it simplified management by providing a framework for decisions.

CEOs readily accepted that strategy should be their main responsibility. During the late 1960s and 1970s many companies established formal planning systems, and the appropriate structure and uses of such systems received much attention from academics.[12] In the early 1970s, Louis Gerstner, who later ran IBM, remarked on how quickly strategic planning had been adopted by companies, noting that, "Writer after writer has hailed this new discipline as the fountainhead of all corporate progress."[13]

Problems with resource allocation

The 1970s cash crisis made the challenge of allocating resources across a portfolio of businesses a critical activity in most diversified companies. It became synonymous with corporate-level strategy: and a preoccupation of CEOs and CFOs. But it was a difficult job, and the growing field of strategy did not have an easy answer. Corporate CEOs needed to understand the relative merits of investment proposals coming from a range of businesses in different sectors, with different time horizons, competitive positions, and risk profiles, not to mention management teams with differing levels of credibility. A company such as ITT had to allocate resources among businesses that included telecommunications, insurance, rental cars, bakeries and construction. With many divisions competing for funds, how could a company be sure it was investing in the best projects for future growth?

Joseph Bower explored in detail how a large, diversified firm allocated resources. His research highlighted the gulf between financial theory, which saw the manager's task as choosing projects with the highest returns, and corporate reality, where all proposed projects showed at least the return required by the corporate hurdle rate for investment. In practice, divisional managers only proposed projects with acceptable forecast returns, and corporate-level managers could not use financial analysis to choose among projects.[14] What they needed was a management technique to help them.

The portfolio planning school

To help companies with this resource allocation challenge, academics and consulting companies developed portfolio planning tools. These tools were based on insights about which businesses offered the most attractive opportunities for investment. They solved the resource allocation problem by allowing corporate managers to direct resources towards such businesses. They also gave insights into which businesses were unattractive. These businesses could then be restructured, sold or closed down.

The precursor of these portfolio planning tools was developed by the Boston Consulting Group (BCG). As a result of work that the company had done helping its clients with business level strategy issues, BCG consultants discovered the experience curve, which was written up and developed by the company's founder, Bruce Henderson (see Figure 2.1).

The experience curve proposed that costs come down in a predictable way as a company gains experience in producing a particular product. Attractive businesses were those with more experience than competitors, and thus lower costs and higher margins. These businesses also offered higher returns on incremental investment – so they were better candidates for further investment and growth. This growth led them to have even lower costs, higher margins and more attractive returns on incremental investment – a virtuous circle.

Figure 2.1: Experience curve: costs decline with cumulative experience (steam turbine production cost example, 1946–1963)

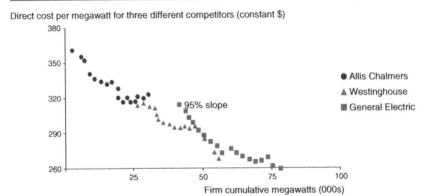

Direct cost per megawatt for three different competitors (constant $)

Note: For each competitor, the cost of production in each year between 1946 and 1963 is shown

Source: Adapted from The Experience Curve-Reviewed (Part III) © 1973, The Boston Consulting Group

The classic example of this was in steam turbines. There were three main competitors in the USA. The data on costs was made public due to an anti-trust suit. In the figure, the cost level of each company in the years from 1946 to 1963 is shown plotted against the cumulative production of that company. Each company is travelling down a similar experience curve but, because GE has the highest market share, it is well ahead of the number two player (Westinghouse), which in turn is well ahead of the number three competitor (Allis Chalmers). GE has an attractive business whereas Allis Chalmers has an unattractive business.[15]

The experience curve suggests that the primary driver of advantage and attractiveness (to Henderson they were virtually synonymous) is relative cumulative experience. If you have twice the experience of a competitor this is likely to give you a significant cost advantage. BCG consultants were busy taking this insight to their clients. Their message was that businesses needed to aim for market leadership, which would lead to greater volumes and greater cumulative experience. The measure they used was relative market share (the market share of the business divided by either the market share of the leading company or, if the business was the market leader, by the market share of the second largest player).

Meanwhile, Bruce Henderson was using the same experience curve insight to help conglomerates with their resource allocation problem. He argued that they should allocate resources so as to create businesses with high relative market share. In the event that it was not possible to become one of the leading players, the business should be sold or closed down. This had a big impact on management thinking. For example, in the 1980s Jack Welch of GE took the idea and turned it into his No. 1 or No. 2 strategy. Businesses in GE were required to develop plans that would take them to the first or second position in their markets; otherwise Jack Welch would change the managers or sell the business.

The growth share matrix

BCG then developed the famous Boston Consulting Group matrix. Individual businesses in a corporate portfolio could be positioned on two dimensions. The bottom axis was relative market share, a proxy for competitive advantage, profitability and cash flow generation. The vertical axis was growth, which reflected the investment needs of the business (see Figure 2.2).

This matrix provided additional insight about which businesses were attractive and how to allocate resources. Businesses that had, or could develop, high market share were attractive. Size and growth were also attractive characteristics of a business, because bigger, faster growing businesses could generate more value than smaller, stagnant ones. Growth was indicated by the position of the business on the vertical axis. Size was indicated by drawing circles proportional to the revenue or assets of the business. This meant that the three

Figure 2.2: The Growth Share matrix

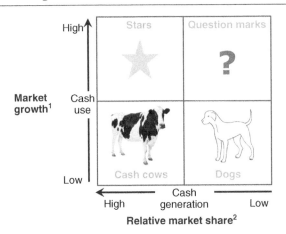

1. Over 3–5 years usually
2. Company's market share/largest competitor's market share

Source: Adapted from Strategy in the 1980s © 1981, The Boston Consulting Group

contributors to attractiveness – size, growth and competitive advantage – could be seen on one chart.[16]

The BCG matrix built on the insights provided by the experience curve. It provided a richer guide to attractiveness and how resources should be invested. Corporates should take the cash generated by the cash cows and invest it in maintaining the leadership position of the stars. Question marks should get cash only if it was possible to turn them into stars, through acquisition or market share gains. Otherwise they should be divested. Dogs should be divested (unless it was possible to consolidate the business with other competitors to create a cash cow). As the stars matured, they would become the next cash cows, creating the cash to fund the next phase of investment into new stars and question marks.

For example, GE's steam turbine business, with its high relative market share, would have been a star during the phase when industry growth was high. During this period it would have needed enough investment to allow it to maintain or grow market share. It would have become a cash cow as industry growth slowed – at which time it would be expected to throw off cash for other businesses.

Over the same period, Allis Chalmers would have slipped from being a question mark to being a dog. While it was a question mark it needed cash to grow not just with the market, but to build market share so as to approach the competitive position of GE. However, by the time growth flattened out, Allis Chalmers had failed to do this. Without radical restructuring, for example a merger with Westinghouse, there would be little future for this business because it would be unlikely to generate sufficient margins or cash to warrant continued investment.

The matrix provided the strategic framework managers needed to allocate resources among their businesses. It also helped them decide which businesses to sell and which to keep. The matrix even had implications for the overall portfolio shape. Henderson assumed that cash needed to be recycled around the corporation, because raising equity was a risky business in volatile capital markets (and the 1970s was an especially volatile time). Therefore, attractive portfolios were those which were balanced, so that the amount of cash used by some businesses was balanced by the cash generated by the others.

Concepts of balance extended beyond cash balancing. Balanced portfolios should have high growth businesses to balance low growth businesses, and high profit businesses to balance businesses where an aggressive strategy might mean periods of low profits. Using these ideas, many companies restructured their portfolios, divesting low growth, low margin, low potential businesses and investing in higher margin or higher growth businesses. Monsanto, for example, used portfolio planning to restructure its portfolio, divesting low growth commodity chemicals businesses and acquiring businesses in higher growth industries such as biotechnology.[17]

The BCG matrix assumed that cumulative experience drove competitive advantage and thus business attractiveness. Hence, market share was the key to success. However, this razor-like focus on market share was challenged by others, including within BCG itself. Other factors were found to be drivers of advantage, such as patents, brand strength, the scale of individual plants or focus on a limited number of product lines.[18] One study suggested that the effect of the experience curve was only 20–40% of that predicted by BCG.[19]

A further refinement to portfolio thinking at BCG came from the insight that the ability to build competitive advantage is not equally prevalent in all industries. The BCG Environments matrix (1981) (Figure 2.3) proposed that there are four different types of industry, based on the potential size of the competitive advantage available to leaders, and how many ways there are to create advantage.

"Volume businesses" are particularly attractive because there are high economies of scale, allowing the leaders to earn par-

Figure 2.3: The Competitive Environments matrix

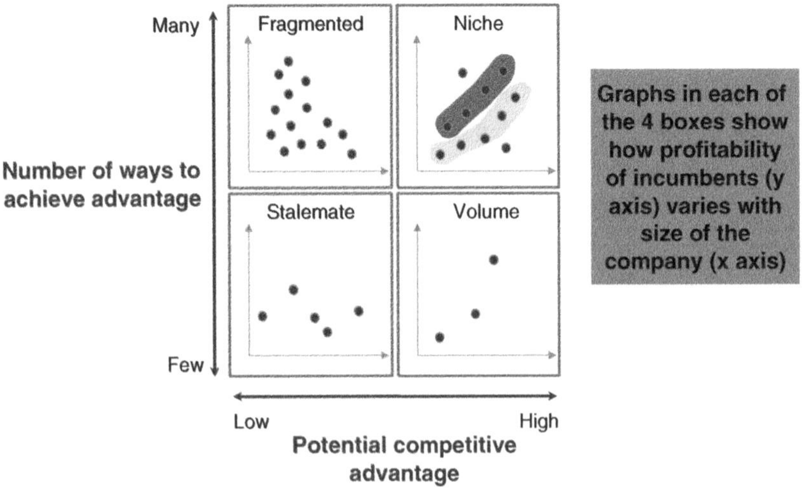

Source: Adapted from The BCG Portfolio Matrix from the Product Portfolio Matrix © 1970, The Boston Consulting Group

ticularly high returns. For example, in disposable diapers there are scale economies in the purchasing, manufacturing, distribution, sales, administration and branding functions – thus making it particularly profitable for the market leaders.

Other industries are attractive because they are "niche" businesses, offering high returns to those who have market share in one or more niches within a broader industry – in effect the industry consists of a number of different volume businesses each competing in a particular niche.[20]

Other industries do not offer significant sources of advantage. No one player can earn superior profits over the long term. Such businesses are called "stalemate" or "fragmented" businesses and are associated with generally lower rates of profitability. The implication for corporate strategy is that attractiveness, and thus portfolio and resource allocation decisions, should not be based solely on growth rate and market share, but also on the characteristics of the industry and the potential for any competitor to make a healthy return.

At one level these developments in strategy, and the associated tools and frameworks, enabled corporate managers to be smarter about identifying attractive businesses, allocating resources and designing appropriate strategies for businesses. However, they also suggested that the sources of business attractiveness were more varied and business specific than suggested by the original BCG matrix. Corporate managers needed a framework for categorising attractiveness that would help them understand the strategic requirements of the business and guide resource allocation. It was BCG's consulting rival McKinsey who proposed an alternative tool that captured the greater complexity that managers needed.

The GE or McKinsey matrix

Fred Gluck, a McKinsey director (eventually to become McKinsey's managing director), was determined to come up with a

Figure 2.4: The GE or McKinsey matrix

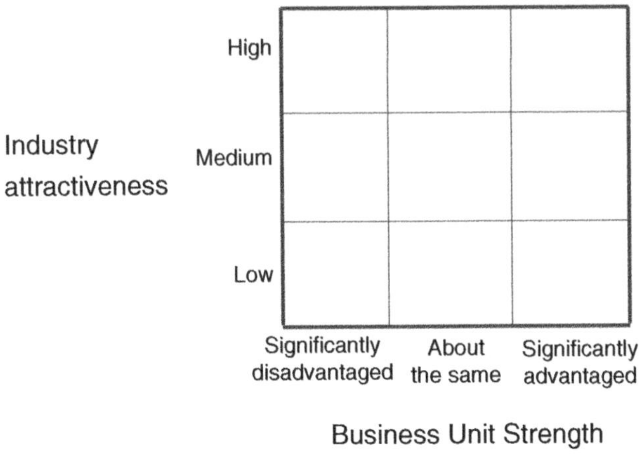

strategy framework that could challenge BCG and its epony-
mous matrix.[21] Working with General Electric in the 1970s,
Gluck came up with a rival matrix (see Figure 2.4), which fac-
tored in some of the developments in thinking during the
1970s.

Rather than plot the precise figure of relative market share
(RMS) on the horizontal axis, Gluck plotted the strength, competitive position or competitive advantage of the business unit.
This was less precise than RMS, but provided a catchall for the
wide range of sources of competitive advantage that were now
acknowledged.

The vertical axis plotted market or industry attractiveness.
This was less precise than the market growth rate used in the
BCG matrix, but it included other dimensions that might make
the market attractive for investment – for example, its size or
its profitability. Being in a large market was good because it
offered more potential for investment. This was of particular
importance for large corporations such as General Electric who
preferred focusing on a few large businesses rather than spreading themselves across many niche businesses.

Profitable markets (a concept that was not included in the BCG matrix) were self-evidently more attractive to invest in than less profitable markets. For example, the average return on capital employed in a market, such as pharmaceuticals, is nearly 30%.[22] The average return in a market, such as airlines, is nearer to 5%. In 1996, Southwest Airlines, one of the world's most successful airlines, earned a return on capital employed of 12%. In the same year, one of the most successful pharmaceutical companies, GlaxoWellcome, earned 55%.

There was also less emphasis on the need for a "balanced" portfolio. Implicit in the application of the BCG matrix was the concept of cash flow balance. However, this idea was not fundamental to the GE/McKinsey matrix.

While the BCG matrix advised managers to "sell Dogs, grow or divest Question Marks, grow Stars and create a balanced portfolio", the GE/McKinsey matrix advised managers to "restructure bottom left, and invest in top right". Businesses on the middle axis could be invested in if cash was available. But there were no explicit prescriptions for "balance".[23] The implicit idea here was that an attractive portfolio was one that provided "sustainable growth", with a mix of established and developing businesses.

The concept of cash flow balance was still important, however. The available cash limited what could be invested in. But it was a constraint on strategy, rather than a core part of the underlying logic. To the extent that stock markets were liquid, this constraint could be relaxed, allowing for a more aggressive investment strategy.

BCG's matrix was more powerful because its axes could readily be quantified. However, in the long run, the vagueness of the axes of the GE/McKinsey matrix was also its strength. They could accommodate an ever expanding view of what made industries attractive – for example, the various factors suggested by Porter's five forces (a framework that was not available when the matrix was first created).[24] According to a BCG study, the two dimensions of the GE/McKinsey matrix are the most popular criteria used by corporate managers to evaluate their business portfolios.[25]

The helicopter view provided by portfolio planning techniques was widely perceived as useful. For example, one CEO explained:

> Portfolio planning became relevant to me as soon as I became CEO. I was finding it very difficult to manage and understand so many different products and markets. I just grabbed at portfolio planning, because it provided me with a way to organise my thinking about our businesses, and the resource allocation issues facing the total company. I became and still am very enthusiastic. I guess you could say that I went for it hook, line, and sinker.[26]

During the 1970s, more and more corporations adopted portfolio planning, with the largest diversified companies being among the earliest adherents. One survey showed that by 1979, 45% of the Fortune 500 companies were using some form of portfolio planning.[27]

Portfolio planning reinforced the virtuous circle of corporate growth and diversification. It helped corporate-level managers correct past diversification mistakes, leading to divestitures of unattractive businesses, and it encouraged a mix of businesses, with different strategic (and cash) characteristics to ensure current performance and future growth.

Problems with portfolio management

Even as an increasing number of corporations turned to portfolio planning, practical problems emerged.[28] Companies discovered that while certain businesses appeared attractive, they were not necessarily easy to manage. It turned out to be extremely difficult, for example, for corporate managers with long experience of managing mature businesses in a particular industry sector to manage new growth businesses in new, dynamic and unfamiliar sectors.

Research on how companies actually used portfolio planning confirmed the difficulties of managing businesses with different strategic characteristics, missions or mandates. Philippe Haspeslagh investigated whether companies adjusted their systems of financial planning, capital investment appraisal, incentive compensation or strategic planning to fit the requirements of their different businesses. The focus of his study was on the role played by corporate-level managers, rather than on specific business-level strategies. He found that companies made few formal changes in their corporate-level systems. But, he also noted that in successful companies managers did make informal attempts to adapt these systems to their different businesses.[29] In another study on the effectiveness of portfolio planning techniques, the authors discovered that cash cows performed better in an organisational context of autonomy while fast-growing businesses benefited from more control. The authors concluded that the administrative context was an important variable in explaining business performance, and that many companies were taking the wrong approach to some of their businesses.[30]

The recognition that different types of businesses needed to be managed in different ways undermined the arguments of both the professional management and portfolio planning schools. Many companies discovered that common systems and approaches, when applied to different kinds of businesses, helped improve some businesses but caused others to underperform. A focus on attractive businesses did not put tight enough boundaries on what types of businesses a particular management team should and should not own, and did not shed enough light on how these businesses should be directed and managed.

1980s: Back to basics

During the 1980s, there was widespread scepticism about the ability of companies to manage and add value to diverse, conglomerate portfolios. Stock market analysts and observers highlighted the existence of a "conglomerate discount" – the degree to which the value of a particular conglomerate was less than the sum of its parts – the opposite of what proponents of the professional management and portfolio planning schools would expect. Raiders such as Carl Icahn and T. Boone Pickens demonstrated that they could acquire even the largest companies, break them up and realise huge profits. This prompted a rethinking of both the role of corporate management in large companies and the kinds of portfolio strategies that were appropriate.

What seemed most obvious about the corporate level in many companies was not its contribution, but its cost. Thus, attention shifted to cutting headquarters costs. Some companies turned central services into profit centres, charged with selling their services to the business units, while other companies disbanded central functions altogether. The pruning of corporate staffs often meant devolving more authority to business divisions.[31]

Companies also trimmed their portfolios. For example, in the 1960s only 1% of US firms refocused, while 25% diversified their portfolios. In contrast, in the 1980s 20% refocused while only 8% diversified.[32] Refocusing was driven by a number of factors. Capital markets, which had rewarded diversifiers in the 1960s, became sceptical. They also became more sophisticated, punishing underperformance and making takeovers more feasible. Managers who had been overoptimistic about their ability to manage diversified portfolios found that they were takeover targets. Rather than have their companies broken up, they discovered the benefits of focusing back onto their core businesses.

Value-based planning

Faced with the threat from corporate raiders and the criticism of academics, chief executives of diversified companies focused on shareholder value. They wanted to do whatever would drive up the value of their shares and reduce the risk of a hostile takeover. Again, consultants came to the rescue and value-based planning techniques were born. These techniques viewed the business as a shareholder might. Managers were encouraged to invest only in businesses where doing so increased their value.[33] The idea of attractive businesses was retained – but taken back to its fundamentals. Any business was attractive, so long as it generated value for shareholders.

Value-based planning, like portfolio planning, offered corporate-level managers a means of evaluating many different businesses using a common framework. Attractive businesses were those that could deliver "economic value added" (a surrogate for share price gains). This provided corporate-level managers with a tool for portfolio planning and capital allocation.

Value-based planning was not just a way of selecting portfolios, it also came with a set of tools for managing businesses. Targets could be set on the basis of what would maximise shareholder return. The specific targets varied according to the particular models used. Some emphasised returns on capital employed above a cost of capital. Others emphasised cash generation. But all provided ways of setting targets, monitoring performance, designing incentive plans and educating managers in techniques that could be applied to a wide range of businesses. So, although value management originated as a way of measuring the attractiveness of a business, it rapidly developed into a more generalisable approach to managing large organisations. As such, value management contributed to both the portfolio planning and the professional management schools.

Value management techniques gained many adherents, especially among American corporations. In 1987, an article in *Fortune* described how "managements have caught the religion. At first reluctant, they pound at the door of consultants who can teach them the way to a higher stock price – a price so high it would thwart even the most determined raider."[34]

But value management also had limitations as a guide to corporate strategy. Like all financial tools, once the hurdle becomes clear, managers learn to manipulate the numbers so that future projects meet the hurdle. Also, it measures the outcome rather than the input. A higher stock price is a reward for creating value. But the key question remained. What sort of portfolios, managed in what sort of ways, would enable corporate-level managers to deliver superior performance?

With hindsight both portfolio matrices and shareholder value techniques were powerful tools for helping managers get out of the mess they had got themselves into. But they did not shine a light on where the real gold might lie.

The synergy school

The synergy school offered a very different approach to the previous two schools. It suggested that corporate strategy should be built round linkages between businesses. If one or more businesses in the portfolio has a common activity or skill, and the cost of the activity or skill is driven by scale, utilisation or learning effects, then there may be benefits to sharing these activities or skills across businesses.[35] Creating these benefits involves designing "linkages". The benefits themselves are "synergies".

The amount of value that can be created depends on the degree to which there are synergies from sharing activities or skills. This differs from the professional management school, which implies that the amount of value that can be created depends on the degree to which the management skills of corporate-level managers are greater than those of business-level managers.

Although the concept of synergy came to the fore in the 1990s, it has an older pedigree, dating back to Edith Penrose's *The Theory of the Growth of the Firm*.[36] Penrose, a Cambridge academic, saw two types of synergy: the sharing of indivisible resources (such as a large manufacturing facility) and the transfer of excess resources that are hard to trade (like excess management time). Igor Ansoff, often referred to as the father of strategic management, was the first author to work the synergy idea into a theory of corporate-level strategy. In his 1965 book, *Corporate Strategy*, he identifies four types of synergy. The first three (sales, operating and investment) relate to sharing parts of the value chain (sales, distribution, purchasing, production processes, plant and equipment and inventory).[37]

The fourth, managerial synergy, suggests that knowledge gained in one business by a management team can be applied to another business – assuming that the problems faced by the new business are similar to the ones faced in the core business.

The concept of synergy provides clear insights into what businesses should be in the portfolio – only those where there are synergies with other businesses. It also suggests how to manage the businesses – identify where the synergies are and design linkages to release them.

Stick to the knitting

The synergy school was given a boost in 1982 by Peters and Waterman's *In Search of Excellence*. It arose as the result of a study conducted at McKinsey as a counterbalance to the types of ideas being promoted by the professional management and portfolio planning schools. Successful corporations, these two McKinsey consultants observed, did not diversify widely. They tended to "stick to the knitting" – specialising in particular industries and focusing intently on improving their knowledge and skills in the areas they knew best. Managers should move away from their core business only if there are large synergies to be had from connecting with another business.[38]

Stick-to-the-knitting advice was in part a reaction against the analytical techniques and impersonal approaches of professional managers and the growing fields of strategic and portfolio planning. Bob Hayes and Bill Abernathy, two Harvard economists, also voiced this concern in their article "Managing Our Way to Economic Decline". In their view, too many American corporations were being run by "pseudo-professional" managers, skilled in finance and law, but lacking in technological expertise or in-depth experience in any particular industry. They warned that portfolios diversified across different industries and businesses were appropriate for fund managers, but not for corporations.[39]

The need for experience and deep knowledge of a business was also emphasised by Henry Mintzberg, a Canadian academic, who criticised the "thin and lifeless" strategies that result from treating businesses as mere positions on a portfolio matrix. He argued that, instead of broad diversity, we need "focused organisations that understand their missions, 'know' the people they serve, and excite the ones they employ; we should be encouraging 'thick' management, deep knowledge, healthy competition and authentic social responsibility".[40]

The widespread conviction that companies should stick to the knitting increased scepticism about the ability of corporations to manage and add value to diverse portfolios. It reinforced the practical pressures created by the corporate raiders and contributed to a wave of retrenching, refocusing and decluttering.

The case for synergy was powerfully made by Dick Rumelt, who showed that multi-business firms whose businesses were somewhat related, as defined by SIC codes, performed better than more diversified firms.[41] He argued that related diversification offered more opportunities for the corporate parent to add value to the businesses. In this way, managers stick to what they know well, and are most likely to be able to exploit synergies. However, some argued that SIC codes were not always a good way to define "relatedness".

Chris Zook, a Bain & Co. consultant, attempted to broaden the definition. He coined the term "adjacency" and argued that there are a large number of factors that can make a business adjacent: customers, products, channels, technologies, geographies, etc.[42] However, companies should step into adjacent areas carefully. Ideally companies should only take on one dimension of difference (customer or product or channel or technology or ...) each time they try a new business. If 90% of the new business is similar to existing businesses, the chances of synergy are much higher and the chances of misunderstandings and mistakes much lower.

Costas Markides and Peter Williamson also explored what defined "relatedness". They argued that the critical measure should be the degree to which businesses can share strategic assets such as brands, suppliers or market knowledge. Drawing on resource theory they argued that these strategic assets have to be valued by customers, rare, imperfectly tradable and costly to imitate.[43] Others have suggested that relatedness should be defined in cognitive terms.[44]

In other words, there have been a number of different attempts to clarify the synergy concept and make it practically useful to managers.

Problems with synergy

One challenge came from academics trying to copy Rumelt's research. Empirical evidence on the performance of companies pursuing more and less related strategies was ambiguous and contradictory. Many studies compared the performance of single-product firms, companies that diversify into related products, markets or technologies, and unrelated conglomerates, but no clear relationship between different diversification strategies and performance was confirmed.

Another challenge came from companies that appeared to stick to a related industry but still encountered significant problems. For example, during the 1980s, companies such as Prudential and Merrill Lynch sought to combine different types of financial services businesses. They discovered that businesses such as insurance, stockbroking and banking, though all in the financial services industry, nonetheless required very different approaches, resources and skills.

A third challenge came from the difficulty many companies had in realising synergies. As one observer commented, synergy benefits "... show an almost unshakeable resolve not to appear when it becomes time for their release".[45]

A fourth challenge came from a study of performance improvements following acquisitions. The researchers concluded that most improvements arise from asset disposals and restructuring rather than from synergies.[46]

A fifth challenge came from Marcus Alexander's "blockages" theory. Alexander, a consultant turned academic, proposed that most synergies happen quite naturally in the free market. The sorts of synergies that justify bringing two businesses under the same ownership are quite rare. These are synergies that can only be released as a result of common ownership: synergies that are "blocked" from occurring between independent companies. "Blocks" include things like laws, such as those against cartels or those that make it hard to share tax benefits, relationship difficulties or strategic differences between managers, skill deficiencies and institutional voids, such as a lack of an efficient capital market. As a result, many related businesses may be able to release synergies without common ownership.[47]

The return of synergy

Despite these problems, by the 1990s synergy became virtually synonymous with corporate-level strategy. Partly this was in response to the failure of diversified companies. Partly it was the result of the prescriptions of prominent academics. Michael Porter, the Harvard strategy guru, viewed the management of interrelationships between businesses as the essence of corporate-level strategy.[48]

Porter argued that diversification would succeed only if it added value to the acquired businesses. The most typical way of doing this was through two types of synergy. The first occurred when business units shared activities that were important sources of competitive advantage: Procter & Gamble's businesses shared a common distribution system and sales force; McKesson had a common warehousing system to serve markets ranging from pharmaceuticals to alcohol. The second type of synergy came from transferring skills between businesses – for example, PepsiCo's branding skills and 3M's technologies.[49]

Porter was not alone. Rosabeth Kanter, another Harvard guru, argued that synergy is the only justification for a multibusiness company.[50] And Friedrich Trautwein, a German academic, found that managers almost always justified diversification moves in terms of the synergies available. He also noted that most of the advice in the management literature on diversification was based on the concept of realising synergies.[51]

Core competences

Despite, or possibly because of, the difficulties managers were having building portfolios around synergies, the synergy school gained huge credibility with the publication, in the *Harvard Business Review*, of an article titled "The Core Competence of the Corporation" by Gary Hamel and C.K. Prahalad, academics from London and Michigan. They argued that the best multi-business companies have a core competence: an organisational skill that is important to the success of every business in the portfolio. This competence is nurtured by corporate-level managers and is present in every business team.

Core competences, they argued, are the glue behind successful multi-business groups. The added value comes from the superiority of the competence, which helps every business succeed. The company should enter businesses that can benefit from or help build the core competence. Corporate-level managers should run the company so as to nurture the core competence.

The corporate portfolio should not be perceived as a group of businesses, but as a collection of such competences. In managing the corporate portfolio, managers ensure that each part draws on and contributes to the core competences the company is seeking to build and exploit. Even a poorly performing business may be contributing to a core competence, and, if managers divest such a business or underinvest in it, they may be undermining some part of their core competences. Businesses that do not benefit from, or contribute to, the core competences should be sold.[52]

Following publication, managers leapt on the idea of core competences and launched many projects to identify their core competences. But after much effort, most companies found it hard to isolate these core competences or to guide their corporate strategies by this light. For example, Texas Instruments attempted to exploit the core competence it had developed in its semiconductors business in areas such as calculators, watches and home computers. It failed in these new areas because its top management had no experience in managing such consumer-oriented businesses.[53] Similarly, Procter & Gamble applied its skills in product innovation and consumer promotion to a soft drinks business, Crush, but eventually divested the business because it ran into unfamiliar problems managing the local bottlers who largely control distribution of soft drinks.[54]

The capital markets school

While academics and consultants were developing different schools of thought about which businesses to buy and how to own them, practitioners were developing their own ideas in parallel. Many managers focused not just on professional management, attractive businesses and generating synergies but also considered whether some businesses could be purchased for a particularly low price, or sold for a particularly high one.

The logic was that capital markets did not always price businesses correctly, creating arbitrage opportunities. For example, James Hanson of Hanson Trust based his corporate strategy partly on buying businesses at a competitive price. One of his most impressive takeovers was that of Imperial Tobacco Group in 1986. Hanson paid £2.5 billion for the group, sold a number of businesses for £2.3 billion, leaving him with the highly profitable tobacco business at a cost of £200 million. Hanson avoided overpaying for acquisitions by identifying "downside risks" that might result in overestimation of the value. Hanson was also willing to sell any business if another company offered him more than it was worth under Hanson ownership. In summary, Hanson was constantly looking for opportunities to take advantage of vagaries in capital markets – buying cheaply, or selling at a high price.

More recently, private equity companies spend considerable time evaluating the price at which they can sell a business. While they do not necessarily look to buy cheaply, they are careful to ensure that they will be able to sell at an attractive multiple. This involves thinking about who might buy, how many buyers there would be, how they would value the business and what prospects the current acquisition target has of being in adequate shape to sell in a few years.

Unlike the previous three schools, few academics or consultants considered this way of thinking a valid approach to corporate strategy. Finance academics tended to espouse the efficient markets hypothesis which proposed that stock prices fully reflected the implications of all publicly available information. This still left the opportunity for those with unique information to spot arbitrage opportunities, but this was difficult to research. Finance academics also tended to research capital markets about which there was lots of information – which were typically US capital markets, where the efficient markets hypothesis was most likely to apply. Testing the idea that, for example, small companies sometimes traded at prices below the value of their future cash flows was very difficult to do – and so received limited attention.

Similarly, the high profile strategy consultants such as BCG or McKinsey, who did much to develop thinking about corporate strategy, tended to believe that shareholder value was driven by the strategies they espoused rather than by anomalies in capital markets. Specialists in value management might have been expected to include arbitrage opportunities as one way to generate shareholder value. However, they tended to espouse the efficient market hypothesis – perhaps partly because this validated their argument that it was possible to predict how management action would lead to changes in share prices.

The investment banks, who might have been interested in developing such theories, tended not to publish them if they had them. Arbitraging capital markets remained something many corporate managers thought they did – but there was limited investigation of whether it was a credible strategy.

One person in particular has brought the idea of arbitraging capital markets as part of corporate strategy to the fore. Warren Buffett's investment strategy has been immensely successful and rests partly on acquiring businesses cheaply. His strategy is based on two assumptions. First, that markets are sometimes overheated (and expensive) and sometimes fearful (and cheap). This is captured in one of his famous mantras – that investors "should try to be fearful when others are greedy and greedy only when others are fearful". Another component of his investment strategy is that stock prices may not fully reflect the long-term value of certain sources of advantage – such as a strong brand in a mature market.

Towards a synthesis

Many of the ideas, practitioners, strategies, researchers and writers previously mentioned can be located broadly in one or other of the four schools. This is perhaps a surprise, as the various viewpoints on what corporate strategy should focus on are not necessarily exclusive. It should be possible to improve business unit performance with a mix of professional management skills *and* synergies. Warren Buffett's success suggests that it is possible to invest in attractive businesses *and* buy them at low prices.

Some have come close to a more integrated perspective – without fully developing the idea. For example, Ansoff's original definition of synergy included both the linkages between businesses and the application of knowledge gained in one business and applied by headquarters managers to another – but this was not developed to consider how a corporate team might develop superior skills and apply them to a range of businesses.

Michael Porter, who emphasised synergies as the basis for most good corporate strategies, noted that restructuring was an alternative – highlighting Hanson Trust as an example. Hanson focused on improving performance in mature businesses. Indeed, part of Hanson's strategy was to avoid any attempt to manage linkages from the corporate level. However, Porter treated restructuring as a special case and it was the only example he identified that fits the professional management school.

Dominant logic and management style

The idea of "dominant logic", proposed by C.K. Prahalad and Richard Bettis, offers one way to integrate the various logics. They argue that "The dominant logic is the lens through which managers see all emerging opportunities (options) for the firm."[55] It is also the lens that guides their management behaviour. For example, managers may believe that success comes from high margins gained by offering customers high service levels. If this "dominant logic" fits the businesses in the portfolio it is likely to add value. The whole is likely to be more than the sum of the parts. But where the dominant logic does not fit the business, the influence from the corporate level can subtract value. Corporate-level managers may push businesses into adding service features that customers do not want, or raising prices to levels that customers are not prepared to pay.

In this view, the dominant logic or management style of the corporate management group is central to the performance of a multi-business firm, and a group of businesses is best managed when the dominant logic of top managers matches the strategic characteristics and requirements of the businesses.

Dominant logic may help explain why some diversification can succeed, and also why many diversification strategies, even those based on synergies, can fail. For example, businesses with opportunities for sharing activities or skills may nonetheless have different dominant logics. Vertical integration is a classic example. Upstream businesses, like farming, typically have different logics (different business models) to midstream businesses, like food manufacturing, which also have different logics to downstream businesses, like food retailing. This can make it difficult for corporate-level managers to realise synergies by vertical integration without risking significant subtracted value.

While the dominant logic concept seemed to explain many experiences, it was hard to apply in a particular company. Managers found it difficult to identify their dominant logic in a way that helped them make decisions. Also, managers were uncomfortable with a concept that appeared to limit their capacity to change. As a result, despite its promise, it never evolved into a professional management technique.

Resource theory

Another promising viewpoint, which integrates the professional management and synergy schools, is the resource-based view of strategy – developed during the 1980s. This theory proposes that it is the unique "resources" owned by companies that provide the basis for competitive advantage.[56] These resources can be physical assets (such as a global network of warehouses), intangible assets (such as a brand) or capabilities (such as a professional management process). Valuable resources are those that are important, superior to competitors, hard to copy or substitute, long lasting and controlled by the company rather than by other parties such as its employees or suppliers. In many cases, resources that meet these tests are the intangible assets or the capabilities, rather than the physical assets which can often be replicated.

David Collis and Cynthia Montgomery, two Harvard professors, brought resource theory to a more managerial audience in the 1990s. Resources, they argued, are the source of competitive advantage for any business unit. They can also be the basis for a corporate-level strategy when the resources can be applied to multiple businesses. Some of these resources are valuable because they create synergies between businesses – for example, a corporate brand, a logistics network, shared research and development, or centralised training and development. But, there are also capabilities that are held by a corporate management team who then apply them to various businesses that are otherwise left to operate autonomously. For example, they describe Cooper Industries, a diversified manufacturer, which created a manufacturing services group, to spread best manufacturing practices across the company. This fits the prescriptions of the professional management school.[57]

Markides and Williamson, mentioned earlier, also use resource theory to blur the boundaries between the professional management and synergy schools. Their view is that a successful corporate strategy is one that allows the different businesses to share a strategic asset – but the definition of a strategic asset is rather broad. For example, Markides describes Boddington, a regional UK brewer, as being successful because its strategic asset was that it excelled at running pubs – a mix of synergies (for example, in purchasing) and professional management skills (corporate managers have superior management skills to individual pub managers).[58]

Resource theory thus offers the basis for a synthesis of two schools of corporate strategy. However, it has never really developed to be used by managers and corporate strategists.

Parenting advantage and adding value

A further contribution was made by Michael Goold and Andrew Campbell in their book, *Strategies and Styles*. They examined a number of different corporate organisations and suggested that their management approach fell into three groups. "Financial Control" companies, such as Hanson Trust or BTR followed an approach consistent with the professional school – using a standard set of financial metrics, processes and associated HR systems to manage business units in a common fashion. Financial Control parents typically did not seek to extract synergies from the businesses they owned. "Strategic Planning" companies, on the other hand, worked closely with business unit managers on the long-term strategy of each business, including the search for synergies. A third style, "Strategic Control", fell between these two more extreme models, and could include elements of both the professional management and synergy schools. The implication is that corporate managers could and did utilise the ideas of both schools – sometimes leaning more towards the prescriptions of one school but frequently mixing the two.[59] This approach provided a way of integrating the insights from both schools, but implied that there were only three primary styles, and in fact two of them were extremes. This did not provide many options for corporate managers to choose between.

These two authors, joined by Marcus Alexander, developed these ideas into the concept of "parenting advantage" – that the goal of any corporate organisation should be to add more value to its businesses than any other owner. Value can be added by a variety of approaches – thus bringing together the ideas of different schools. For example, ABB generated synergies by integrating small companies into a global network, and applied professional management techniques, such as a ruthless approach to cutting overhead costs.[60] Goold et al. also focused on the issue of subtracted value, mirroring concerns raised by Prahalad's concept of dominant logic and Zook's concept of adjacency, and by researchers who had observed the many ways in which multi-nationals failed to generate the performance levels they expected from their strategies.

The idea of "parenting" to "add value" pulls together the approaches by the professional management and synergy schools. However, it does not integrate the ideas of the other two schools. Adding value implies that managers should not worry about the underlying attractiveness of their businesses. In practice corporate managers spend a lot of time seeking attractive industries or niches where they can invest. Those who are successful in developing attractive businesses can generate significant value for shareholders even if they are not the best parents of the businesses.

A recent survey indicated that while parenting advantage is a widely used concept, it is competing with a number of the concepts developed by the portfolio management school – such as competitive advantage, industry profitability and value management.[61] It appears that, at least from the point of view of practitioners, parenting advantage is part of the answer, but not all of it.

Goold et al. also largely ignored the arbitrage opportunities offered by capital markets inefficiencies.

Practitioners

While there have been some attempts to develop more integrated theories about corporate strategy, practitioners have been combining these different approaches to corporate strategy and putting them into practice.

We have already mentioned Warren Buffett. Berkshire Hathaway's corporate strategy is based partly on buying attractive businesses – for example, companies with strong consumer brands in relatively mature markets. It also creates value by arbitraging capital markets. For example, Buffett waits to buy an attractive business at a point when it is undervalued. He also invests in insurance companies which provides him access to low cost capital and buys low beta stocks, which have historically been undervalued by capital markets.[62]

Since the 1990s, private equity has provided a highly successful new model for strategists to evaluate. Given the booms and busts within private equity, opinion varies on whether private equity offers significant lessons for the long term. Some argue that private equity has thrived primarily because of temporary advantages, such as a lower tax rates. However, where it has succeeded, private equity is best explained by a mix of the four schools.

Private equity firms buy to sell. They acquire good businesses that can be made more attractive (portfolio planning school) and drive improvements largely through a combination of target setting and incentives (professional management school). Some have argued that the only management skill that private equity brings is financial engineering – replacing equity with mezzanine debt. Even if this is true, it is still a professional management skill that is applicable to any business that does not have a well-designed financial structure.

Private equity companies are very concerned to buy businesses which can be sold at a high multiple in a few years – for example, because there are a number of potential well-funded acquirers. They also exploited the market for cheap debt especially in the early 2000s (capital markets school).

Private equity firms rarely make any attempt to generate synergies among their portfolio companies. But they do create synergies within a portfolio company through bolt-on acquisitions (synergies school).

International strategy

In this review of thinking on corporate-level strategy, we have not included work by academics and consultants whose primary focus is international strategy. This is because much of the work on international strategy is focused at the business level rather than at the corporate level. However, the reverse is also true. It is possible to see international strategy as almost completely overlapping with and hence a special case of corporate-level strategy: the issue is the choice of countries and how to manage them rather than the choice of businesses and how to manage them.

Rather than extend this chapter to cover international strategy ideas, we address them in the Appendix. There we show how the two sets of ideas have evolved in parallel and where each can contribute something to the other.

Conclusions

Corporate strategy seeks to answer two questions: Which businesses should be owned, and how should they be managed for maximum performance? Thinking in the past has been influenced by four broad schools of thought, each of which offers valuable insights into what makes for a successful corporate strategy. The writers and researchers in one school often ignore or understate the insights of the others – although some have suggested how these four perspectives might be more integrated or used together.

The three logics, we argue, build on and expand the insights of the four "schools". They offer three ways in which corporate strategy can be evaluated and developed.

The proposition that corporate groups need to add value through some combination of professional management skills, specialist skills tailored to a sector or type of business and linkages that create synergies is not disputed. Since Ansoff, managers in corporate-level jobs have been searching for the best ways to add value. This proposition is our "added value logic". It combines the insights from both the professional management and the synergy schools and adds in the observation that corporate headquarters frequently subtracts value.

The proposition that it is preferable to own attractive businesses that have competitive advantage in profitable markets is also not disputed. Owning a portfolio that allows you to make significant investments into growing businesses that offer high returns is clearly better than the alternative. This proposition is our "business logic". It derives from the portfolio planning school and the excellent work consultants and academics have done to understand what drives high profitability.

The proposition that capital markets offer opportunities for value-creating arbitrage is less broadly supported by research and more debated – but we know that it plays a role in many corporate strategies. While some still argue that capital markets are efficient, the roller coaster ride through the late 1990s and first 10 years of the twenty-first century has laid the capital market's strengths and weaknesses on the table. It has also led to new theories about the behavioural dimension of capital markets, which explain why the market can overvalue and undervalue companies. These theories are the basis of our "capital markets logic". Companies, we argue, need to take into account the state of the capital markets when they are developing corporate-level strategies.

What follows therefore is built on solid ground. It has been hard earned from 50 years of experience, driven by theory and by trial and error. We now believe we know the core principles that managers should use to drive their corporate-level strategies.

Notes

[1] This chapter draws heavily on Michael Goold and Kathleen Luchs, "Why Diversify? Four Decades of Management Thinking", *Academy of Management Executive*, Vol. 7, No. 3, 1993. Many passages are taken verbatim from this article, although they are not indicated by quotation marks.

[2] Kenneth R. Andrews, "Product Diversification and the Public Interest", *Harvard Business Review*, July 1951, 91–107; "Toward Professionalism in Business Management", *Harvard Business Review*, March–April 1969, 49.60.

[3] Peter Drucker, *The Practice of Management* (New York, 1955; reissued Pan Books, 1968), 21.

[4] Robert L. Katz, "Skills of an Effective Administrator", *Harvard Business Review*, January–February 1955, 37.

[5] David N. Judelson, "The Conglomerate-Corporate Form of the Future", *Michigan Business Review*, July 1969, 8–12; reprinted in John W. Bonge and Bruce P. Coleman, *Concepts for Corporate Strategy* (New York, NY: Macmillan, 1972), 458.

[6] Harold Geneen, with Alvin Moscow, *Managing* (New York, NY: Doubleday, 1984).

[7] Norman Berg, "Textron, Inc.", HBS Case Study, 373–387, 1973, 16.

[8] Kenneth R. Andrews, "Product Diversification and the Public Interest", *Harvard Business Review*, July 1951, 98.

[9] Robert S. Attiyeh, "Where Next for Conglomerates?" *Business Horizons*, December 1969, 39–44; reprinted in John W. Bonge and Bruce P. Coleman, *Concepts for Corporate Strategy* (New York, NY: Macmillan, 1972); Geneen, op. cit., 43.

[10] Peter Drucker, "Long-Range Planning: Challenge to Management Science", *Management Science*, Vol. 5, No. 3, 1959, 238–249; Igor Ansoff, *Corporate Strategy* (New York: McGraw-Hill, 1965); Alfred P. Sloan, *My Years with General Motors* (New York: Doubleday, 1963) (reissued by Penguin Books, 1986); Alfred D. Chandler, Jr., *Strategy and Structure* (Cambridge: MIT, 1962) (reissued 1982); Myles L. Mace, "The President and Corporate Planning", *Harvard Business Review*, January–February 1965, 49–62.

[11] C. Roland Christensen and others, *Business Policy: Text and Cases* (Richard D. Irwin, 1965).

[12] R.F. Vancil and P. Lorange, "Strategic Planning in Diversified Companies", *Harvard Business Review*, January–February 1975, 81–90; Peter Lorange and Richard F. Vancil, *Strategic Planning Systems* (New Jersey: Prentice-Hall, 1977); K.A. Ringbakk, "Organized Planning in Major U.S. Companies", *Long Range Planning*, Vol. 2, No. 2, December 1969, 46–57; Norman A. Berg, "Strategic Planning in Conglomerate Companies", *Harvard Business Review*, May–June 1965, 79–92.

[13] Louis V. Gerstner, "Can Strategic Management Pay Off?" *Business Horizons*, Vol. 15, No. 6, December 1972, 5.

[14] Joseph L. Bower, *Managing the Resource Allocation Process* (Harvard Business School Press, 1970), Harvard Business School Classics Edition, 1986.

[15] C.W. Stern and M.S. Deimler, eds, *The Boston Consulting Group on Strategy* (Wiley: New Jersey, 2006), 12–14, copied from a BCG Perspective, Bruce Henderson, 1973.

[16] Stern and Deimler, op. cit., 35–37, BCG Perspective, Bruce Henderson, 1970.

[17] Richard G. Hamermesh, *Making Strategy Work* (New York: John Wiley & Sons, 1986).

[18] Stern and Deimler, op. cit., 48–51, BCG Perspective, Business Environments, Michael Goold, 1979.

[19] Robert Buzzell and Bradley Gale, *The PIMS Principle: Linking Strategy to Performance* (The Free Press, 1987).

[20] Stern and Deimler, op. cit., 56–59, BCG Perspective, Business Environments, Dick Lockeridge, 1981.

[21] Walter Kiechel III, *The Lords of Strategy* (Harvard Business Press: Boston, 2010).

[22] Michael Porter, "The Five Competitive Forces that Shape Strategy", *Harvard Business Review*, January 2008, 79–93.

[23] https://www.mckinseyquarterly.com/wrapper.aspx?ar=2198&story=true&url=http%3a%2f%2fwww.mckinseyquarterly.com%2fEnduring_ideas_The_GE-McKinsey_nine-box_matrix_2198%3fpagenum%3d1%23interactive_ninebox&pgn=frameworks_ninebox

[24] Michael Porter published his two seminal books, *Competitive Strategy* and *Competitive Advantage* in 1980 and 1985, respectively. They came after both the BCG and McKinsey matrixes, but developed the concepts of these two strategy tools to a much greater level of detail and rigour. *Competitive Strategy* showed how industry structure (the five forces) influenced industry profitability. *Competitive Advantage* codified and developed much of the thinking about this topic that firms such as BCG had developed in the 1970s, and formalised the idea of the value chain as a way of analysing competitive advantage.

[25] Ulrich Pidun, Harald Rubner, Matthias Kruehler, Robert Untiedt and Michael Nippa, "Corporate Portfolio Management: Theory and Practice", *Journal of Applied Corporate Finance*, Vol. 23, No. 1, Winter 2011, 63–76.

[26] Richard G. Hamermesh, *Making Strategy Work* (New York: John Wiley & Sons, 1986).

[27] Philippe Haspeslagh, "Portfolio Planning: Uses and Limits", *Harvard Business Review*, January–February 1982, 58–73.

[28] Richard A. Bettis and William K. Hall, "The Business Portfolio Approach – Where It Falls Down in Practice", *Long Range Planning*, Vol. 16, No. 2, April 1983, 95–104.

[29] Haspeslagh, op. cit.

[30] Richard G. Hamermesh and Roderick E. White, "Manage Beyond Portfolio Analysis", *Harvard Business Review*, January–February 1984, 103–109.

[31] Rosabeth Moss Kanter, *When Giants Learn to Dance* (London: Simon & Schuster, 1989), 94; Thomas More, "Goodbye, Corporate Staff", *Fortune*, December 21, 1987.

[32] C. Markides, "Corporate Refocusing", *Business Strategy Review*, Spring 1993, Vol. 4, No. 1, 1–15.

[33] Alfred Rappaport, *Creating Shareholder Value: The New Standard for Business Performance* (New York, NY: Free Press, 1986);Bernard C. Reimann, *Managing for Value* (Oxford: Basil Blackwell, 1987).

[34] John J. Curran, "Are Stocks Too High?", *Fortune*, September 28, 1987, 24.

[35] Michael Porter, *Competitive Advantage* (New York: The Free Press, 1985), 328.

[36] Edith Penrose, *The Theory of the Growth of the Firm* (New York: John Wiley and Sons, 1959).

[37] Igor Ansofff, *Corporate Strategy* (New York, NY: McGraw-Hill, 1965).

[38] Thomas J. Peters and Robert H. Waterman, *In Search of Excellence* (New York, NY: Free Press, 1982).

[39] Bob Hayes and Bill Abernathy, "Managing Our Way to Economic Decline", *Harvard Business Review*, July–August 1980, 67–77.

[40] Henry Mintzberg, *Mintzberg on Management* (New York, NY: Free Press, 1989), 373.

[41] Richard Rumelt, "Strategy, Structure and Economic Performance", Division of Research, Graduate School of Business Administration, Harvard University, 1974.

[42] Chris Zook, *Profit from the Core* (Boston, MA: Harvard Business School Press, 2001).

[43] C. Markides and P. Williamson, "Corporate Diversification and Organisational Structure: A Resource Based View", *Academy of Management Journal*, 1996, Vol. 39, No. 2, 340–367.

[44] D. Collis and C. Montgomery, *Corporate Strategy: Resources and the Scope of the Firm* (Burr Ridge, IL: Irwin, 1996).

[45] Richard Reed and George A. Luffman, "Diversification: the Growing Confusion", *Strategic Management Journal*, Vol. 7, 1986, 34.

[46] S. Chatterjee, "Sources of Value in Takeovers: Synergy or Restructuring", *Strategic Management Journal*, Vol. 13, No. 4, May 1992, 267–286.

[47] M. Goold, A. Campbell and M. Alexander, *Corporate-Level Strategy* (Wiley: New York, 1994). The blockage ideas were further developed in A. Campbell and M. Goold, *Synergy* (Persus Books, 1998).

[48] Michael E. Porter, *Competitive Advantage* (New York, NY: Free Press, 1985).

[49] From Michael E. Porter, "Competitive Advantage to Corporate Strategy", *Harvard Business Review*, May 1987.

[50] Kanter, op. cit., 90.

[51] Frederich Trautwin, "Merger Motives and Merger Prescriptions", *Strategic Management Journal*, Vol. 11, 1990, 283–295.

[52] C.K. Prahalad, and Gary Hamel, "The Core Competence of the Corporation", *Harvard Business Review*, May–June 1989, 63–76.

[53] C.K. Prahalad and R.A. Bettis, "The Dominant Logic: A New Linkage between Diversity and Performance", *Strategic Management Journal*, Vol. 7, 1986, 495.

[54] Patricia Winters, "Crush Fails to Fit on P&G Shelf", *Advertising Age*, July 10, 1989.

[55] C.K. Prahalad, "The Blinders of Dominant Logic", *Long Range Planning*, Vol. 37, 2004, 171–179.

[56] Robert M. Grant, "The Resource-Based Theory of Competitive Advantage: Implications for Strategy Formulation", *California Management Review*, Spring 1991, 114–135.

[57] David Collis and Cynthia Montgomery, "Competing on Resources: Strategy in the 1990s", *Harvard Business Review*, Vol. 73, No. 4, July–August 1995, 118–128.

[58] C. Markides, "To Diversify or Not to Diversify", *Harvard Business Review*, November–December 1997, 93–99.

[59] M. Goold and A. Campbell, *Strategies and Styles* (Oxford: Basil Blackwell, 1987).

[60] Goold, Campbell and Alexander, op. cit.

[61] Pidun et al., op. cit.

[62] The Secrets of Buffett's Success, *The Economist*, September 29, 2012.

PART II

PORTFOLIO STRATEGY: WHERE TO INVEST AND WHAT TO AVOID

CHAPTER THREE

HOW TO FIND GOOD BUSINESSES AND AVOID BAD BUSINESSES

As explained in Chapter 2, the consultants BCG showed that the best businesses to own are those with high relative market share: these businesses typically earn higher margins than competitors; they have competitive advantage. When these businesses are growing they can often fund their growth out of retained profits. When they mature, they generate large amounts of free cash flow. BCG went on to show that relative market share is only one way to earn higher margins, other factors such as technology or location can give competitive advantage and so drive attractive margins.

Another dimension that leads to attractive profits is the appeal of the market. Michael Porter, the Harvard Business School strategy guru, developed the five-forces framework to help identify attractive markets. The five factors that determine the average profitability of a group of competitors in a market are competitive rivalry, the power of customers to bargain down prices, the constraint that substitute products place on price levels, the power of suppliers to bargain down margins by pushing up costs and the threat that new entrants pose to the price structure of the market.[1]

By combining market attractiveness and competitive advantage, it is possible to create a framework for assessing business attractiveness. Of course, the attractiveness of a particular business to a particular company may be influenced by more factors than the average profitability of the market and the competitive advantage that the business has in the market. Growth is typically an important factor to most management teams. Size of the market is typically another factor. But the overall message of business logic is that it is better to own attractive businesses than unattractive businesses. Attractive businesses earn higher margins, generate more cash flow, offer more opportunities for growth and suffer less during downturns.

The Haniel Group in Germany is a family-owned company with over 50,000 employees. It operates in businesses ranging from trading and recycling of raw materials for the stainless steel industry through to hypermarkets. Included in the public description of its "group strategy" is the following: "All divisions operate within the trade and services industries – yet their business models are very different. Even in terms of customer groups, there are hardly any overlaps … Markets with above-average opportunities for growth in which the Corporate Divisions can take up a leading position are attractive for Haniel[2] … Responsibility for the operating business rests with the five divisions, all of which occupy market-leading positions."[3]

In other words, Haniel seeks to invest in businesses which are leaders in their segments, and operate in markets with high growth opportunities. Haniel does not specify a focus beyond that of "trade and services". Haniel leaves the businesses to operate in a highly autonomous fashion, without significant involvement from the corporate centre. Indeed, the corporate team is very small. Its main responsibilities are split between a finance manager and the chairman of the management board, who is also head of HR and Strategy. Reporting to him are functions for Corporate Development/M & A, Corporate Communications, Internal Audit, Shareholders and Sustainability (including Corporate Responsibility) and Corporate Legal. Because the corporate centre does not have much involvement with the businesses, it may not even fully own them. For example, one of its businesses, Metro, is a publicly quoted retailer in which Haniel holds a significant share.

Haniel is an example of a company driven mainly by business logic. The goal is to own attractive businesses. This involves:

- Acquiring and supporting the strategies of attractive businesses. Haniel invests in "Markets with above-average opportunities for growth" – for example, businesses with opportunities to expand into Eastern Europe and Asia.
- Investing in businesses with unattractive competitive positions, if the management team in the business is able to turn the business around. For example, Haniel entered the German pharmaceutical wholesaling business in the early 1980s. However, the pharma business became increasingly global, threatening the position of national wholesalers. At that point, Haniel could have divested the business. Instead, it decided to back the strategy of the management team, which was to build a leading position in the European pharmaceutical wholesaling industry, by acquiring and merging with other businesses.
- Disposing of, or liquidating, businesses that are unattractive, and where the management team in the business does not have a viable plan to make the business attractive. Over the years, Haniel has divested itself of many businesses. For example, in 2006 it divested itself of Belfor, the global leader in restoration of properties that have suffered fire and flood damage. The business generated a pre-tax profit of only 34 million euros on turnover of 673 million euros with a workforce of 3000.

A company that uses only business logic to guide its strategy is often referred to as a holding company or investment company. Its main role is to decide which businesses to hold, which to divest and in which to invest. It is like an active fund manager that acquires a controlling share of its investments. One of the most consistently successful companies of all time, Berkshire Hathaway run by Warren Buffet, is heavily driven by business logic. The importance of investing in good businesses is illustrated by his comment that, "It's far better to buy a wonderful company at a fair price than a fair company at a wonderful price." Another quote describes his views about unattractive businesses: "When a management with a reputation for brilliance tackles a business with a reputation for bad economics, it is the reputation of the business that remains intact."[4]

Since future returns are heavily influenced by the attractiveness of the businesses in a corporate portfolio, most companies use business logic, at least in part, to guide their corporate strategy. In the rest of this chapter, we will describe the tool that strategists can use to assess business attractiveness and we will discuss some of the challenges of using this tool.

The tool is a matrix that has two axes: market profitability and competitive advantage.

Market profitability

Market profitability is one dimension of business attractiveness. It varies widely across different markets and different industries (see Figure 3.1 – note, we generally use the term "markets", but "industries" is also often used). In a more profitable market it is easier to earn high returns on both existing capital and incremental investments. If a company has a range of businesses it can invest in, it will generate better returns if it chooses to invest in those that are in more profitable markets – all else being equal.

For example, in 2009 the CEO of Hamworthy, a manufacturer of pumps and gas systems for ships, was under pressure.

Figure 3.1: Differences in market or industry profitability

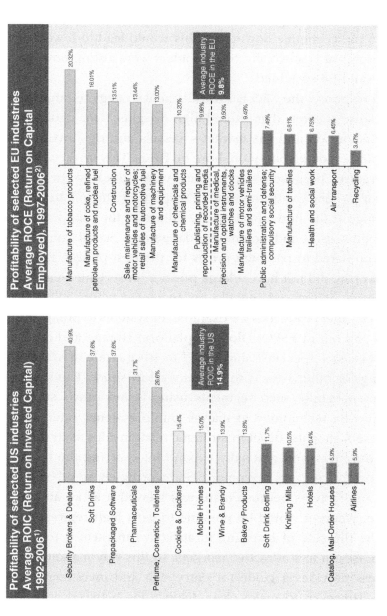

Sources:1) Porter, HBR, January 2008; 2) ESMT analysis Burger, Rocholl

Sales and profits were at record highs, but ship builders, which were the core customers for Hamworthy's four business divisions, were expected to reduce their production significantly due to the economic downturn. This would lead to lower sales and profits at Hamworthy. Shareholders were asking how earnings could be sustained.

In response, the CEO launched a new strategy to target new "specialist" markets that offered high margins.[5] One choice was the offshore oil and gas market – vessels and rigs involved in pumping crude oil out of offshore oil fields. This market offered high returns because pump systems were critical to the operation of drilling platforms and transporting the oil to shore. Shutting off the flow of oil due to failure of the pump systems was both costly and potentially dangerous. So oil companies were prepared to pay high prices for the best pumps. Because Hamworthy did not have a large position in serving oil and gas customers, it focused initially on segments where it had the most credible products – for example, in systems to pump crude oil in and out of FSPOs (floating platform storage and offloading vessels) – specialist ships used to store crude at sea while waiting for other vessels to take the oil to shore. The strategy was to penetrate such segments using Hamworthy's superior and proven technology in marine pump systems, build share in these segments, develop stronger relationships with oil and gas customers, and gradually expand into serving the broader needs of oil and gas customers. Hamworthy chose oil and gas pumping systems because managers viewed it as an attractive market where it would be possible to earn high returns.

The flip side of investing in attractive markets is to divest businesses in less attractive markets. In this way market attractiveness provides a guide for entry, exit and investment decisions. However, to make clear distinctions between attractive and unattractive markets it is necessary to have a clear dividing line. This is the cost of capital.

A market where the average competitor earns a return on capital for new investments that is less than the cost of capital is unattractive. A market where the average competitor earns a return on capital on new investments that is more than the cost of capital is attractive. A market where the average competitor earns around the cost of capital is somewhere between the two.

The airline industry is an example of an unattractive market (as shown in Figure 3.1). Warren Buffett eloquently points this out:

> If a capitalist had been present at Kitty Hawk back in the early 1900s, he should have shot Orville Wright. He would have saved his progeny money. But seriously, the airline business has been extraordinary. It has eaten up capital over the past century like almost no other business because people seem to keep coming back to it and putting fresh money in. You've got huge fixed costs, you've got strong labor unions, and you've got commodity pricing. That is not a great recipe for success. I have an 800 number now that I call if I get the urge to buy an airline stock. I call at two in the morning and I say: "My name is Warren, and I'm an aeroholic." And then they talk me down.[6]

Like the airline industry, the pharma industry also has huge fixed costs, but its products are highly differentiated. Most drugs target a particular condition or disease – greatly reducing or eliminating the competition between different drugs. The health benefits from the drug are highly valued by doctors and patients alike. Companies with valued drugs are able to charge very high prices – so long as the unique characteristics of each drug can be protected through patents. As a result, average returns are high – over 30% for US pharma companies over a recent 15-year period, versus 6% for airlines.

Competitive advantage

Companies within the same market perform very differently. Even the airline business has higher performing companies, such as Southwest Airlines and Ryanair. For example, in the mid-1990s Southwest Airlines made an average return on invested capital of about 12% versus the industry average of 6%. In pharmaceuticals, Glaxo Wellcome made a return of over 50% versus the pharmaceutical average of about 30%.[7] Despite the extremes of airlines versus pharmaceuticals, many studies have indicated that the differences in profitability between competitors in a market are more significant than the differences between markets.[8]

Differences in performance are due to advantages that some businesses have over their competitors. For example, Hamworthy aimed to have businesses with superior technology. They competed primarily in markets where performance was more important to customers than price. In these markets, the business with the best technology would be likely to win the contract even if its prices were higher than competitors. Following this strategy, Hamworthy focused on making acquisitions of businesses with special technology. For example, they acquired businesses specialising in ship design and ballast water treatment.[9]

Part of the advantage that a business has resides in its management team. In the case of Hamworthy, it lacked certain key skills – particularly in oil and gas and in China – both important markets. In response it hired in new managers. Hiring new managers at Hamworthy was aimed at filling gaps – but at some companies it is absolutely core to the success of the strategy. An example was at Egg, an internet banking venture. The manager hired to run Egg was Mike Harris, who had previously started up First Direct, the UK's first telephone banking operation. He and the team he gathered around him were head and shoulders above the management teams of the other internet banks at that time.[10]

Competitive advantage, whether it comes from technology, market share, the management team or any of a wide range of sources, translates into either lower operating costs or higher prices or lower capital costs or all three. Hence, we can measure relative competitive advantage by measuring relative returns on capital employed.[11] We have to be careful with these measurements because they can be clouded by historic accounting policies. Ideally, we want to compare returns on capital using replacement cost accounting to ensure we are comparing apples with apples. But, often, at least initially, we have to make do with data that companies report to stock exchanges and governments. When we have the relevant data, we can judge whether the business has significantly higher returns, about the same level of return or significantly lower returns compared to the average in its market.

The Business Attractiveness matrix (Figure 3.2) is used to display both average market profitability and relative competitive

Figure 3.2: The Business Attractiveness matrix

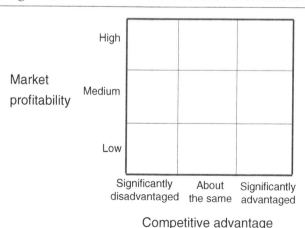

advantage. A business that falls in the top right corner is in an attractive market, like pharmaceuticals, and has a significant competitive advantage, like Glaxo Wellcome. From the perspective of a long-term investor, this is an ideal business to own: it is likely to produce good returns for many years, unless there are major changes in the market or competitive situation. Of course, as we know, there were big changes in both these dimensions in the first 10 years of the twenty-first century. This made it difficult for Glaxo Wellcome (now GlaxoSmithKline) to deliver the performance that was expected.

A business that falls in the bottom left corner is in an unattractive market, like airlines, and has a weak competitive position, like Alitalia. From the perspective of a long-term investor, it is a bad business to own. It is likely to produce losses and demand additional capital to maintain its business – a problem that Warren Buffet spotted.

Businesses in the middle boxes have differing degrees of market profitability and competitive advantage. In most cases, if the business is to the right of the middle diagonal, it is attractive: owners are likely to get above average returns. If it is to the left of the middle diagonal, it is unattractive: owners are likely to get below average returns. However, each business in these middle boxes needs to be analysed carefully before judgements are made.

Figure 3.3 positions some of the Hamworthy businesses on this matrix.

For Hamworthy, the vertical axis represents the average profitability of all competitors in the market segment that each business competes in; so it is different for each business. It is important to focus on the segment rather than the entire market – because profitability can vary widely across different segments. One of Hamworthy's core businesses was providing specialist marine pump systems for use in ships. Barriers to entry were high, with several specialised niches in which only a few suppliers had the necessary technology and track record to be credible. During the boom in building new ships, returns were healthy, although not spectacular, because the buyers – ship builders and the future owners of those ships – were large, powerful and hard negotiators.

Figure 3.3: Business Attractiveness matrix for Hamworthy

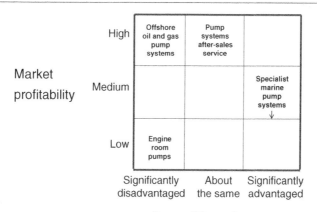

However, in 2009 this market was in a cyclical downturn where all competitors were feeling the squeeze. New orders were less than half the level they had been at the peak in 2007. Buyers were often able to negotiate lower prices than in the past. Hence, average profitability for all competitors had fallen somewhat and was heading further down as the market contracted. Overall, this business is aligned to the middle of the vertical axis, with a downwards arrow indicating the negative trend in average profitability.

Other segments offered higher profitability. The supply of pump systems after-sales service was a more profitable and stable business than the sale of new pumps – particularly during a downturn in the shipping market. The offshore oil and gas sector was booming and also offered higher average returns.

Some segments had lower average margins. For example, a portion of Hamworthy's business consisted of supplying relatively unspecialised engine room pumps used to pump bilge water or other basic liquids. There were many potential suppliers for these pumps. Because of their commodity nature, competition for orders was based primarily on price. Buyers were strong negotiators and very interested in saving costs where they could.

The horizontal axis represents the competitive advantage, as measured by the profitability of the business relative to the average of competitors in this segment. Each of the four Hamworthy businesses discussed above can be positioned on this axis to provide their position on the matrix:

- In specialist marine pump systems, Hamworthy had a strong position and was earning returns higher than the average for the segment.
- In after-sales service, Hamworthy did not have quite as strong a position, as it had not focused so much on the area and faced more competitors.
- In offshore oil and gas, Hamworthy was currently less profitable than competitors. Although it targeted profitable niches, it had to spend proportionally more than competitors on research, product development and building up the business.
- In engine room pumps, Hamworthy was disadvantaged because, as a supplier of specialist pumps, it was higher cost than several of the competitors in this segment.

Businesses in the three top right boxes are clearly attractive. For example, in after-sales service for pump systems, Hamworthy's strategy was to grow and invest.[12]

Businesses in the bottom left corner are clearly unattractive. Such businesses should normally be restructured, closed or sold. Hamworthy would likely have selected one of these options for its engine room pumps business, were it not for the access this business gave to the more profitable business of supplying after-sales services, and the boost it gave to overall factory utilisation.

But what if a business is on the borderline – in the top left or bottom right part of the matrix?

Weak businesses in attractive markets

Opportunities in the top left-hand corner are in many ways the most difficult to characterise as attractive or unattractive, because they can be either of these depending on how they develop. They offer the highest levels of both return and risk.

Doing nothing is rarely an option because market attractiveness typically declines as a market matures. A weak business in an attractive market might earn healthy returns in the early growth stages, but these will likely decline as the market matures and competitive rivalry increases.

However, if it is possible to shift the business to the right, then profitability can be increased significantly. If the business improves its competitive position, profits will rise and so may the price earnings multiple. But there are several challenges and risks involved in doing so.

The first risk is that, despite a lot of investment of time and money, the business fails to overtake its rivals – or its rivals fight back with aggressive tactics that lower the overall profitability of the market. For example, to develop a substantial oil and gas business Hamworthy would have had to invest significantly in research and development, product development and building relationships with oil and gas companies.[13] Moreover, other competitors could have resisted Hamworthy by bidding aggressively on contracts that Hamworthy sought to win. Building a competitive position equal in strength to its core marine business would have taken several years.

This risk is typically lower in a market that is fast growing – as rivals will be able to grow even as your business gains market share, thus lowering the risk of an aggressive competitive response. It is harder to move a business from top left to top right when the market is slow growing. One strategy, therefore, is to grow businesses in this position if the market is fast growing, but divest them if the market is mature. Another possible strategy, adopted by Hamworthy in oil and gas markets, is to focus on niches where it is possible to rapidly build a credible position based on existing capabilities – rather than try to make advances on a broader front.

Another challenge in trying to improve a weak business is that it may not have the capabilities to execute the required transformation. For example, Hamworthy had "... four quite autonomous business areas, and its corporate culture is characterised by a strong entrepreneurial spirit".[14] Therefore, to execute the strategy of growing its presence in offshore oil and gas, it had to either acquire a business already in oil and gas, or set up a new business unit, or rely on its existing business unit management teams to hire new managers, invest appropriately and develop new market positions. It chose the latter option because the existing businesses had the products and technologies required. However, this meant relying heavily on the capabilities of its existing business unit managers – few of whom had extensive experience of the offshore business. In addition, these business unit managers were all busy dealing with the consequences of a significant downturn in their core marine markets.

Another option is to sell a business in this quadrant. For example, Invensys is a British multinational engineering and information technology company. It has a variety of businesses, one of which was a business providing a variety of control systems for mainline, metro and freight railways. However, because the business was subscale, it needed to grow to become competitive. Because no suitable candidate for acquisition was available, Invensys instead sold the business to Siemens, at a healthy premium.

In summary, businesses in the top left quadrant offer particularly high levels of risk and return. Investing in these businesses is risky. But, if it is possible to shift a business from this quadrant to the top right-hand quadrant, returns can be very attractive.

Strong businesses in unattractive markets

These businesses will typically still return above or around the cost of capital. For example, Ryanair, a strong competitor in a very tough market, made an average return on equity of 10% between 2006 and 2011, including one year that was loss making.

A company owning such a business should ensure that it receives enough investment to maintain its strong position, but that it delivers any excess cash back for reinvestment in higher returning opportunities.

This was the case for Hamworthy's core marine businesses. Profitability for the segment as a whole was falling, but it was strongly positioned. The challenge was to minimise investment into the business while retaining a strong competitive position. Capital expenditure and employee numbers were trimmed, but expenditure on acquisitions and research and development were increased.

Ryanair is famous for its focus on controlling costs. For example, new pilots have to pay for their training and uniforms and have been known to arrive at work on their first day to find that the company no longer needs their services. It is adept at getting free publicity rather than advertising. But, at the same time it invests in new planes and engines to ensure it can operate with low fuel costs and a good on-time record.

Overall, compared to businesses in the top left-hand corner, there are relatively few options for generating high returns for a business in the bottom right-hand corner, but also lower risks in continuing to own such businesses, so long as they do not require big bets or face discontinuities in the external environment.

Growth

For many management teams, growth is as important as profitability. Haniel targets "Markets with above-average opportunities for growth." Hamworthy also seeks growth, targeting "... markets with long-term growth prospects".[15] Indeed, it owes its current position to its historic strategy of pursuing growth markets. It established itself initially by serving the UK's ship building industry. As that industry declined it moved to Japan and then South Korea as those countries became the growth markets for ship building. More recently it entered the Chinese market as that country built share in the ship building business.

Growth is attractive for simple compounding reasons. A company growing at 10% per annum will, after 10 years, be worth nearly twice as much as a similar company growing at 5% per annum (see Figure 3.4). Growth is a major driver of shareholder value. It also provides career opportunities, and opportunities for pay increases as responsibilities widen. Everyone loves growth.

But growth is a two-edged sword. High growth in a market that offers returns above the cost of capital is the ideal. But

Figure 3.4: Why grow? $100 growing at 5%, 10% and 15% for 10 years

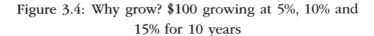

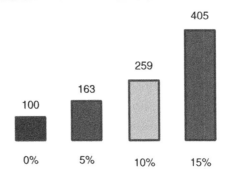

high growth in a market that offers returns below the cost of capital is worse than no growth at all: with every extra percentage of growth the business is destroying the wealth of its owners faster and faster. It is also sucking managers into dead end careers. Figure 3.5 captures this two-edged aspect of growth. The best position on this simple matrix is the top right box – box B. But, box D is not the worst position to be in. The worst position on the matrix is box A – high growth in a market that gives returns below the cost of capital – for example, the airline industry.

Figure 3.5: Where will your growth come from?

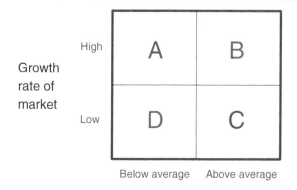

Frequently, it is necessary to invest in a low return, high growth market because returns are expected to improve in the future. The period of low returns is an entry ticket. Hamworthy was prepared to invest in building its oil and gas business because of the prospects for long-term growth.

To represent growth on the Business Attractiveness matrix, each business can be plotted with a different colour showing the growth rate – red/dark grey, amber/light grey or green/mid grey for low, medium and high growth rates. This can be done to indicate market growth, current growth rate of the

Figure 3.6: Business Attractiveness matrix for Hamworthy with growth added

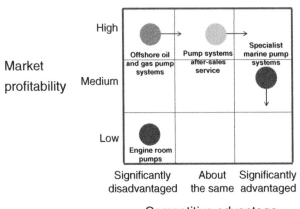

business or overall growth prospects. Figure 3.6 updates the earlier figure of the Hamworthy businesses with colours corresponding to the short-term growth prospects for each segment. Oil and gas offers the highest growth prospects because the market is growing and Hamworthy can build share. Pump systems after-sales service is a relatively stable business – but Hamworthy can grow by building share so it is shown as orange. The other two businesses are red because the market is entering a cyclical downturn and it would be impractical for Hamworthy to increase its market share.

Arrows are also included to represent changes in position that are expected in the future. Hamworthy is intending to grow its share and competitive advantage in serving oil and gas customers, and in winning after-sales service business for its core marine pumps.

Size

Another factor that is often considered, when companies are deciding where to invest, is the size of the market, and more specifically the size of the business in the market. Bigger markets offer more opportunity for investment. If the company is large, like GE, managers are looking for large businesses to invest in. Market size can therefore be included as a dimension of attractiveness.

However, like growth, market size is two edged. A big market is only more attractive than a small market if it is possible to earn returns above the cost of capital. When returns are below the cost of capital, size is a disadvantage. The larger the business the more wealth is being destroyed.

We can represent size on the Business Attractiveness matrix by making the circles different sizes. Normally, we would size the circles according to sales or market size (sales is useful for mature businesses, but market size gives more indication of growth prospects in emerging industries). It is also possible to use other measures of size, such as capital employed, value at risk, profits or value.

Figure 3.7 updates the previous figure, plotting the approximate size of the Hamworthy businesses along with their growth colours and the changes expected in the near future.

Figure 3.7: Business Attractiveness matrix for Hamworthy with size added

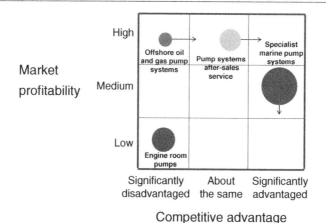

One reason for not exiting the core marine business is that it is still a substantial part of the business. It would not be viable to enter the oil and gas business without the foundation of Hamworthy's presence in the marine business.

What to plot in the matrix

The Business Attractiveness matrix acts as a useful visual summary of the factors that need to be taken into account when using business logic. It can be used to structure a "quick and dirty" view of where different businesses are positioned, whether they are currently in the portfolio or a prospective investment or acquisition.

However, a practical issue concerns what to plot in the matrix. This raises the question of what is a business. Is a single product a business? Is a single location a business? Is the whole company just one business? To illustrate the challenges, consider the situation at Hamworthy. In 2009 it was organised into four business divisions – Pump Systems, Gas Systems, Water Systems and Inert Gas Systems. This structure had been created partly to make it easier to sell off bits of the business if that turned out to be a value-creating strategy. The company had recently entered the oil and gas market, focusing on particular applications such as FPSOs, using technologies and products from its Pump Systems and Gas Systems divisions. Each of its business divisions was a global business, although the company wanted particularly to increase its business in China. It also wanted to grow its share of after-sales service markets. So what should be plotted on the matrix? In other words, how should the business be segmented? According to the current organisational structure? By market served? By application? By technology or product? By country? By bundling new products with after-sales service, or separating them out?

The answer is that it is normally useful to use the Business Attractiveness matrix at multiple levels of analysis. Typically, you start at a high level, to provide an overall diagnostic. You then "unpeel the onion" by segmenting down to finer levels of detail in order to focus on particular choices that have to be made.

For example, the first level at Hamworthy might involve plotting the four business divisions. At the next level, it might make sense to focus just on one division, such as Pump Systems, and plot the different market segments and applications served or the different geographies it operates in.

The process of unpeeling the onion – using the matrix to plot the company's current activities and planned future activities at different levels of detail – can continue as far as it is useful for the decisions that are being taken. Often it is helpful to try to go at least one level below the decision that is being considered, to see if there are insights to be gained at this extra level of granularity. For example, if the decision is about whether and how to expand in China, then it will be helpful to look at China's position on the matrix compared to other opportunities for investment, such as oil and gas or inert gas systems or Korea. At a lower level of granularity, it may also be helpful to plot different products or applications within China on the matrix to see if there are parts of the Chinese business that are more attractive than others.[16]

As the analysis is taken down to lower levels of detail, the work needed to assess average market profitability and relative competitive advantage becomes harder. Not only are there difficult issues of measuring profitability within your own business due to cost allocations – for example, how to allocate the costs of research and development, or a shared sales force across different product lines – but there is also the difficulty of getting competitor information at the same level of granularity. Normally, it is necessary to make big assumptions, at least for the purposes of making an initial plot. It is often worth doing an initial "best guess" of the position on the matrix, and then deciding how much further analysis is warranted to confirm or challenge this best guess.

In most cases, even with a significant amount of analysis, the position on the axes is based on some qualitative judgements as well as some fact-based judgements. Therefore, it is a good idea to check the reasonableness of the positions against the high-level financial information for each business division and for the company as a whole. If the company as a whole is struggling to make returns above the cost of capital, it is not credible to place all its business in the top right of the matrix. If a division is making high returns, it is not credible to place its largest business to the left of the diagonal.

There are other practical challenges when using the Business Attractiveness matrix, which are addressed on the book's website: www.corporatelevelstrategy.info.

Summary

One way to develop a corporate portfolio is by acquiring and building attractive businesses. The Business Attractiveness matrix is a useful tool for summarising attractiveness. Its primary dimensions are market profitability and competitive advantage, but it is also possible to add in additional dimensions of attractiveness, such as growth and market size. Businesses in the top right are attractive and those in the bottom left are unattractive. Those in the top left can be attractive if they can be pushed to the right by improving their competitive position. Those in the bottom right are normally harder to move – but their returns can be above the cost of capital if they have sufficient competitive advantage.

An important first step is to segment the business at a level of detail that helps you make the decision you are considering. Often it is useful to do the analysis at more than one level of detail to see if more detail brings more insights.

Notes

[1] Michael Porter, "The Five Competitive Forces that Shape Strategy", *Harvard Business Review*, January 2008.

[2] http://www.haniel.com/en/group/strategy/

[3] http://www.haniel.com/en/group/profile/

[4] http://www.brainyquote.com/quotes/authors/w/warren_buffett.html

[5] See, for example, Hamworthy annual report, 2009, page 2.

[6] http://www.fool.com/investing/general/2012/05/23/if-you-have-to-invest-in-airlines-dont.aspx, quoting from a 2002 interview with Warren Buffett.

[7] Southwest Airlines and Glaxo Wellcome 1996 Annual Reports.

[8] Gabriel Hawawini, Venkat Subramanian and Paul Verdin, "Is Performance Driven by Industry or Firm-specific Effects?" *Strategic Management Journal*, Vol. 24, 2003, 1–16; Anita McGahan and Michael Porter, "How Much does Industry Matter, Really?" *Strategic Management Journal*, Vol. 18 (Summer Special Edition), 1997, 15–30.

[9] Hamworthy, op. cit., 17.

[10] A. Campbell and R. Park, *The Growth Gamble* (Nicholas Brearley: London, 2005).

[11] To be more precise, the relative return on capital employed should be measured by the spread earned above the cost of capital for the business, because some businesses may have an advantage from a lower cost of capital. In some cases, the advantage from being able to charge higher prices can be used to grow faster than the

competition. A full analysis of competitive advantage therefore needs to review changes in market share.

[12] Hamworthy, op. cit., 17.

[13] Hamworthy, op. cit., 24.

[14] Lena Barner-Rasmussen, "Making Perfect Sense", *Twentyfour7*, Issue 2, 2012, 28–31.

[15] Hamworthy, op. cit., 17.

[16] Andrew Campbell, Phil Renshaw and Staffan Engstrom, "The Black and White and Grey of Strategy", *Journal of Strategy and Management*, Vol. 3, No. 4, 2010, 344–351.

CHAPTER FOUR

HOW TO MAKE BUSINESSES MORE SUCCESSFUL

Every owner of a business would like to make the business more successful. But the idea of added value as a prime criterion for helping decide which businesses to invest in did not emerge properly until the mid-1990s.

The concept is simple. A company should aim to invest in businesses or markets where it can add value: where its influence and support will help make the business concerned more successful. The test is whether the parent company can help the business grow faster, realise higher prices, reduce operating costs or increase asset utilisation?

The reverse is also true. If the parent company cannot add value in at least one of these ways, it should not seek to have a presence in this market because it will impose an overhead burden on the business concerned, causing it to perform less well than an equivalent independent company.

Of course, any larger company is not only competing against focused, independent companies. It is also competing against other large companies. So, adding value relative to an independent company may not be enough. The higher objective is to add more value than other parent companies. In other words, companies should develop into new areas where they have an added value advantage (or parenting advantage). They will have an added value advantage if they possess some superior skills or resources, which they can deploy to help this business be more successful.

What is value?

The term "added value" presumes an understanding of the word "value". So, it may be useful to devote a couple of paragraphs to making sure this word is understood.

In its purest sense value is "net present value": the flow of future net cash generated by the business, discounted to today's value. However, in a broader sense, value is whatever the leaders of the company value. In other words, it is determined by the objectives of the organisation. In the case of a business school, one objective may be to get articles published in top management journals. So, one form of "added value" is anything that helps ensure that more articles are published per year or that fewer resources are used in publishing the same number of articles. In this broader sense, value is a much more squishy term. But the concept of added value is still meaningful. It is the ability to achieve objectives faster, more fully or with fewer resources.

In continental Europe and in some other countries, there is an established tradition of defining value in these broader terms. Leaders of businesses frequently include objectives such as continued survival, growth, benefits to society and impact on the environment. It is possible to use this broader definition of value alongside all the ideas in this book. The concepts are the same. It is just the measure of value that is a little different. However, for the purposes of simplicity, we will use value in its narrower definition: as net present value – the discounted valuation of all future cash flows. Those who find the broader definition of value more powerful should not reject the ideas in this book, but rather rework them using the broader measure.

The language of added value, using the narrower definition, is particularly helpful when thinking about acquisitions.
It suggests that a company should acquire another business
only if it can create more discounted cash flow from owning
the new business than the current owners. This may come
from improving the acquired business or from synergies with
or improvements to existing businesses that can only be delivered by acquiring the new business. The extra cash flow is
needed to be able to pay the current owners a fair price and
expect to have some surplus left over after taking account of
the costs of completing the transaction and integrating the new
business.

However, just creating some extra cash flow may not
be enough. Buyers compete with other companies for acquisitions. To be able to outbid other companies, buyers need to
be able to create more "extra cash flow" than others can.
This is the concept of added value advantage or parenting
advantage.

The language of added value – extra cash flow – can also
be used to help think about green field investments. While
the first question should be about business advantage: what
advantage will this green field investment have versus its competitors? It is also useful to think ahead: once established, will
there be any extra cash flow as a result of owning this new
business? Will the parent organisation be able to add value to
the new business or will the new business be able to contribute
anything to other businesses in the portfolio? If there is some
extra cash flow, how does it compare to the extra cash flow
that might be created by another owner?

It only makes sense for a company to start a new business
if the company has something of value to contribute or to gain.
And it only makes sense to retain ownership of the new business if the continuing value added is greater than the value
added that can be created by other parent companies.

Figure 4.1: Parent as value adding middleman

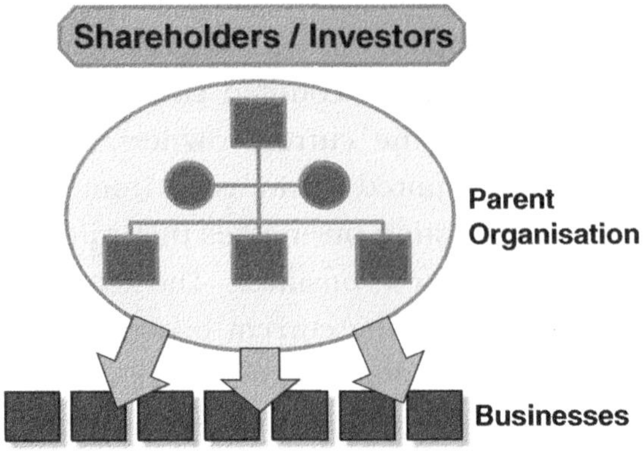

The cost of corporate headquarters

Added value is needed to offset the costs of the management layer above the business divisions. This layer, which we refer to as corporate headquarters or the parent company, is a middleman sitting between the business divisions and the investors (see Figure 4.1). This layer, and sometimes there are multiple layers, has a cost, not just in terms of its direct expenses but also in terms of the time it absorbs of the managers who are running the business divisions. For this "parenting" layer to make economic sense, it must generate some additional value that at least offsets its costs. If not, investors would gain more from separate investments in each business as independent companies.

To use the example from Chapter 1, Blacklock, owner of Carlsen and CIW, needed to add enough value to offset its costs. If not, the shareholders of Blacklock would be better off if the company were broken into two independent businesses without the extra costs of a shared corporate headquarters.

Interestingly, shortly before Molsand acquired Blacklock, the chief executive, Jan Morris, was himself concerned about the added value of Blacklock. As a result of this concern, he decided to reduce the costs by collapsing the Blacklock level of the organisation and the CIW level. He became both chief executive of CIW and chief executive of Blacklock, saving the cost of one executive and some finance and support functions. For example, CIW and Blacklock shared the same director of human resources.

His concerns were well placed. Following the acquisition by Molsand, the Blacklock level was eliminated altogether. The Blacklock level was replaced by the Molsand level, so CIW and Carlsen still had a parent company. But the added costs in the Molsand organisation were significantly less than the costs of the Blacklock level, even after Jan Morris had reduced them. Of course, Molsand did not buy Blacklock just to save the overhead costs. Molsand managers believed they could add value as well (see Chapter 7).

Blacklock was an acquisition target partly because it was seen not to be adding sufficient value to justify its costs. But it was also an acquisition target because it was not adding as much value to Carlsen and CIW as other companies, such as Molsand and Vantex, thought they could add. As a result, Molsand was prepared to pay a large premium to own CIW and Carlsen.

The heartland matrix

The financial cost of the corporate headquarters is not the only reason added value is necessary. Corporate headquarters also subtracts value more directly. Subtracted value is something managers readily recognise. They refer to interference, bureaucracy, delays, ineffective services and time wasting. There are few managers who cannot provide rich stories of things done by their corporate centre that subtracted value.

Subtracted value often comes from the same sources as added value. Added value can come from wise guidance, from

a parent company brand, from technical expertise, from relationships with important stakeholders, from financial strength,
from shared sales forces and from many other sources (see
Chapters 7 and 8). Subtracted value can come from inappropriate guidance, from an unhelpful parent company brand, from
poor technical expertise, from bad relationships with important
stakeholders, from insufficient financial strength, from poorly
integrated sales forces and from many other sources (see
Chapter 9).

The dimensions of added value and subtracted value can
be combined to form a matrix – the Heartland matrix. This
matrix was first developed by Michael Goold, Andrew Campbell
and Marcus Alexander, all of Ashridge Business School. It was
called the Ashridge Portfolio Display.[1] They were the first to
spot that added value and subtracted value exist in most companies most of the time. Successful groups are those where the
balance between them is positive (see Figure 4.2).

Figure 4.2: The Heartland matrix

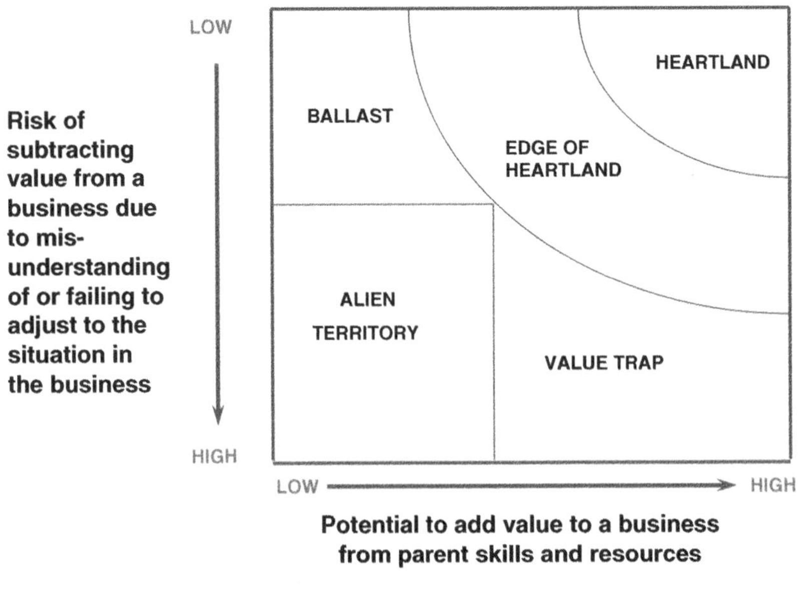

Potential to add value to a business
from parent skills and resources

Both axes measure from low to high. The measure is the percentage impact on net present value or profitability or market capitalisation. Low is close to zero. High could be an increase of 50% or more (or decrease on the subtracted value axis). The lines separating different parts of the matrix are conceptual more than mathematical.

If the subtracted value is likely to be low and the potential for added value is high, the business is in the company's "heartland". In other words there is a good fit between the business and its parent company.

The **heartland** of Procter & Gamble is fast moving consumer goods, where investments in R&D, global distribution and international brands give advantage. The heartland of 3M is products that build on the company's core technologies such as its coatings capabilities. The heartland of LVMH is luxury brands in fashion, leather goods, perfumes, cosmetics, watches, jewellery, wines and spirits. The heartland for a private equity company might be established businesses that have not been well managed for cash flow. These different parent companies each add a lot of value to businesses in their heartland and subtract only a little. Typically, they help to increase profits in these businesses by 50% or 100% or more.

If the subtracted value is likely to be high and the potential for added value is low, the business unit is in "alien territory". The fit is bad, and the company should consider selling or closing this activity. In the years when diversification was popular (1960s to 1980s), many companies invested in businesses that proved to be in **alien territory**. The companies had entered new industries that would provide growth potential. The driving logic had been business attractiveness (see Chapter 3). Exxon entered the electric motor industry. BP entered IT software. BAT (British American Tobacco) entered financial services. All proved to be alien territory: there was little added value and plenty of subtracted value. For example, BAT sold its investment in the financial services company Eagle Star for less than they had paid a few years earlier and after accumulating almost £2 billion of losses.

If the subtracted value is likely to be low and the potential for added value is low, the business is "ballast". **Ballast** businesses are ones that the managers in headquarters understand well. The businesses will probably have been part of the company for many years. They are well run, and hence there is little opportunity for headquarters to add value. The disadvantage of ballast businesses is that they can consume the scarce time of headquarters managers without resulting in any extra value. For this reason they should be candidates for selling. The advantage of ballast businesses is that they are usually stable and reliable. They provide solidity and bulk to the larger company. Sometimes they are retained for these reasons or because there may be opportunities to add value in the future. Often, however, they are retained because of loyalties and attachments that are not justified against a metric of discounted future cash flows.

Ballast businesses are common in diversified companies. Louis Vuitton is probably a ballast business in LVMH. Louis Vuitton would perform just as well as an independent company, and there are few benefits for the other brands of having Louis Vuitton in the portfolio. GE's aero engines business is probably a ballast business within GE for the same reasons.

If the subtracted value is likely to be high and the potential for added value is high, the business is a "value trap". It is a **value trap** because, tempted by the potential for added value, managers can underestimate the risk of subtracted value. The result is frequently net negative: the subtracted value proves to be greater than the added value. It is normally best to exit these businesses. The only reason to retain a value trap is to learn how to reduce the subtracted value so that the activity can be "raised" to edge of heartland.

Minerals proved to be a value trap for oil companies in the 1980s. In the early 1980s, most of the oil companies acquired mining and minerals businesses in the belief that their skills at exploration, major project management and government relations would enable them to add value to minerals companies. While some of these skills were helpful, the net result was negative: minerals companies owned by oil businesses made losses at a time when equivalent independent companies made profits. By the end of the 1980s, the oil companies had all sold their minerals divisions.

Elizabeth Arden, the high fashion perfume brand, proved to be a value trap for Unilever, whose heritage was mass-market products. Unilever managers, however, recognised the risks and, at least initially, took care to limit subtracted value. For the first two years of ownership, managers at Unilever were not allowed to contact managers at Elizabeth Arden unless they had permission from a gatekeeper. This created a bottleneck that allowed Elizabeth Arden to operate in a fairly autonomous fashion.

However, after eight years, Unilever sold Elizabeth Arden in a private equity deal. In the following 18 months, released from constraints imposed by Unilever, the new owners were able to double the company's profit margins as well as increase its sales growth.

Edge-of-heartland is a space in the matrix where the balance between added value and subtracted value is unclear. There is some added value, but there is also likely to be some subtracted value. If the company becomes good at adding value and avoiding subtracted value, the business will become a heartland business. If it does not, it may become ballast, alien territory or value trap. So the edge-of-heartland space exists more as a temporary home for businesses that have the potential to become part of heartland.

When Unilever bought Elizabeth Arden, managers would have positioned it in edge-of-heartland rather than value trap.

They would have expected to be able to add value from combining Elizabeth Arden with their other cosmetics businesses, and they would have believed that they could limit any subtracted value. As it turned out, Elizabeth Arden slipped into the value trap space, possibly even into alien territory. Added value was much less than expected, and, over time, once the gate keeper was removed, Unilever's bureaucracy began to smother Elizabeth Arden.

When British Airways launched the low cost airline GO, managers would have expected it to be in edge-of-heartland. The leaders of Daimler would have expected Chrysler to have been in edge-of-heartland. HP thought that Autonomy was edge-of-heartland. But, in all of these examples, the acquiring company failed to create as much added value as they expected, and succeeded in subtracting much more than they expected. GO and Chrysler were subsequently sold: GO to easyJet and Chrysler to a private equity buyer. HP, having written down $8 billion of its investment in Autonomy, may well do the same.

Of course, there are examples of edge-of-heartland businesses moving successfully into heartland. The move by professional auditing firms into tax and management consulting is one example. The edge-of-heartland experiment, which started for many firms in the 1970s, quickly became part of heartland. Subsequently, regulation caused many auditing firms to exit management consulting, not because it was in ballast or alien territory but because regulators were concerned that it could compromise the independence of the auditor's opinion.

The same is true of the move by car companies, like Volkswagen or General Motors, into financial services. While there are synergies through the financing of car purchases, it seemed likely that there would be significant subtracted value because the normal management systems for a car company would not suit a financial services business. However, most car companies have found ways of adding more value than they subtract. Their financial services arms are often the most profitable part of the company.

Other examples of successful investments into edge-of-heartland businesses are HP into computers, Intel into micro-processors or IBM into consulting. All of these companies made tentative investments into businesses that were different from their existing core. Over time, as they learnt to add value and avoid subtracted value, the businesses became heartland.

Using the heartland matrix to guide strategy

The Heartland matrix is conceptually strong but practically weak. As the description of edge-of-heartland businesses reveals, it is hard, ahead of time, to calculate in which quadrant a business lies. In part, this reflects reality: it was hard to know in advance whether the management team at British Airways would be able to create significant added value with its investment in GO; and it was hard to know how much value would be subtracted. It was hard to predict that car companies would create net added value from their investments in financial services. It was hard to predict that Daimler would fail to add value to Chrysler or that IBM would succeed in consulting. It was hard to know whether Lenovo would be a good owner of mobile phone and tablet businesses alongside its personal computer businesses, especially when compared to Apple or Samsung. For this reason, the edge-of-heartland space is large.

Since it is hard to assess in advance where a business will lie on the matrix, there is a danger that this framework is more useful for describing what happened than for predicting what will happen. So how can managers use the Heartland matrix to guide decision making?

First, managers can use the matrix to **plot existing business divisions**. There is no precise calculation for doing this. It is a judgement. But the judgements should be well informed.

They should be based on feedback from the managers in the division, as well as on examples of value added and value subtracted. Fortunately, the judgements do not need to be fine grained. The comparison is with the discounted cash flow or profit or market capitalisation that would occur if the division were an independent company. For added value, only broad brush judgements are needed. Does the performance of the division (in profit or cash flow or market capitalisation) improve by 10% or 50% or 100% as a result of being part of the larger company? A similar broad-brush judgement is required for subtracted value. Does the performance of the division (in profit or cash flow or market capitalisation) suffer by 10% or 20% or 50% as a result of being part of the larger company?

If the numbers are small, around the 10% level, the division is ballast. If both subtracted value and added value are large, 30% or more of added value and 20% or more of subtracted value, the division is in value trap space. If added value is large and subtracted value is small the division is in heartland. If subtracted value is large and added value is small the division is in alien territory.

Inevitably, politics and self-interest can influence these judgements. But the benefit of the Heartland matrix is the discussion it stimulates as much as the precise plotting of individual businesses. Where there are disagreements, more analysis can be done.

Business divisions that are clearly in alien territory should be sold. For the other positionings, the discussion should focus on how to minimise subtracted value (value trap and edge-of-heartland) and how to increase added value (ballast and edge-of-heartland).

The benefit of the ballast and value trap categorisations is that they signal caution. The ballast categorisation warns managers to be cautious about investing time in "parenting" the division, because the management costs may not be recovered in added value. The value trap categorisation warns managers to be cautious about interfering and influencing managers in the division, because this may subtract more value than it adds.

The categorisations also encourage managers to monitor added and subtracted value more closely than they might otherwise. This is especially important for business divisions in edge-of-heartland and in value trap space. As the examples of Elizabeth Arden, Chrysler and GO illustrate, it is easy for a company to add less value than it expects and subtract more.

The second way of using the matrix is to **plot potential acquisitions and new business ventures** on the matrix. This is clearly harder than plotting existing businesses, and requires even more judgement. The default position is edge-of-heartland.

Even with these businesses, it is often possible to make an estimate of the potential to add value. The analysis is similar to the work needed when estimating improvements and synergies for an acquisition. It is never fully precise, and the amount of value that is actually realised often falls short of the potential. But, it is not usually difficult to decide whether the added value is likely to be large (i.e. more than 50%) relative to the investment being made.

What is particularly hard to estimate is the likely significance of subtracted value. This is because managers cannot know what they do not know, and it is usually what they do not know that is the main cause of subtracted value. One solution to this problem is to compare the critical success factors of the new business with the critical success factors of the core businesses. If more than half of them are different, there is a large risk of subtracted value (see Table 4.1).

But, however much analysis is done, plotting new businesses on the matrix requires judgement, and the judgement will often be that the business is in the edge-of-heartland space. The benefit of the matrix is that it encourages managers to focus

Table 4.1 Comparing critical success factors (example)

Critical success factors	Core business: restaurants	Proposed new business: local hotels
Skills at designing the brand	High	Medium
Skills at communicating the brand	High	Medium
Cooking and chefing skills	High	Medium
Service management skills	High	High
Consistency across sites	High	Low
Supply chain management	High	Low
Selling skills	Low	High
Balancing different profit centres	Low	High

on maximising added value and minimising subtracted value, with the intention of moving the business into heartland.

Attempts have been made to give more precision to the Heartland matrix by calibrating the axes. In particular, an attempt was made at Shell to use the matrix to review the portfolio of businesses in one of Shell's divisions (see www .corporatelevelstrategy.info). However, the matrix is probably more useful as a conceptual model than as a mathematical model.

Combining the heartland and business attractiveness matrices

The Heartland matrix can be combined with the Business Attractiveness matrix to help synthesise the messages coming from the first two logics (Figure 4.3).

On the vertical axis of the combined matrix the parent company is rated as an owner. Is the company clearly a superior

Figure 4.3:

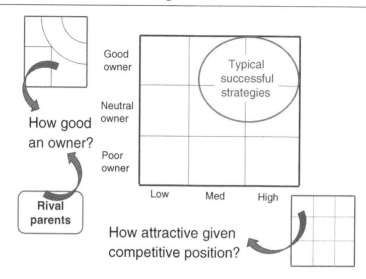

owner (i.e. can add more value than other parents), clearly an inferior owner (i.e. is likely to add less value and subtract more value than other parents) or about the same? Mercedes was clearly "about the same" or "inferior" as an owner of Chrysler. Molsand believed that it was clearly a superior owner of Blacklock's businesses. HP has proved to be an inferior owner of Autonomy (at least at the time of writing).

On the horizontal axis the business concerned is rated in terms of its overall attractiveness. If it falls into the three boxes in the top right of the Business Attractiveness matrix, it is rated as high attractiveness. If it falls into the three boxes in the bottom left, it is rated as low attractiveness. If it falls into the three boxes on the diagonal from top left to bottom right, it is rated medium attractiveness. Chrysler would have been low attractiveness. Carlsen, within Blacklock, would have been rated high attractiveness.

The four boxes in the top right of this combined matrix identify the businesses that are part of typical successful corporate-level strategies. These are reasonably attractive businesses for which the parent company is a reasonably good owner. But there are some other spaces on this matrix that are worth some attention.

The top left box describes unattractive businesses that the parent company is particularly good at owning. In certain circumstances this can be a viable strategy, especially if the parent company is able to make the businesses more attractive by improving their competitive position. For example, local food brands are typically divested by big international food companies, like Unilever and Nestlé, because they are less attractive than brands that have international potential. A parent company with a local focus can buy these brands at reasonable prices, integrate marketing, logistics, selling and back office costs within a country and give these orphan brands new life.

The two lower boxes on the extreme right are also interesting. These capture highly attractive businesses that the parent company is not very good at parenting. However, if they can be acquired for reasonable prices, it may still be worth experimenting to find out if it is possible to build the needed parenting skills. The businesses are so attractive that it is worth investing in the skills needed to be a superior parent.

We will discuss some more of the situations where the two logics are not aligned in Chapter 6. In Chapter 13, we will focus on the challenge of building new parenting skills.

Summary

This chapter has focused on the added value logic for helping make decisions about which businesses and markets to invest in and which to avoid or exit. Added value logic steers companies towards investing in businesses that will benefit significantly from being part of the company or that will contribute significantly to the success of other businesses in the company.

The Heartland matrix is a way of helping with these judgements. It encourages managers to think about both added and subtracted value. Since both exist simultaneously most of the time, it is the net added value that should drive decisions.

The Heartland matrix is conceptually powerful, but can be hard to use in practice because both axes are difficult to calibrate and difficult to assess. We have described some of the ways in which the matrix can be used to aid managers as they make these difficult judgements. We have also shown how the Heartland matrix can be combined with the Business Attractiveness matrix to give an integrated view of the situation.

Note

[1] Michael Goold, Andrew Campbell and Marcus Alexander, *Corporate Level Strategy* (John Wiley & Sons, 1994).

Chapter Five

How to Buy Low and Sell High

Markets are dependent on buyers and sellers. The price in the market is the price at which buyers match sellers. This is how capital markets establish the price of companies' shares. If markets had complete and accurate information, this price would be equal to the "fundamental" or "true" value of the company. But they rarely possess such perfect information.

Markets therefore create opportunities to buy businesses for less than they are worth and to sell businesses for more than they are worth. Capital markets logic suggests that companies should buy businesses when the capital markets are undervaluing them, and sell businesses when capital markets are overvaluing them: in other words, buy low and sell high.

For example, UBM is a company that organises tradeshows and provides marketing services, information and media services. In the mid-2000s there were two alternative business models in this industry. One consisted of offering exhibitions and a range of complementary services. Another focused more on offering digital services. The second model was seen as more attractive, and thus attracted many competitors, bidding up the price of acquisitions in this sector. UBM, however, focused on the exhibitions business model. This made it possible for the company to acquire businesses at good prices.

UBM's corporate strategy was driven partly by capital markets logic.

Capital markets can also be a constraint on strategy. A business that you want to buy may be overpriced. Or a business that you want to sell may only be sellable at less than its true value. For example, Mexican Foods decided to shift its focus from private label products to branded products because it anticipated reduced margins in private label products. But the company decided not to sell its private label products businesses because the prices it was offered were well below its estimate of the cash flow it could get from these businesses.

Therefore, when making portfolio decisions or developing a portfolio strategy, it is important to consider the capital markets and the price of the businesses you are interested in buying or selling.

Typically, the markets will price a business at close to its true value. This is because those valuing the company (executives, analysts, shareholders, traders, investment bankers and potential investors) often have considerable information about the company, its markets and its environment. They are also highly motivated to use all this information to arrive at an accurate valuation. This is the efficient markets hypothesis.

Beating the market, by finding a business that is priced significantly under or over its fair value, is difficult. For example, studies repeatedly find that fund managers, who are meant to be experts in identifying under- or overpriced stocks, on average perform no better than the market.[1] Indeed, because they incur certain costs that are passed on to their customers, on average they typically *under*perform the market.

Unfortunately, it is also easy to persuade yourself that a business is mispriced, when it is not. Because there are so many assumptions required, it is easy to get a valuation wrong. The main assumption is about expected future cash flows. These cash flows are estimated and then discounted back to the present, using a discount rate that is itself an estimate of the cost of capital. Since this analysis requires estimates about the future and estimates about the cost of capital, different people can arrive at different valuations. So there is no way of telling in advance what exactly the true value is. As a result, it is hard to know, beforehand, when you have made a mistake.

Therefore, to be confident that a business is mispriced by the capital markets, it is important to consider three questions:

1. **Are there good reasons why the capital markets might misprice this business?** The default position should be that the market has it about right. Only if there is some reason for you to believe the markets are wrong should you believe the business is mispriced.

2. **Do you have the superior insight and capabilities required to take advantage of any mispricing?** Even if there is a chance that the market has it wrong, you need to have superior information, and be a superior analyst, to spot whether a specific business is, in fact, over- or underpriced. You also need to have the capabilities required to negotiate and close the deal.

3. **Does the financial analysis suggest that the level of mispricing is significant?** If there are good reasons why capital markets might misprice a business, and you do have superior insights and valuation skills, it is important to determine whether the mispricing is trivial or significant. This requires doing some financial analysis to roughly scale the level of mispricing. For example, if financial analysis suggests that the business is priced at only 50% of its true value then there is clearly an opportunity to buy cheap. Because of the range of assumptions required to come up with this estimate, it is important not to be in thrall to the numbers. The goal of the financial analysis is to roughly scale the opportunity, not to come up with a precise valuation.

The rest of this chapter is structured around these three questions. We conclude with a few comments on how capital markets logic is used in practice.

Are there good reasons why capital markets might misprice this business?

The likelihood that the market might misprice a business depends on a number of factors, including: the relative number of buyers and sellers, the characteristics of buyers and sellers, differences in the information available to different buyers, the way the deal is structured and the deal process.

The number of buyers and sellers

Prices tend to be lower when there are very few buyers relative to the number of sellers, and vice versa.

For example, Sara Lee wanted to sell their Western European personal wash and hand soap business. This was a substantial business with market share of about 25%. However, few companies were in a position to acquire and add value to such a business. The most likely corporate buyers were P&G, Unilever and Colgate, but P&G already had a 12% market share and so was unable to bid, due to competition law. No major PE companies were bidding, because the deal was done in 2009, when there was limited availability of bank debt.

In the end, Unilever was able to acquire the business at a moderate price because there was only one other credible bidder.

The quantity of buyers is determined by a number of factors. One is the general landscape of corporations, private equity companies and potential investors. Another is the nature of the business that is up for sale. Some businesses are too big to attract a large number of buyers (this was the case for Sara Lee's European business). Some are too small. Some are too spread across multiple segments to appeal to many buyers. Some businesses have significant risks attached to them, such as lawsuits or unfunded pension liabilities, which deter some buyers. Some businesses are too unattractive.

Conversely, some businesses attract a large number of buyers. Such businesses have a greater chance of selling at a significant premium to their value. Only a very determined, and possibly irrational, buyer is likely to win the bidding.

The number of sellers can also vary. In some cases, the seller has a unique business: there are no equivalents. In other cases, there are many, similar businesses for sale from many sellers. For example, when Tesco began acquiring small local retailers, to create a chain of local grocery stores, there were many potential sellers.

The number of buyers and sellers is likely to vary over time. For example, it was described earlier how UBM was able to acquire exhibition companies at low prices. This was because most of UBM's corporate competitors were targeting digital services companies. However, over time these competitors began to take more interest in the exhibition companies that UBM was focusing on. This drove up the price of acquisitions.

The characteristics of buyers and sellers

Buyers vary in their characteristics – for example, their motivation, skills and general approach to valuation, and hence in the likelihood that they will pay a particularly high price for a business. Some are motivated to pay as low a price as possible; while others are motivated to win the deal whatever the cost. Some are more sophisticated than others. Some are conservative in their outlook – only valuing more highly predictable cash flows of the business; while others are more willing to add in other potential cash flows, such as the value of future options. Some are highly rational; while others are more prone to bouts of irrational exuberance.

For example, consider two buyers for a US retail business that has been put up for sale. One is a privately held financial holding company, looking to earn a market return for its owners who are also its managers. It could invest its money on the stock market, but is looking to earn a small extra margin by acquiring whole companies. It is interested only in the cash flows that the business will deliver. It evaluates the company carefully, based on the available data. It is willing to pay up to the value of the company, but no more. Since the managers have a strong motivation to negotiate as low a price as possible and make this kind of investment regularly, they are unlikely to make a major mistake.

Another potential buyer is the management team of a mid-sized, publicly quoted European retailer which has grown organically in its home market. The company has plenty of cash flow, but its core business is in decline. The business it is looking to buy is a rare opportunity to enter a new but related business. The management team is very enthusiastic about the opportunity. The managers have not done any deals of this size before. The CEO is a charismatic character who has vowed to find a way to restore the company to growth.

It is pretty clear that the second management team is more likely to pay too high a price for the business. While the two teams are caricatures, experience suggests that they are not extreme cases. The existence of the second type of buyer is one reason why private equity companies make a lot of effort to make the businesses they want to sell appeal to what they term "strategic" buyers. They know that strategic buyers are likely to pay more than "financial" buyers. Financial buyers care only about the cash and will tend to value the business only on projected cash flows, making predictions for the future based heavily on current performance. Strategic buyers are more likely to take this value and then add something for the extra value they believe they will be able to add. Frequently, the "something extra" is optimistic and the strategic buyer pays too much.

Indeed, there are many examples of even the most experienced and successful executives paying too much for acquisitions that they were excessively keen to make. Derek Rayner, CEO of Marks and Spencer, paid too much to acquire Brooks Brothers, despite being warned by his finance team.[2] Sir Fred Goodwin, CEO of Royal Bank of Scotland, paid too much for ABN Amro. Daimler Benz paid too much for Chrysler. HP paid too much for Autonomy.

So far we have described situations in which buyers overvalue businesses. But they can also undervalue them. For example, in bear markets, the very same buyers, who were happy to pay high prices for acquisitions when the market was bullish, become extremely cautious and negative in their outlook. While caution is warranted at such times, they may become overly conservative and not want to bid at all. Part of Warren Buffett's strategy is to study companies in detail and to identify moments when their stocks are priced below his estimate of their value. "The best thing that happens to us is when a great company gets into temporary trouble ... We want to buy them when they're on the operating table."[3]

Just as buyers vary in the likelihood that they will pay over the odds, sellers vary in the likelihood that they will sell cheaply. Sometimes sellers will only sell if they receive a price in excess of the value of keeping the business. Sometimes, however, they will want to get rid of a business even if it means taking a low price – for example, when a new CEO arrives and wants to sell off the "mistakes" of his or her predecessor.

The overall message here is that the characteristics of both buyers and sellers can lead to differences in their tendency to misprice businesses. This gives opportunities for other buyers and sellers to profit.

Differences in the information available to buyers

Another situation in which the market may misprice a company is when different buyers have very different information. If a business is private, small, poorly covered by analysts and in a capital market where there are limited requirements to provide standard information, buyers may have to rely on their own unreliable sources. For example, evidence from the USA suggests that small companies are more likely to be mispriced than large companies.[4] Public information about smaller companies is limited, and so it is more likely that buyers will bid too high or too low. This is one of the reasons why UBM, the company mentioned earlier, focused on smaller, niche markets.

Another example is that of the "winner's curse", which was first described in the 1970s. When oil companies bid for exploration leases, the price of the winning bid was often at such a high level that it was difficult to make an adequate return. This occurred even when there were relatively few bidders, and when those bidders were trying hard to make a rational bid, based purely on the projected future cash flows from the property. A group of managers at ARCO (a US oil company) published a seminal article on why such assets or businesses can be overvalued. They suggested that the problem arose because each of the bidders had different information about the value of the business – in this case, how much oil was under the ground.

A bidder with perfect information knows how much to bid. However, bidders for oil leases each have their confidential geological data, interpreted by their own analysts. This means that each bidder will have a different view of how much oil is available. The one who estimates the most oil will tend to win the bid. But the reality is that the amount of oil available is the same for all bidders. The winners will typically have overestimated the amount of oil, even though they have tried to be as objective as possible: the winner's curse.[5]

The same can occur in equity markets. For example, if several companies are bidding for a business whose value is determined by the growth prospects for its primary product, the bidder who wins the bid is likely to be the one with the most optimistic growth forecast. If this is based on a unique insight it may result in a value-creating acquisition. But, if it is the result of overoptimism, or a lack of insight about threats to the market, then it will result in a value-destroying bid: the winner's curse.

Deal process

The deal process can also affect the chance of a business being mispriced. At one extreme, a business may be sold through an auction where the winner needs to outbid several competitors over a number of rounds. Such a process increases the chances of an eager buyer overbidding.

At the other extreme, even if there are several potential bidders, the seller may adopt a process that increases the chance of a low price. For example, the seller may approach only one buyer, and try to negotiate a private sale. This may be because the seller wants the sale to be confidential or wants to ensure that the business goes to someone perceived to be a good owner.

Another type of deal process that can result in mispricing is when the seller wants to offload the business quickly. For example, when Texas Utilities' European energy business got into serious financial difficulty, shortly after the Enron debacle, the US managers needed to offload it quickly. E.ON, a European utility, was able to purchase the business at a low price partly because it was one of the few companies willing to make an offer quickly. Also, because E.ON was in similar businesses it could be confident of valuing the complex contracts that had caused the financial problems. When there is an eager seller and only one confident buyer the chances are high that the business is sold for below its true value.

Do you have the superior insight and capabilities required to take advantage of any mispricing?

Identifying that the market is likely to misprice a business is an important first step. But it is not enough. You also need to be better able to take advantage of the situation. You need to have unique, valuable information and insights into how to interpret the information. You need to be able to turn these insights into accurate valuations. You need to be able to structure, finance and negotiate deals. If you do not have superior capabilities in these areas, then it will be hard for you to take advantage of the situation.

For example, when various buyers are bidding for an oil lease, but with limited and different information, you are unlikely to acquire it at a reasonable price. If you have no better information, insight or skill in valuing oil leases than other players, you can still bid. But, to reduce the risk of overpaying, you have to bid at below the value you believe the business to be worth. You then have to hope that your bid is below the true value and all other players submit bids that are below your bid. Your chance of winning a bid is low.

If, however, you have superior information, you have a better chance of success. If you have negative information, at least you can avoid buying the well. If you have positive information, you may be able to outbid others and still acquire the well at below its true value.

You are more likely to have superior information if you are dealing with businesses close to your heartland. For example, in the case of acquiring oil fields, you have an advantage if the auction is for a plot adjacent to one of your existing fields, or the geology is particularly complex but something that you have particular experience in dealing with. UBM has superior insights and information about the media sectors it competes in and can therefore be more confident about whether an acquisition is cheap or expensive. Mining companies are more likely to have superior knowledge of the value of mines than oil companies.

The importance of familiarity is underlined by academic studies. For example, insiders appear to make better than average decisions about when to buy their own company's stock. This is true whether they are buying for their own account[6] or using the company's cash to repurchase company stock.[7] They are also better than the average investor at spotting when their company is overvalued – as they tend to issue new equity when the price is at or near a peak.[8] By extension, it is also likely that some executives have superior skills in evaluating companies that they do not yet own, but which trade in their industry.

However, it is wise to avoid being overconfident about whether you have superior information or not – particularly if there are many industry competitors, specialist investors, fund managers, private equity companies and analysts who are also looking at the target company. It is all too easy to believe that you have special insight when, in fact, you do not. For example, managers at one company described to us how "We always used to think the teenage scribblers in the City were way off in the valuation they placed upon us, and that, based on our own detailed plans, we could see a big mis-valuation. But they turned out to be right more often than us."

Corporate teams should be particularly wary of thinking that they can spot when the overall market is mispriced. Studies of investors' ability to achieve high returns by identifying when the market as a whole is over- or undervalued suggest that this is very difficult to do (see sidebar).

A common pitfall in looking for mispricing opportunities

There is a belief that it is possible to spot when stocks are generally over or undervalued. The implication is that you should buy stocks when markets are cheap, and sell when markets are highly priced. However, in practice this strategy is not only difficult to execute, but appears not to deliver higher returns.

This might seem surprising. There is a documented tendency for markets to create bubbles in which rising prices create healthy returns, which generate optimism, encouraging more investment and raising prices further – until the bubble bursts. Consider the figure below, which shows the Schiller P/E ratio for the US stock market for more than 100 years.[9] The price paid for the earnings generated by a typical stock has been highly volatile over time – suggesting that markets may go through periods where they over- or underprice stocks.

Schiller price/earnings ratio

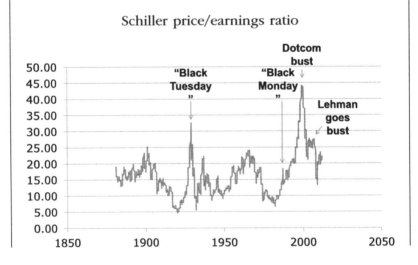

While some of these fluctuations might be justified on the basis of differences in expected future growth rates, or changes in the real cost of capital, it appears difficult to explain the magnitude of these boom bust cycles through rational modelling.[10] Schiller's explanation is that markets suffer from periods of "irrational exuberance".

But, while volatility undoubtedly exists, it is hard to spot when a market is about to turn. For example, in 1993 you might have thought the market was at a high point based on historical multiples – with the P/E ratio rising above 20. But, if you had sold out of the market, vowing not to get back in until the p/E fell well below 20, you would have missed a long period in which your investment would have delivered attractive returns.

Elroy Dimson, Paul Marsh and Mike Staunton of London Business School researched the benefits of a switch strategy versus a hold strategy. They calculated the return that investors would have made if they had invested when markets were trading at low multiples relative to historical levels, and divested into treasury bills when markets were at high multiples. So, for example, an investor in 1930 would decide whether to switch to treasury bills or not based on data available on multiples and returns in all the years leading up to 1930.

The results are surprising. Investors, on average, make less money by switching than by holding. This is true across all of the 20 countries they surveyed (see figure below). The red (light grey) bars show the average annual real return that would result from remaining invested in the stock market the whole time. The blue (dark grey) bars show the results of trying to switch in and out of the market based on whether it appears to be over- or undervalued.

Any benefits of avoiding stock market crashes are outweighed by the costs of being out of the market when share prices are rising. It is also partly because returns on treasury

Real returns: 1900–2012. (Source: Elroy Dimson, Paul Marsh and Mike Staunton, DMS database)

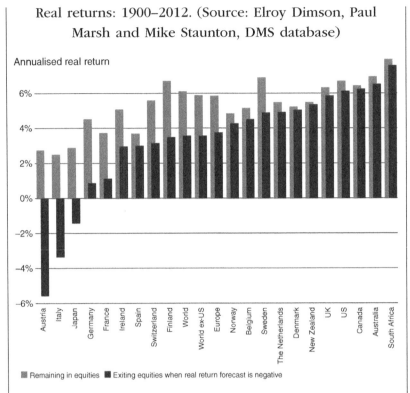

Annualised real return

■ Remaining in equities ■ Exiting equities when real return forecast is negative

bills during boom years are often low. Interestingly, the UK and the USA are two markets where the switching strategy almost works – but even in these markets it fails.

The authors conclude that it is hard to arbitrage the stock market. They suggest that some strategies do seem to offer some potential – but they require the investor to have a great deal of courage, a high level of sophistication, a long time horizon and an appetite for risk. Few corporate managers will want to bet their company on such strategies. If they feel they have such skills, they should probably seek employment with a hedge fund or investment company.[11]

The implication is that, when applying capital markets logic, corporate managers should not try to second-guess the price level of the overall stock market. Rather, they should focus on spotting whether individual companies are mispriced.

Does the financial analysis suggest that the level of mispricing is significant?

If you believe that a business has been mispriced, and that you have unique capabilities that allow you to take advantage of the situation, it is worth checking your assumptions with some financial analysis. This should be done in combination with the thinking described above, rather than as a separate exercise. The goal is to quantify the size of the mispricing to see if it is trivial and should be ignored, or significant enough to be considered when making the decision.

The exact analysis required depends on the situation – for example, whether you are considering buying, holding or selling. For simplicity, we consider here just one situation – in which you are deciding whether to sell an unattractive business to which you do not add much value. However, the basic approach is similar, whatever the situation. A more detailed description is given on our website: www.corporatelevelstrategy.info.

You need to start by understanding the conditions in the capital markets. Assume that, in this case, you think the business you want to sell will not attract many buyers; that those it does attract will be "financial" buyers; and that all buyers will have access to good information about the business and will analyse it rationally. This leads you to conclude that the business is likely to be priced rationally based on the information available. It is unlikely to sell for a premium.

Then you need to consider whether you have superior capabilities or insights that would allow you to value the business better than the buyers. Assume that, in this case, you have unique insights into the business that will not be available to buyers. In particular, you know that the performance of the business will deteriorate from today's level in a way that is not obvious to buyers. This means that the true value of the business is likely to be lower than the price that an outsider would calculate.

The financial analysis can help by bringing all your thinking together, so that you can make a judgement about whether to sell or not. Three steps are required.

First, calculate the value to you of retaining the business. This is done with a conventional analysis, discounting the projected future cash flows of the business. You will need to make a large number of assumptions about such things as market attractiveness, competitive advantage, growth rates, margins, capital requirements, etc. Therefore, it is sensible to come up with a range of scenarios for the valuation.

Second, estimate a range of prices that buyers might be likely to pay. This could come from a number of sources. The price earnings ratios paid in previous, similar transactions are a typical starting point. More detailed modelling could involve estimating how potential buyers might value the acquisition. In some industries there are particular models, such as the price per barrel of reserves for an oil company, the price per room for hotels or the price per subscriber for a magazine. In other industries there are typical premiums to current market price. Again, a range of estimates, rather than a precise number, is more useful.

Perhaps, at this stage, the numbers give a clear answer. For example, if, under most reasonable scenarios, the business is worth less to you than the lowest price you expect buyers to offer, then you will sell.

Often, the analysis is less conclusive. When this happens, it can be helpful to identify the key assumptions that drive the valuations. It may be useful to do more work on these assumptions. Ultimately, however, the decision should not be made on what the financial analysis says, but on your judgement about these key assumptions.

Of course, when selling, the solution is often to put the business up for sale and see what happens. If you get offered more than you think the business is worth to you, sell. If not, hold. Doing the analysis first can arm you for the sale process and it can help you avoid unnecessary disappointment.

Fair value matrix

The results of the analyses described in this chapter can be summarised on the matrix shown in Figure 5.1. The vertical axis is the estimated market price that the business could achieve. The horizontal axis is the value of the business under your ownership. The goal is not to position the business precisely, but to decide in which of the three broad areas it lies. The position of a particular business will not be a point, but an area on the chart, illustrating the range of credible prices and valuations.

When capital markets price businesses "about right" (the "fair value corridor" in the middle of the figure) you can apply the conclusions drawn from the previous two logics. For example, if you own an attractive business for which you are the best owner, you should keep it.

Figure 5.1: Fair Value matrix

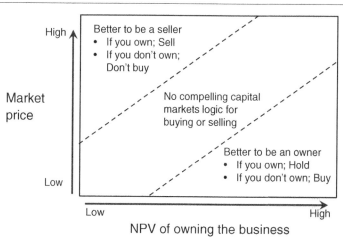

However, if the market price of a business is likely to be significantly higher than the value of the business under your ownership (top left), you should consider selling it or not buying it, even if you believe it to be attractive and you are convinced you would be a good owner. If the market price is significantly lower than net present value (NPV) (bottom right), you should consider holding or buying, even if you believe that the business is unattractive and you are not the best owner. How to deal with such situations is discussed further in the following chapter.

What level of difference between the market price and NPV is "significant" is tricky to define. In mature businesses, where you can be somewhat confident of valuations, a figure around 20% is a useful rule of thumb. In practice, the analysis is often not so precise – so that the final decision is likely to be more based on strategic judgement, informed by financial analysis, rather than the other way around.

Using capital markets logic proactively

In many cases, capital markets logic is used primarily to check a decision that has provisionally been made using a combination of the other two logics. For example, if you find an acquisition that is both attractive and to which you can add value, you then apply capital markets logic to see if you can buy it for a reasonable price. However, capital markets logic can be used more proactively – as a primary element of your portfolio strategy, driving what businesses are bought and sold.

One proactive strategy is to look to buy companies when they are cheap. Barry Diller built Interactive Corp following the dot.com bust. He spotted that dot.com businesses were out of favour. This meant that their share prices were artificially low. They were also finding it difficult to raise money for expansion.

Diller had sold a cable business for $10 billion and had plenty of cash. He therefore acquired businesses like Expedia and Hotels.com at low prices (capital markets logic). He then invested more money in these businesses to help them expand at a time when their competitors were short of capital (added value logic).

This combination of capital markets and added value logic is a natural pairing. For example, the more internet businesses Diller bought using capital markets logic, the more he learnt about how to add value to those businesses – for example, by helping them negotiate better deals with suppliers. The more he learnt about how to improve the performance of the businesses he owned, the better able he was to spot other undervalued internet businesses.

Another way to use capital markets logic proactively is to think about how to get a high price for a business you want to sell. For example, as has already been mentioned, private equity companies will take extensive steps to ensure that businesses they own will be attractive to a number of buyers – preferably ones who might pay over the odds for the business. They will not invest in things that might put off buyers – for example, factories, offices or new ventures that these new owners might want to close down. They will market their businesses to potential buyers who might not otherwise have considered the business – for example, promoting European businesses to American buyers who might otherwise have overlooked them. They may structure the deal to appeal to particular buyers – for example, agreeing to sell only a share in the business if the buyer is concerned about its future prospects. They may play up the threat of selling to a competitor who could use this entry point to attack the targeted purchaser. In other words, they do not simply analyse the price a business will obtain, they proactively manage it.

UBS (a global bank) has a dedicated unit that specialises in selling businesses – the "Exclusive Sales and Divestments Group". From experience in carrying out over 270 deals, it has learnt how to get the best price for a client's business, even when there is a lack of "competitive tension". Internal analysis shows that in 30% of the deals, the winner paid more than 10% above the offer of the second bidder. In another 25% of their deals, the final winner raised its offer even though it was the only bidder.

Summary

Like business logic, capital markets logic is mainly an investment logic not a management logic. It is the logic used by fund managers looking after a portfolio of investments. It is the logic Warren Buffett uses to make investment decisions in Berkshire Hathaway. In his own words, "... Ben Graham taught me that 'Price is what you pay; value is what you get.' Whether we're talking about socks or stocks, I like buying quality merchandise when it is marked down."[12]

Directly or indirectly capital markets logic affects all mergers and acquisitions. Companies estimate the value of a business they want to buy, and stop bidding if the price goes above this level. They estimate the value of businesses they want to sell and only accept prices above this value.

Often, capital markets logic will not provide clear guidance. In such cases, the other two logics should drive the decision. At other times, capital markets logic will be so persuasive that it may cause you to make a decision that is in opposition to the conclusion drawn from the other two logics. At still other times, when a particular sector becomes over- or undervalued, it may proactively drive corporate strategy.

In general, capital markets logic should be used with caution. It is all too easy to persuade yourself that a business is over- or underpriced when, in fact, the market has it about right. Experience and academic studies suggest that it is hard to second guess the market. Many managers think they have better information and insight when they do not. Capital markets logic should therefore be used carefully – following the approach laid out in this chapter.

Notes

[1] Edwin Elton and Martin Gruber, "Mutual Funds", in George Constantinides, Milton Harris and Rene Stultz (Eds.), *Financial Markets and Asset Pricing: Handbook of the Economics of Finance* (North Holland, 2012); Garrett Quigley and Rex Sinquefield, "Performance of UK Equity Unit Trusts", *Journal of Asset Management*, 2000; Mark Rhodes, "Past Imperfect? The Performance of UK Equity Managed Funds", Occasional Paper Series 9, Financial Services Authority (FSA), 2000.

[2] Sydney Finkelstein, Jo Whitehead and Andrew Campbell, *Think Again: Why Good Leaders Make Bad Decisions and How to Keep it From Happening to You* (Cambridge: Harvard Business Press, 2008).

[3] *The Warren Buffett Way* (Wiley) eu.wiley.com/WileyCDA/Section/id-817935.html.

[4] The particular evidence for this is that insiders in large companies are not better at valuing them than the market, but insiders in smaller companies are – see Josef Lakonishok and Inmoo Lee, "Are Insiders' Trades Informative?" *Review of Financial Studies*, Vol. 14, No. 1, 2001, 79–111.

[5] E.C. Capen, R.V. Clapp and W.M. Campbell, "Competitive Bidding in High-Risk Situations", *Journal of Petroleum Technology*, 23, 1971, 641–653.

[6] Leslie Jeng, Andrew Metrick and Richard Zeckhauser, "Estimating the returns to insider trading: A performance-evaluation perspective," *The Review of Economics and Statistics*, 85, 2003, 453–471.

[7] David Ikenberry, Josef Lakonishok and Theo Vermaelen, "Market Underreaction to Open Market Share Repurchases", *Journal of Financial Economics*, Vol. 39, Nos 2–3, October–November 1995, 181–208.

[8] Tim Loughran and Jay R. Ritter, "The New Issues Puzzle", *Journal of Finance*, Vol. 50, No. 1, March 1995, 23–51.

[9] The Schiller P/E ratio, developed by Yale Professor Robert Schiller, is obtained by dividing the S&P 500 by the average inflation-adjusted earnings from the previous 10 years.

[10] Mark Kamstra, "Pricing Firms on the Basis of Fundamentals", Federal Reserve Bank of Atlanta, *Economic Review*, First Quarter, 2003.

[11] Elroy Dimson, Paul Marsh and Mike Staunton, "Mean Reversion", *Credit Suisse Global Investment Returns Yearbook*, 2013, 17–27.

[12] Berkshire Hathaway, Chairman's letter, 2008.

CHAPTER SIX

MAKING DECISIONS ABOUT WHERE TO INVEST AND WHAT TO AVOID

The three logics can be combined to decide where to invest, where to cut back, where to buy and where to exit – in other words, to make portfolio decisions. Because each logic contributes something to the decision, we recommend that managers keep all three in mind when making decisions. Typically, managers start with one of the logics and come to the others later. For example, managers at Apple might start by looking for attractive product categories to enter (business logic), focusing the search on areas where they can add some value (value added logic). If acquisitions are required, they are evaluated to determine whether they are affordable (capital markets logic).

Companies with very clear value added strategies, such as Danaher, may start from a different position. Managers at Danaher will look for businesses to which they can add value (value added logic), and which are available at reasonable prices (capital markets logic). When they have found an affordable target they will check its attractiveness (business logic). If it is a real turkey it may not be worth acquiring because, even under their ownership, it will not generate adequate cash flow to justify the cost. But, if it is a reasonable business, they will proceed with the deal, confident that their ability to add value will make the business worth more than they will pay for it.

When deciding whether to invest heavily in an existing business, most managers start by assessing the attractiveness of the business (business logic), then consider what they have to do to add value (value added logic). They may only consider the price they could get for the business (capital markets logic) tangentially or if someone approaches them to buy the business.

When selling, some managers will start by identifying businesses that are not performing well (business logic) or that they do not understand well (value added logic) and then evaluate what price they might be able to get (capital markets logic). Others may be open to opportunities to sell any business if the price is attractive (capital markets logic).

What counts most is not the specific approach used, but that all three logics are used, to evaluate all reasonable options.

Decision making when logics conflict

The simplest situation is one where all three logics are aligned. The business is attractive, we can add value to it and it is cheap. Alternatively, the business is not attractive, we subtract value and it will fetch a good price. In such cases the decision is easy. But often the three logics are not aligned – for example, an attractive business to which we can add value is selling for a high price. Or, an unattractive business, to which we can add little value, but which is likely to sell for a low price.

In situations when the three logics are not aligned, some careful consideration is typically required. There are many such situations. Suppose, for example, we evaluate an existing business or potential acquisition using three possible categorisations for each of the three logics (see Figure 6.1). The categorisation for each is either green (suggesting the business

Figure 6.1: Many different combinations of "green, red, amber" possible

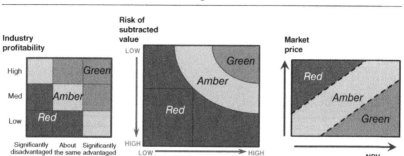

should be retained or acquired), red (suggesting the business should be sold, or not be acquired) or amber (neutral or inconclusive). There are 27 combinations, each of which needs a potentially different approach.

We will not attempt to discuss all 27 situations. Instead, we will focus on a few common ones. Those interested in a more comprehensive description of how to deal with all different situations can visit the website: www.corporatelevelstrategy.info. Here we also give advice to managers facing a common growth challenge: the core business is becoming less attractive, but the adjacent growth sectors are expensive to get into and the company is unlikely to be a good parent.

You can add value but the business is unattractive

Most management teams try to avoid unattractive businesses: ones with low margins, weak positions and limited growth prospects. But what if you are good at adding value to these businesses, as in Figure 6.2 below? The default answer is to focus on what you are good at.

Consider the case of Grupo Bimbo, a $10.8 billion Mexican baking giant, the world's largest bread manufacturing company. It operates in a tough business: bakery products. These products have notoriously low margins, partly because customers

Figure 6.2: You can add value to an unattractive business

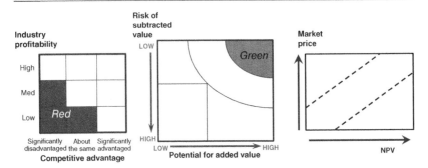

are price sensitive, partly because supermarkets have a lot of bargaining power and partly because there are many competitors.[1] Operating margins for 2011 were only 8% and return on equity 11%. Some competitors, such as Hostess Brands, have gone bankrupt. Other industry participants, such as Sara Lee in the USA or Hovis in the UK, have been in gradual decline.[2] However, Grupo Bimbo's stock price has gone up 700% since 2000, and revenues have nearly doubled in the past five years.[3]

Grupo Bimbo's secret is that it adds a lot of value to the bakery businesses it owns. It has a strong focus on operations. For example, it is particularly skilled at optimising delivery routes for its trucks. Each truck carries a computer to help the optimization process.[4] The company is skilled at optimising oven utilisation in its 100 plants. Much of the machinery used in its factories is developed and manufactured in its industrial division. It also produces a significant portion of the plastic packaging used on its products.

Grupo Bimbo brings an innovative approach to a very traditional industry. It introduced Spaniards to sliced loaves and pioneered the packaging of bread in clear cellophane. It also transfers best practices around the world. For example, it uses tricycle delivery bikes in Chinese cities where streets are too narrow for trucks, a practice it first developed in Latin America.

Using its ability to add value to low return businesses has allowed Grupo Bimbo to acquire other bakery companies such as Weston Foods Inc. (Sara Lee's American baking operations) and sections of Hostess Brands' bread business out of bankruptcy.[5] It is now the largest baker in the USA.[6, 7] Such businesses are often available at reasonable prices, because other potential owners regard them as unattractive.

Grupo Bimbo is an example of acquiring and investing in unattractive businesses. Dow Corning is an example of holding onto a business that became unattractive. Dow Corning is the global leader in silicone-based products. As the industry matured, parts of it came under attack from competitors selling at low prices. Dow Corning had been adding value to its businesses through high investment in R&D, and by sharing technical support, sales forces and logistics. Unfortunately, while these activities helped deliver high service levels and high margins in most product categories, they also added cost. This meant that Dow Corning became unprofitable in the low price segment.

Dow Corning's response was to create a new division, Xiameter, acting below the level of the corporate parent, with its own brand and sales force. Xiameter sells 350 of the most commoditised silicone compounds at a 10–15% discount, with strict terms for customers (such as a requirement to use the internet to order and track orders) and a stripped-down, low cost approach. The rest of the business continues under the traditional approach. Xiameter and the other businesses share Dow Corning's sophisticated IT and logistics system. The modification in parenting style has been highly successful – in 2010 Dow Corning sales were $6 billion, up from below $2.5 billion in 2001, and the company achieved a turnaround from losses to $866 million in profits.[8]

Dow Corning is an unusual example of dual corporate strategies – one that adds value to highly attractive businesses and one that adds value to less attractive businesses. It is challenging to pull off but provides greater opportunities for value creation and growth if successful. Less dramatic forms of dual strategies are possible. For example, Procter and Gamble has split its sales force into two groups, one for high income and one for low income markets – the latter selling cheaper products such as Luvs diapers and Gain detergent.[9]

Before leaving this section it is important to highlight a major risk with buying or holding unattractive businesses. Typically, unattractive businesses do not provide a reasonable return on incremental investments. Hence, the added value needs to be sufficient to overcome this major disadvantage.

Whether a particular situation generates significant value for shareholders will, therefore, depend on the numbers: What is the price at which businesses can be bought? What further investment is required to maintain the business? What will be the returns on this investment? If some are likely to be below the cost of capital, what is the net return on investment?

Attractive business where you do not add value

Every manager likes an attractive business, one with high margins that has a competitive advantage. But what if you are

Figure 6.3: Attractive business where you do not add value

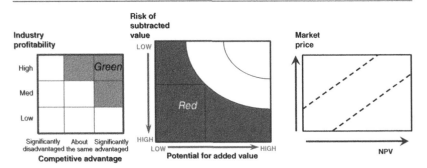

not good at adding value to this business? The default answer is to learn fast how to add value. But it is not always possible.

When Rolls-Royce acquired the marine business of Vickers, it acquired a number of different businesses, one of which was the Ulstein offshore ship business. This small Norwegian business made components and systems for vessels used to supply oil rigs – a technically demanding environment in which ships, in the middle of very heavy seas, have to remain within a few metres of the rig.

Rolls-Royce could see that, from the perspective of business logic, this was an attractive business. The value of such a vessel to an oil company is very high and there were few competitors able to design and build them. However, Rolls-Royce added little immediate value to Ulstein. To become a strong competitor, Ulstein would need to broaden its products, add niche technology capabilities and sell globally. Rolls-Royce did not have a management team with the industry expertise required.

To address the management gap, Rolls-Royce hired a new head for its marine businesses, who put together a team of managers to lead this effort. He drew from Ulstein, Rolls-Royce and outside. This team contained insights and skills that could add value to the growing portfolio of marine businesses. For example, Rolls-Royce corporate managers understood the potential value that could be created from offering ship owners not just components (such as diesel engines) but systems (such as complete drive systems including electronic controls). They also understood the potential value that could come from offering long-term service support to ship operators. They had learned this from their experience in civil aerospace and defence.

Rolls-Royce's marine business has grown from about £750 million revenues in 2000, the year after the acquisition, to over £2500 million in 2010. Today, Rolls-Royce is a leading competitor in this segment. But, to get there it had to develop many of the parenting skills needed to turn the vision into a reality.

Another example is that of E.ON, the European power and gas company, which entered the renewables business by investing in a number of wind farms. These were attractive businesses, operating with secure revenues under government subsidy schemes. At the time, E.ON was not able to add significant value to these businesses, but thought that it could in the future, by building up a large portfolio of wind farms and extracting economies of scale. Purchasing scale could be used to lower costs (as the purchase of equipment is the major element of total cost), and the process of bidding, designing, building and operating could be standardised to lower costs and improve performance. Some value could also be generated by providing a strong balance sheet and by introducing managers in the new business to E.ON contacts across Europe.

While E.ON had a vision of how it could add value to the renewables business, it had to create the capabilities required, as few of these were available in house. It hired a new CEO, Frank Mastieux, from outside, who built up a team capable of adding value to the wind farm businesses. Some of the team came from existing E.ON businesses, some from outside and some from the various acquisitions. Today, the renewables business is one of the core areas where E.ON is focusing new investment.

It is even possible to enter renewables without an added value strategy. Many companies have chosen to take advantage of the guaranteed returns, including Warren Buffett,[10] Sir Richard Branson, the private equity company Terra Firma and even Google, whose Director of Green Business Operations stated, "It's a way of helping us to diversify our cash, put it into businesses that can earn good returns and that aren't correlated to other investments ..."[11] While we do not consider cash diversification a valid logic (shareholders are in a better position to do this), we support the objective "earn good returns".

As we will point out in Chapter 14, developing new parenting skills is not an easy thing to do. It often requires significant changes in people and a willingness to let go of past habits and processes. It is easy to presume that a company will be able to learn to be a good parent, especially when the business is attractive. Failure is three or four times more common than success.

One way to seize the challenge and hence help managers decide whether to try or not to try is to focus on the rival parents. For Rolls-Royce's marine businesses and for E.ON's renewable businesses, the rival parents were not obviously superior at adding value; hence, the challenge of developing good enough parenting skills was worth the risk. In many other cases, it is not.

Another reason for entering an attractive business, even when you are not a good owner, is because you plan to resell the business rather than hold onto it.

In 1990, Mannesmann, a steel company, bid for a mobile phone licence in Germany. Because the market was growing and only a few licences were being issued, Mannesmann's management could see that it was highly probable that companies owning a licence would do well. Mannesmann's concerns about lacking a management team with relevant experience were outweighed by the prospect of very high returns.

As the business evolved, however, it became clear that Mannesmann was not the most value-adding owner of such a business. Mannesmann eventually sold its mobile networks business to Vodafone for over £100 billion, at a significant profit on its investment.

A parallel example is Cellnet in the UK, a mobile phone network which was originally developed by Securicor, a security company. Securicor was a poor owner of a mobile phone company – operating at half the profit margins of its UK rival, Vodafone. But, it was still an attractive investment for Securicor, because returns were high and, when Securicor sold the business to its partner, BT, it received over £3 billion from its initial investment of just £4 million.[12]

Attractive, heartland businesses which are overpriced

When you find an attractive business that you can add value to, your instinct is to hold onto it or to acquire it. But, what if the price in the capital markets is higher than the net present value (NPV) of owning the business – perhaps because the business is in a hot sector? Should you sell? If you are considering acquiring, should you withdraw from bidding? The default answer is different depending on whether you are looking to acquire or whether you already own the business, and whether the reason for the overvaluation in the capital markets is likely to be temporary or permanent.

If you are looking to acquire, the default answer is not to. Either change the strategy so that you do not need to buy the business, or wait until the capital markets correct themselves. However, there are tactics that you can employ if you want to proceed with the acquisition. For example, if both your company

Figure 6.4: An attractive business to which you add value, but which is overpriced in capital markets

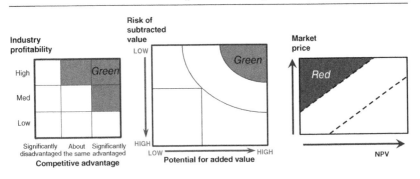

and the target are trading at high multiples relative to historic levels (and especially if your multiple is particularly high), you can make the acquisition with equity rather than with cash, or issue new shares and use the cash to buy the acquisition. This results in paying for an overpriced asset with overpriced equity.[13]

Another tactic to cope with high prices is to structure the deal to reduce the risk that you overpay. A common approach is to use an "earn-out formula". This can work if the seller believes the business is worth more than the buyer. An earn-out allows both to see the deal as attractive due to different assessments of its future prospects. In the event that the business performs to the seller's expectations, both sides are happy. In the event that it performs to the buyer's expectations, at least the buyer is happy.

If you are looking to hold, and you are a superior owner, but the price which you could receive from selling the business is higher than the NPV, the default answer is to hold. You should be wary about allowing your strategy to be buffeted by the vagaries of the capital markets. The overvaluation is likely to be temporary.

However, there are some conditions when you should consider selling. Maybe the premium the buyer is offering is too big to ignore. Maybe the cash will help you overcome a shortage of funding that is preventing you from investing in other parts of your portfolio. Maybe you believe there is a chance of selling now and repurchasing later if the business fails to perform to the new owner's expectations.

Where the overvaluation is likely to be permanent, and you want to retain the business, there are tactics that can ease the problem. For example, the business can be set up with a separate stock market quotation, yet still be majority owned by the existing parent company. This was the solution for many mining companies that owned gold mining businesses. Gold mining companies traditionally had market capitalisations higher than their NPVs. A company, like Anglo American, which for many years owned a gold mining business, maintained a separate stock market quotation for this business.

Further tactics and advice on how to select the most appropriate ones are provided on the website: www.corporatelevelstrategy.info.

Unattractive businesses you own, where you are subtracting value, but which can only be sold at below NPV

Managers with unattractive businesses to which they cannot add value will normally sell. But, what if you cannot get a price that matches the value to you of retaining the business? The default position is to construct a way of selling.

Many companies will simply keep such a business and wait until they can offload it at a better price. But, as the seller, there are some tactics that can be used to increase the price offered by buyers. Which tactic is most appropriate will depend on the reason for the low price – be it a lack of buyers, the nature of those buyers, the information they have about the business or the deal process. For example, a mining company wanted to

Figure 6.5: An unattractive business from which you subtract value, but which is priced below NPV

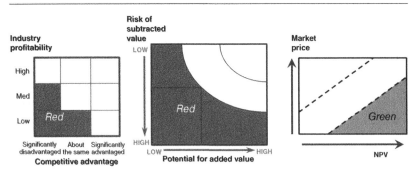

dispose of a combined smelter and cast house (a facility in which the metal from the smelter is cast into semi-finished products). Unfortunately, there were very few interested buyers. Relatively few companies wanted to purchase the combined smelter and cast house. The problem was made worse because the smelter had committed to buying electricity from the local power utility at a high price.

To deal with the situation, the mining company restructured the deal into three separate parts. The cast house could now be sold to a company who wanted to use their own metal as an input. The power contract for the smelter (a commitment to buy electricity at a fixed price for a 20-year period) was sold back to the utility. The smelter was left as an independent asset that could be sold or, if the reserve price was not reached, shut down. Unbundling the business into separate parts turned it into a more saleable proposition and improved overall NPV.

Another way to increase price is to redesign the deal process. For example, when Tesco divested its Japanese operation, it had to pay the buyer, Aeon, £40 million to take it off its hands. To make the best of a bad situation, it divided the deal process into two stages. In the first stage it transferred 50% of the business, with the intention of selling the rest at a later date. This allowed the buyer and seller, who had different views about the value of the business, to reach an agreement. If the business performs well, Tesco will be able to get a better price for the remaining 50% share.

What to do also depends on the risks of subtracted value. If the current owner neither adds nor subtracts much value the business is "ballast". Retaining it for a while is unlikely to reduce its value. The sale process need not be rushed.

For example, a natural resources company owned an aluminium business. Aluminium was, at that time, not an attractive business due to global overcapacity. Also, the company was not a particularly good owner of aluminium businesses. Unfortunately, the business could not be sold at a sufficiently attractive price. Better parents had their own challenges at the time and were not keen to acquire the business.

Fortunately, the company had a partner in this business, who was the operator of the joint venture. Since the partner acted as the parent, there was little risk that the natural resources company would subtract value. So, the company decided to hold on to its share, and look for an opportunity to offload the investment in the future.

If subtracted value is high, the pressure for an urgent disposal is higher. Retaining the business means it will sell for less in the future. Moreover, the parent company may be distracted by the need to deal with continuing problems and frictions. Getting rid of it speedily – using whatever tactics you can to maximise the price – is likely to be the least bad solution. This appears to have been the case for Tesco in Japan.

Running the numbers

Financial analysis can provide some additional help when the logics are not aligned by integrating the insights from the three logics into one calculation. However, caution is needed. In our experience, financial analysis is best used to support or to test strategic logic, rather than to replace it. Because financial analysis depends on estimates of what will happen in the future, it can easily mislead.

The example shown in Figure 6.6 is for a current business. Assume both business logic and value added logic suggest that you should keep the business: the business is attractive and you can add significant value to it. However, you also feel that the capital markets may attribute a high value to the business: the three logics may not be aligned. So you want to check the financials.

Figure 6.6: Calculating the net present value of retaining a business

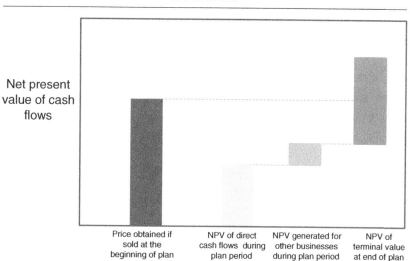

The first column shows the price you would be likely to get for the business today. The next column values the cash flows that you expect the business to generate over the plan period, based on the attractiveness of the business and your ability to add value to it. The third column gives the value of any cash flows that come from other businesses in your company as a result of retaining this business. Often this column is zero. The fourth column is the discounted value of the business at the end of the plan period, based on some estimate of its "terminal value".

If the top of the fourth column is higher than the top of the first column, you should keep the business. If it is lower, you should consider selling: the premium that the capital markets are giving the business is likely to be greater than the value you can generate by holding onto it.

The financial analysis brings together the insights from the three logics and focuses attention on where further analysis is required. If keeping the business is clearly more value creating than selling it under all reasonable assumptions, then the choice is clear. However, the business may only create more value under certain assumptions. In such cases the analysis highlights the key assumptions that drive the net value. For example, these might be about future growth rates of the market, or how much extra value can be generated from synergies with other businesses. This indicates which assumptions need further investigation, analysis, discussion and judgement.

Summary

Portfolio strategy requires all three logics. If all three are either "green" or "red", then the choice is clear. But, when there is a mix, the decision has to be carefully weighed.

This chapter has discussed four out of the 27 possible situations. Three relate to decisions about whether to own a business (whether you hold it already or are seeking to acquire it).

If the business is unattractive, the company must be particularly good at adding value to choose to own it.

If the company does not add value then there are two conditions under which owning the business may make sense. One is that you can develop adequate parenting skills. Another is that the business is so attractive that you can generate high returns for a while and then sell to a better owner. However, in both situations, you need to be confident that rival parents do not have a significant advantage over you.

Possibly the hardest of the three occurs when the capital markets overvalue a business, to which you are a good parent. In certain cases, holding onto the business or finding a way to buy it can still make sense.

The fourth situation concerns disposals. If the price you will get is low, there are some tactics that may alleviate the situation – although you may have to hold on to the business until the market turns.

In all these situations it can be helpful to model the combined impact of the three logics using financial analysis. But beware of allowing the financial analysis to drive your thinking. Strategy should come first and financial analysis used to check and validate the strategy.

Notes

[1] Michael Porter, "The Five Forces that Shape Competitive Strategy", *Harvard Business Review*, January 2008, 79–93. In Porter's study, the US bakery products industry was found to have an average return on invested capital of 13.8%, which was below the average for the USA.

[2] http://online.wsj.com/news/articles/SB10001424052748704635704575604162311064370, Ilan Brat and Anjali Cordeiro, "Sara Lee Profit Falls, Sells Bakery Unit for $959 Million", *Wall Street Journal* online, Nov 10, 2010.

[3] http://finance.yahoo.com/echarts?s=BIMBOA.MX+Interactive#symbol=bimboa.mx;range=my;compare=^dji;indicator=volume;charttype=area;crosshair=on;ohlcvalues=0;logscale=off;source=undefined

[4] http://blogs.hbr.org/2012/10/how-the-worlds-largest-bakery-puts-execution-before-strategy/, Mauro F. Guillén and Esteban García-Canal, "How the World's Largest Bakery Puts Execution Before Strategy", *Harvard Business Review*, Oct 2, 2012.

[5] http://www.atlasadvisors.com/headline/grupobimbo-beefsteak/

[6] "The Best since Sliced Bread", *Economist*, January 19, 2013.

[7] http://en.wikipedia.org/wiki/Grupo_Bimbo

[8] Xiameter case study and teaching note, IMD, 2011.

[9] "Gold-hunting in a Frugal Age", *Economist*, December 15, 2012.

[10] http://www.renewableenergyworld.com/rea/news/article/2013/01/new-ways-to-invest-in-solar-like-buffett, "New Ways to Invest in Solar Like Buffett".

[11] http://www.greenbiz.com/print/45944, "Why Google Invests in Clean Energy", Marc Gunther, 2/1/2012.

[12] http://news.bbc.co.uk/2/hi/business/404792.stm, "BT Gobbles up Cellnet", July 27, 1999.

[13] Ming Donga, David Hirshleiferb, Scott Richardsonc and Siew Hong Teoh, "Does Investor Misvaluation Drive the Takeover Market?" Working paper, September 28, 2003. As further supporting evidence for this, companies that buy with cash outperform those that buy with equity. This is likely because equity is only used when it is overvalued relative to the market (and, in particular, to the target). As a consequence, the company tends to underperform relative to the market after making the acquisition. See N.G. Travlos, "Corporate Takeover Bids, Method of Payment and Bidding Firms' Stock Returns", *Journal of Finance*, Vol. 42, 1987, 943–963, and also Mark Mitchell, Todd Pulvino and Erik Stafford, "Price Pressure around Mergers," *Journal of Finance*, American Finance Association, Vol. 59, No. 1, 2004, 31–63.

PART III

WAYS OF ADDING AND SUBTRACTING VALUE FROM CORPORATE HEADQUARTERS

In Part II, we described the three logics for making portfolio decisions. We wanted to show the importance of these logics and how they can be used together to help make better decisions. We did not have space to explore any of the logics in much detail.

Business logic is fully explored in most business strategy books because it is a foundation of business-level strategy thinking. The same is true for capital markets logic. Understanding capital markets is a foundation of finance theory thinking. As a result, we will not spend more time on these two logics.

There are fewer books and articles dedicated to added value logic. This is because added value logic is unique to corporate-level strategy. Hence, it is appropriate that we have a special part of this book in which we explore added and subtracted value in more detail.

There is also an additional reason for giving more attention to added value logic. Added value logic is the prime driver of decisions about how corporate headquarters should manage its businesses. It is the prime driver of decisions about centralisation and decentralisation, what functions and activities should exist at headquarters, how the organisation should be structured and how much interaction is required among business divisions. Hence, a deeper understanding of added and subtracted value is necessary before we get to Part IV of this book – management strategy.

In Part III, we will look at examples of added value and subtracted value and the conditions that need to exist for either to occur. We will also share tools and techniques for helping managers identify the sources of added value that are relevant to their company.

CHAPTER SEVEN

TEN SOURCES OF VALUE FROM DIRECT INFLUENCE

Corporate headquarters can add value in two ways: directly by influencing or supporting individual business divisions, or less directly by encouraging coordination across divisions. We will call the first "vertical added value" because the value comes vertically down the hierarchy from corporate headquarters. This is our focus in this chapter. The second type we will call "horizontal added value" because it is about encouraging horizontal relationships and coordination.

Vertical added value happens when corporate-level managers guide, direct, impose, persuade or incentivise managers in the business divisions in ways that cause the business divisions to perform better than they would have performed without this hierarchical influence. Vertical added value can be created by a parent company even for a single business. It does not depend on the existence of a portfolio of businesses. If the managers in the parent company have skills that the business managers do not have, know something that the business managers do not know or own something of value that the business managers do not possess, then there is the potential to create vertical added value.

Horizontal added value is the focus of the next chapter. It comes from sharing between businesses. It requires the existence of multiple businesses or operating units. It is created when one division gets help or strategic ideas or good practice from another division. It is also created when the corporate level exploits bargaining power or economies of scale or skill across a number of business divisions.

Many situations involve both vertical value and horizontal value. For example, when the executive vice president of group marketing sets up a group marketing committee, the objective is often to create both vertical value and horizontal value. Vertical value comes from the central policies and guidance that are agreed and communicated during the meetings. Horizontal value comes from the sharing of ideas and good practice that happens during the meetings. It also comes from agreements among businesses to work together on common challenges, such as a common IT system for managing customer relationships. Finally, horizontal value can come from relationships between marketing managers in different businesses that the meetings help create.

Of course, a group marketing committee can also subtract value, which is the subject of Chapter 9. The executive vice president of group marketing can set inappropriate policies and give unhelpful guidance; ideas exchanged between businesses can prove to be damaging rather than helpful; the meetings and relationships can take up scarce executive time and delay decisions; and arrangements to share an IT system can lead to compromises and delays that reduce effectiveness.

Vertical added value happens when the corporate level influences or helps managers running businesses in ways that cause them to perform better than they would have done without the influence or help. This often involves using superior authority to "persuade" or "impose" targets, people, processes, policies, actions or plans onto the managers running businesses. For example, Molsand managers (described in Chapter 1) imposed a number of changes on CIW, its newly acquired wire division. They changed managers. They launched a major cost reduction effort. They changed the structure from regional business units to global functions. They made these changes in order to make savings in management and administrative costs of about $100 million. They also expected to improve the speed of decision making, and the effectiveness of product development work. If these changes achieve these objectives, they will more than double the value of CIW.

There are a large number of sources of vertical value. Where the source of value is obvious, we will give a simple example or two. Where the source of the value is harder to grasp or has multiple dimensions to it, we will give three or four examples to help illustrate the nature of the value. In each case, we will also try to explain why the opportunity to add value might exist. The list that follows is not intended to be complete. Its purpose is to show some of the main sources of vertical value, and to stimulate thinking more widely. The source of vertical value that generates advantage for your company, that enables you to outbid another company for an acquisition, may not even be mentioned in this list. This is because advantage comes from doing things differently and finding new ways of adding value.

People decisions

The corporate level can add value by removing less competent managers and replacing them with more competent managers. This is what happened at CIW following the acquisition by Molsand. Most of the top managers in CIW left the business following the acquisition. Some of the replacements were managers who had proven their skills in other Molsand businesses. But some were hired from outside. The Molsand team, unconstrained by loyalties and previous decisions, was able to make an objective assessment of the management talent needed to run the business. They also were looking for managers who would perform well under Molsand's fast-paced management approach. If the new managers prove to be more competent than the previous managers, these decisions will add value.

It is worth considering under what conditions corporate-level involvement in people decisions is likely to add value. Value will be added if corporate-level involvement results in removing weak managers or appointing better quality managers than would have happened without the involvement. As in the CIW case, the corporate level often has a more objective perspective, making it easier to spot weak managers and take action. Sometimes headquarters managers have some particular skill at finding or selecting good talent for a particular type of business or function. We would expect that Procter & Gamble is good at choosing product managers for businesses involved in global consumer brands. Also, a chief information officer may know better than managers in the business divisions whether the heads of IT in the business divisions are good quality, and where to find replacements for those who are not.

Many companies devote considerable effort to creating a pool of talent within the company that is better quality than typically available to independent companies not part of a corporate group. This is an example of a source of added value that is partly horizontal value and partly vertical value. We will discuss it further in the next chapter.

Strategies

The corporate level can add value by improving strategies. Molsand, for example, changed the strategy at CIW: to be more global and less regional. If this change is wise, it will add value.

One of the famous examples of strategic added value is Emerson Electric. Under CEO Chuck Knight, the company devoted considerable management effort to its strategy conferences. Each business division would spend one day, followed by a dinner, in an intensive dialogue with Chuck Knight about its strategy. Businesses were expected to spend three months preparing for these days. There were 70 required charts and analyses. The events were so important that Knight would never schedule two on consecutive days. With 40 business units, it took him six months to get through all the strategy conferences.

At the strategy conference, Knight would be challenging – looking for weak spots in the thinking presented to him. Strategy was viewed as a "contact sport". So Knight was not shy in pointing out weaknesses.

The added value came in four ways. First, managers worked much harder on strategy than in most companies. Even if only to avoid having weaknesses in their plans pointed out by Knight. Second, the required charts, such as a chart that distinguished between revenue gains and losses from inflation, new products, new markets and other sources, forced managers into a more detailed examination of their business than was usual. Third, following the rigorous challenge by Knight, managers were more committed and aligned than in most companies. Fourth, Knight was often able to add value in the dialogue, usually drawing on insights he had gained from other strategy conferences. The following day, he would write a short note to the head of the business identifying the three action points that had come out of the conference.

Interactive Corp, owner of internet businesses like Expedia and Hotels.com, had a profound influence on the strategies of these businesses. The CEO, Barry Diller, encouraged his businesses to double or triple the amount they spent on advertising and to be more ambitious in negotiating discounts from the hotels, airlines and travel companies that listed on their sites.

So, when is corporate-level influence on strategy likely to add value? The simple answer is, when headquarters managers know something about the market or the competitors or the sources of advantage or the operations that the managers in the businesses do not know. By definition, this is likely to be quite rare. The business managers will spend more time on their business and be closer to the markets and competitors and technologies than headquarters managers. So, it is normally hard for headquarters managers to add value unless they have had some experiences earlier in their careers that enable them to see what the business managers cannot see. This probably explains some of the added value at Molsand and Interactive Corp. The other possibility is that they are exposed to other similar businesses as a result of their corporate-level job, which gives them a perspective not available to the business-level managers. This probably explains some of Chuck Knight's contributions at Emerson.

Targets

The corporate level can add value by helping the businesses set better targets.

Molsand, for example, reset the performance targets for both Carlsen and CIW. At CIW, Molsand set new targets for costs. At Carlsen, Molsand asked the management team to identify three breakthrough projects, each of which would make a significant impact on performance. The projects could not be part of business-as-usual. If Molsand managers are right in judging that the previous targets were not ambitious enough, this action will add value: it will get the managers in these companies to achieve more than they would have done without the new targets.

Barry Diller at Interactive Corp set targets for higher discounts from suppliers. He observed that many young internet companies started by begging suppliers, like airlines or hotels, to list on their site. Once the internet company became established, managers were reluctant to go back to their original suppliers and demand larger discounts. So Diller set targets for higher discounts. He also offered to join the negotiations himself, if the managers were reluctant to push for major discounts. Diller found that he could typically double the level of discounts.

Jack Welch, CEO of GE during the 1980s and 1990s, was probably most famous for his No. 1 or No. 2 targets. He demanded that each business develop a strategy to become No. 1 or No. 2 in its global market. Businesses that could not reach this target were to be sold. He recognised that many of GE's businesses were successful within the USA but had insufficient international ambition. Anticipating global competition, he added value by driving the managers of his businesses to globalise before their competitors. This example is an illustration of the overlap between strategies and targets. A carefully chosen target can help create a much improved strategy.

Dow Chemical Company runs cyclical chemical businesses. The down cycle is caused when competitors add capacity at the same time. Excess capacity causes prices to drop, even while volumes continue to grow with economic activity. The up-cycle happens when capacity is constrained. Prices can rise sharply.

The cycle means that business units are often making significantly more money or significantly less money than budgeted. This can distract managers from the hard graft of cost management. When times are good, they focus on new developments, on planning new capacity and on satisfying their best customers. Because profits are high, they do not worry much about costs. When times are bad, when prices fall, managers frantically cut back costs and delay discretionary expenditures in an attempt to remain profitable.

Yet long-term advantage is determined by a plant's long-term cost position, which is, in part, a function of how well the managers have driven costs down, raised productivity and debottlenecked capacity. To keep managers focused on this long-term objective, despite the cycle, Dow used a target-setting process called bottom-of-the-cycle planning.

Because it is possible to predict with some accuracy the price that is likely to be reached at the bottom of the next cycle (even though the timing of this bottom is hard to predict), the corporate planners are able to set cost targets. They set the target at a level that would ensure the businesses would be profitable at the bottom of the next cycle. These targets add value by ensuring that managers focused on cost reduction, even in good times.

As with strategy, it is rare that headquarters managers are able to set targets for their business divisions that add value. To do so, headquarters managers must know better than business managers what the targets should be, or they must understand the pressures on business managers that can cause them to focus on the wrong targets.

Performance management

The corporate level can add value by introducing a powerful performance management process. While most companies have some bonus scheme or incentive structure to reinforce targets, some make performance management a source of particular added value.

Granada, a UK company that had businesses in television broadcasting, hotels, catering and TV rentals, had a particular approach to performance management, which the CEO called "unreasonable targets". The process of setting targets took three or four months to ensure full commitment from the businesses. Then the CEO monitored performance every month to make sure the businesses delivered what they had promised. Most of his time was devoted to this performance management approach.

During the year, the CEO would spend a few days in the field, travelling with repair engineers, working in a catering unit or working with a crew making a TV programme. From these experiences, he would spot opportunities for improvement. For example, when travelling with engineers, he found that each fault involved an average of two visits, so he estimated how much could be saved if the engineers fixed the fault with only one visit. When working on a TV programme, he noticed that many of the actors and crew were not doing anything most of the time. So he estimated how much costs could be reduced with better planning.

From these coalface experiences and his knowledge of each business's financial performance, he would come up with a performance target for the following year. He recognised that his targets would seem unreasonable to the managers in the business units. So he designed a process of planning and then budgeting that would gradually, over a four-month period, get the managers comfortable with the targets and confident that they could meet them. He then followed up in detail every month, holding managers to account against these targets. The result was that managers often did achieve a performance level that they initially thought was unreasonable.

Private equity companies also believe that performance management is a powerful way to add value. However, rather than using unreasonable targets, private equity companies typically use incentives as the main driver of performance. Managers in the businesses can often become rich if they succeed in delivering high performance. Their payment may include bonuses but normally comes mainly from equity holdings that only pay out when the business is sold. Moreover, the managers have often mortgaged their houses to buy the equity. So, if the business starts to perform poorly, the managers stand to lose something really important. This combination of carrot and stick can motivate managers to focus on what is important, work harder and perform better.

When is it likely that a performance management process will add value? When the headquarters managers are able to design a process that causes business managers to be more motivated and more focused on the important actions than they would have been in an independent company. Again, this is a tough hurdle. Most corporate parents have performance management processes, but few of these processes are more motivating for managers than running an independent company. Value is normally added only when headquarters managers understand why the business managers are likely to lack motivation or be distracted by inappropriate targets, and design a process to correct the bias.

Policies and standards

The corporate level can add value by setting policies and standards in areas other than performance.

Lord Hanson of Hanson Trust, a large London-based conglomerate, famously had a policy that every capital expenditure request greater than £1000 required his personal signature. He observed that managers often had good processes for controlling expenses, but were less effective at controlling capital expenditures. By insisting that requests for small amounts of capital needed his signature, he ensured that managers lower down would think hard before they spent money on capital items. As a result, he was able to keep capital expenditures low, and return on capital high. Alongside other policies and influences, this focus on capital expenditures often enabled him to double the return on assets from the businesses he acquired.

In another company the CEO was concerned that the managers of his businesses were relying excessively on consultants.

Rather than backing their own judgement, business managers were using consultants to develop the analysis and recommendations that would help them sell their ideas up the hierarchy. The CEO was concerned that this was adding significant costs and delays. As a result, he made a policy that all proposals to hire consultants required his signature. While this policy almost certainly added value by reducing the cost of consultants and speeding the decision process, it could be argued that it was just offsetting a source of subtracted value – a hierarchy that demanded consultant-quality analyses and recommendations.

A typical area for corporate policy is pay structures. These pay policies normally exist either to help businesses keep salary costs under control or to encourage movement of people across businesses. As we will point out in the chapter on subtracted value, the net result is often negative not positive. However, in one logistics company, the pay policies existed to stop managers in the businesses from making mistakes. Experienced managers at the corporate centre had noticed that managers at the business level often found it difficult to hire capable talent: the logistics industry is one where talent shortages are quite common.

To try to solve the problem, the business managers were offering higher salaries. Unfortunately, the higher salaries were undermining the competitiveness of the businesses without solving the talent shortage. By imposing pay limits for different grades, corporate managers were preventing managers in the businesses from making this mistake. The policy forced the managers to find more creative ways of solving their talent shortages.

Unfortunately, policies and standards are often sources of subtracted value rather than added value. It is easy for headquarters managers to impose policies and standards that suit corporate headquarters but are not helpful to the business divisions. Hence, it is important to understand why the corporate-level policies will have a beneficial influence. In all three of the examples, managers in the businesses were liable to make the wrong decisions because of the circumstances they faced. The corporate policies were designed to help improve these decisions.

Relationships

Headquarters managers can add value to businesses through the relationships they have with influential stakeholders.

Belmiro D'Azavedo, founder and CEO of Sonae, Portugal's largest private company, was one of Europe's leading businessmen. As a result, he had relationships with other business leaders in Portugal and across Europe, as well as with senior members of the Portuguese government. He could use these relationships to help his businesses and to set up new businesses. For example, as mobile telephony expanded, he set up a business to compete with Portugal Telecom, the dominant supplier, which was government owned. He arranged a joint venture with France Telecom, who provided the technical support. He lobbied his political contacts to allow more competition within the Portuguese market. As the business grew, he was able to give the business additional help through his contacts inside and outside Portugal.

The CEO of a military equipment company commented that one of the main ways in which he added value came from his knowledge of and ability to work with Arab governments. Since 50% of the sales of his businesses were to Arab governments, his contacts and skills helped the businesses get more contracts and at higher margins.

In the banking sector, banks have relationships with the central bank and with other regulators. These are important relationships that can have a significant impact on the bank's business divisions. Headquarters managers, therefore, devote considerable time to developing relationships with these stake-holders, supported by a team at the centre focused on regula-tory issues.

For some relationships, such as with the government or regulators, central involvement is required for governance reasons, whether the involvement adds value or not. Hence, it is important to pinpoint the source of added value. Why is the business division able to perform better than it would as an independent company? Often the answer is that a larger company can get more attention from these critical stakeholders and can have more weight of influence over them. Sometimes it is a skill issue. A headquarters manager is better at handling these relationships.

Technology or products

The corporate level can add value by providing technology that is core to the success of its businesses.

3M, the coatings technology company, is structured into global product divisions, and within the divisions the structure is primarily by product. However, many of the technologies that underpin 3M's success are applied across the product divisions. The corporate technology function has created a number of "technology centres", each of which is responsible for develop-ing a particular technology. These centres create vertical added value because they provide technology that can be used by the business divisions. But they also create horizontal value because they encourage business divisions to share knowledge in related areas, and they ensure that the cost of developing the technol-ogy is shared across more than one business division. These centres may report to one division or to the group head of technology, but they have a remit that spans the whole company. They are expected to provide leadership across 3M in their chosen technology.

Pharmaceutical companies are mainly organised by geography. This is because the laws, medical practices and medical structures differ from one country or region to another. But, the geographic business divisions do not have responsibility for the full value chain of activities. The geographic units are typically responsible for marketing and sales. Research is centralised to reduce duplication of effort in different regions, and to help discover and patent compounds that will create advantage. Regulatory approval is also typically centralised because the skills involved are specialist ones. In other words, centralised management of research and regulatory approval adds value to the regional business divisions.

CIW, the wire company, was also structured by region before the acquisition by Molsand. Sales, marketing, manufacturing and logistics were all controlled by the regions. But technology and product management was a central function. Central control of products and the technology helped reduce duplication of effort, ensured sufficient resources were devoted to new technologies and helped provide some standardisation across regions, which was particularly helpful when serving global customers.

As with relationships, technology is an area where added value through centralisation is often possible. Duplication can be reduced, cross-fertilisation can be easier and scarce resources can be allocated to the most profitable projects.

Relationships and technology and the next two categories, expertise and brand, are all examples of added value by corporate headquarters that is both vertical and horizontal. It is vertical because the corporate level controls the relationship or technology or brand and passes the benefit onto the business divisions. It is horizontal because it would make little sense to centralise control of the relationship or technology or brand if the company only had one business division.

However, centralisation should not be chosen without careful thought. Technology that is developed close to the customer is often better than technology that is developed in an ivory tower. The benefits from reduced duplication, critical mass and better use of scarce resources need to be balanced against the loss of performance that can come from less contact with the market and longer channels of communication.

Expertise

The corporate level can add value by providing expertise that is not available to the businesses.

Cooper Industries, a diversified manufacturing company, started in oil tools serving oil companies in the Gulf of Mexico. When oil drilling in the Gulf began to decline, Cooper Industries decided it wanted to become the most efficient competitor in oil tool manufacturing, so it could be the survivor in a contracting industry.

Managers went to Japan to learn the latest efficiency techniques from companies like Toyota: just-in-time, total quality and cell-based manufacturing. Using these techniques, Cooper began to outperform in the oil tool industry. It became one of the survivors.

Managers then began to wonder whether the same skills could be applied in other manufacturing businesses. This started a 10-year growth path through acquisition. Cooper bought companies in which managers were not applying the latest techniques. They would frequently move the factory from the north to the south to avoid union problems. They would send in a central team of manufacturing experts to redesign the factory layout and to install just-in-time and total quality processes. The result was often a doubling of margins alongside gains in market share.

Apple has a particular corporate skill at product development (see more details about Apple in Chapter 12). Steve Jobs, when he was in charge of Apple, personally led the weekly product development meetings. These meetings involved all the senior managers concerned with new products. By setting high standards for product excellence and customer usability, and by being willing to abandon or delay products that were unlikely to meet the standards, and by injecting energy into the process every week, Steve Jobs was able to preside over a series of product breakthroughs that transformed Apple from an also ran into an industry leader.

The range of areas where corporate-level expertise can add value is large. For example, most companies will have a central treasury department with special expertise in handling foreign exchange hedging. They will also have a tax team that works on sophisticated tax challenges. These are skills not normally available to the business divisions. Moreover, good tax planning can add a significant amount to profits after tax.

A more unusual area of corporate skill is Virgin's skill at using public relations in place of advertising as a way of getting brand exposure. Whether it is by getting Richard Branson to dress up in a bride's dress or by publicly challenging other companies in ways that get press coverage, Virgin helps its businesses get exposure, enabling them to cut their top-line advertising costs.

Nike is good at signing leading sports men and women, a source of added value that is both about expertise and also about relationships. Nike's success is not only about paying more money to these sports personalities. It is also about Nike's commitment to research, its willingness to invest in talent early and its policy of building deep relationships with these sports stars. The group chief executive gets involved, often becoming personal friends with Nike's leading endorsers.

It is easy for corporate headquarters to presume that it has better expertise than business divisions when it does not. It is also easy for the centralisation of expertise to deskill business divisions in ways that undermines their performance. So any decision to provide central expertise needs to be taken with care considering, both the benefits and disadvantages.

Brand

The corporate level can add value by developing and providing a brand that helps its businesses succeed.

Virgin Group is a portfolio of businesses built round a brand. The group consists of an airline, a financial services business, a business that runs a UK rail franchise and many other seemingly unrelated activities. The group started as a music record label. As the group evolved around Richard Branson's unique skills as an entrepreneur, managers concluded that the integrating core was the brand.

As a result, a separate legal entity was created to own and build the brand. Each business in the family pays a licence fee to the brand company for the use of the brand, and commits to the brand rules and controls. The brand values are things like "value for money", "fun", "young", "anti-establishment". Virgin Group has found that there is a significant segment of the population who identify with these values across a range of product areas, especially those where there are established competitors acting as an oligopoly.

Tata, the Indian conglomerate, built a corporate brand that stands for integrity and honesty – an advantage in some parts of the Indian market. Tata's brand values have been influenced by the company's tradition of philanthropy and by its progressive human resource strategies, such as a minimum working week and maternity pay. In 2013, its brand was estimated to be worth $18 billion, making it the leading brand in India and

39th in the world. This gives its businesses a significant advantage with a range of stakeholders.

Other companies such as IBM, L'Oréal, Microsoft, Nestlé and Shell all add value at the corporate level by the way they manage their brands. Nestlé and L'Oréal are particularly interesting because they compete with companies like P&G and Unilever that do not add as much value to their business divisions through managing a corporate brand. P&G and Unilever focus more on individual product brands, such as Gillette or Sunsilk. The corporate brand is in the background. Nestlé and L'Oréal use the corporate brand much more prominently, with L'Oréal's tag line "because I am worth it" or Nestlé's brand names such as Nescafé and Nespresso.

As product brands have been stretched across categories, such as Gillette or Dove entering the deodorant category, it has become necessary, even in P&G and Unilever, to manage these cross-category brands at a level above the category-focused business divisions. The added value is the consistency with which the brand is used and the added exposure that is possible from combining budgets.

There is no easy analysis that will show when a central brand can add value and when it cannot. As is clear from the example of Nestlé versus Unilever, sharing a brand may appear to be an obvious source of value, yet still fail to deliver significant advantage in the market place.

Financial engineering

In addition to areas of expertise, like foreign exchange hedging, the corporate finance function can have special skills in managing the balance sheet and improving return on equity. Debt is a cheaper form of funding than equity, so finding ways of increasing debt as a percentage of total financing, without significantly raising risk, is often an opportunity for corporate levels to add value.

Raising money secured against specific assets is one way of doing this. While business divisions could do this themselves, they would typically not normally have the expertise. For example, some airlines have explored the potential for raising additional debt secured against the rights these businesses had to landing slots at Heathrow and other congested airports.

Another form of financial engineering is the use of mezzanine debt. This is debt with less security. At liquidation, mezzanine debt gets paid out only after the senior debt has been paid. It is higher risk, and hence earns a higher return. But the cost can still be less than the cost of equity. Private equity firms have been particularly aggressive in using this kind of debt to reduce equity as a percentage of total financing, and hence increase return on equity.

Another way that the financial function can add value is by using company size to lower the cost of debt. By offering banks a parent company guarantee, it is often possible to reduce the cost of debt by a few basis points. For large companies, with reliable cash flows, it is also possible to disintermediate the banks and issue debt instruments directly to the market. This is a further way of reducing the cost of debt.

Vertical value mirages

The list of sources of vertical value is not complete. It is just illustrative. So, if you have an idea for added value, which is not covered by the illustrations above, how do you decide whether it makes sense or not? This is an important question because many ideas for added value are mirages: they sound good, but actually deliver no improvement in performance.

A typical mirage is "capital allocation". Many managers will say that the main task of the corporate level is to allocate capital among the business divisions. By implication they are also saying that allocation adds value: without capital the businesses could do little. However, if we unpick this thought and compare with the alternative – the business divisions as independent companies – we can see that it is a mirage.

As independent companies, the business divisions, in normal capital market conditions, should be able to raise the capital they need, assuming they have sensible plans. Hence, the act of providing them with capital adds no value to an independent company unless there are capital market shortages or misunderstandings that are restricting finance to the business.

But, managers argue, it is the act of allocation, giving some divisions more and others less, that adds value. Here again we can expose the mirage. Each business should have a plan that will optimise its performance; and that plan will require some capital. If the corporate level allocates less than the plan requires, the corporate level is subtracting value: it is making the business perform less well than it would as an independent company. If the corporate level allocates more capital than the plan requires, it is also subtracting value: it is allocating capital that will not earn a full return. So allocating capital by giving some businesses more than their plans require and others less, subtracts rather than adds value.

Managers also argue that capital allocation is important because the corporate level does not have enough capital to support the plans of all the business divisions. So it needs to choose which divisions to cut back. This implies that the corporate level will have to subtract some value from some of its businesses. The capital allocation process is just a way to figure out how to subtract as little value as possible. This is not adding value. This is subtracting value. Moreover, there is an alternative: raise more money or sell something so that the corporate level can support all good plans.

We use the example of capital allocation to illustrate how tricky it can be to know whether a corporate activity really does add value. It is only by thinking hard about what would happen (what does happen) in independent companies that it is possible to distinguish between mirages and real added value.

In the right circumstances, capital allocation can add value. If corporate managers know better than the business managers what amount of capital will optimise the performance of the business, they can guide the businesses to better plans. Also, at certain times in the business cycle or in some less developed countries, capital markets can be biased or ineffective. In these circumstances access to capital can be a source of added value. Inevitably, these are quite rare situations. But they do exist.

As we have already explained, Lord Hanson learnt that mature businesses typically spend more on capital investments than they need to. By giving them tough targets, and by making them apply to him personally for any amount of capital over £1000, he found that he could raise their performance.

Jack Welch at GE concluded that his businesses were under-investing in globalisation. By demanding that they aim for the No. 1 or No. 2 global position, and by providing the capital to support these strategies, he helped them perform much better than they would have without his influence.

Barry Diller at Interactive Corp acquired internet businesses at a time when online businesses were out of favour with capital markets. These businesses could not easily raise the capital they needed to finance their expansion. By allocating more capital to these businesses than their competitors could, Diller added significant value.

When added value is real

If the business divisions are run by competent and energetic managers, who are working hard to optimise the performance of their businesses, there will usually be relatively few opportunities for the corporate headquarters to add significant vertical value. In most cases, the managers of the businesses should be in the best position to decide how to get the best out of their businesses. Headquarters managers, well removed from the coalface, are unlikely to have much to contribute.

Hence, it is useful to have some tests for checking whether an idea for added value is likely to be valid:

1. Is there any reason to suppose that the business divisions would perform significantly less well in this area if they were independent companies? If so, why?
2. Is the proposed approach one that will help raise performance in the area of attention? Does it address the reason why?
3. Is there good reason to suppose that the people taking action on this topic at the corporate level know what they are doing and can set the right targets, give the right guidance or provide the right resources and support without significant subtracted value?

Armed with these three questions, it is often possible to cut in half the typical list that comes out of an exercise to define the added value of corporate headquarters.

There is also a fourth more demanding question, which is about whether the source of added value gives parenting advantage: whether headquarters managers will do a better job than their corporate-level rivals. Many sources of added value are plain vanilla, such as tax or treasury expertise. They are needed, but they are unlikely to help the company outperform its corporate rivals:

4. Is there any reason to suppose that headquarters managers have an advantage that will enable them to create more value from this topic (and subtract less value) than other competing corporate groups?

Managers who can give positive answers to all four questions are likely to have a source of added value that gives them parenting advantage.

CHAPTER EIGHT

NINE SOURCES OF VALUE FROM COORDINATING ACROSS BUSINESS DIVISIONS

The previous chapter explained the difference between vertical value and horizontal value, and pointed out that the two sources of value are often intertwined within a particular corporate initiative. The chapter then gave examples of different types of vertical value and provided a way for managers to distinguish between mirages and real sources of vertical value.

In this chapter we give examples of types of horizontal value: ways in which headquarters creates value by encouraging coordination across divisions. For highly integrated companies, like Apple or CIW or Nokia, horizontal value is core to their corporate strategy. It is also completely intertwined with vertical value. Thinking about vertical and horizontal value as separate categories is almost unhelpful. So readers should recognise that this separation of categories may be more helpful for communicating different types of added value than it is for thinking about the challenges facing integrated companies. In integrated companies, it is often more useful just to focus on the sources of added value, rather than to distinguish between vertical and horizontal types.

As before, the list that follows is not comprehensive. It is illustrative. Examples are provided to illuminate the categories and we try to explain why the opportunity to create horizontal value exists. Throughout we will also provide words of caution: horizontal value is often presumed more than delivered.

One face to the customer

The corporate level can add value by coordinating shared customers or clients across businesses or geographies.

When a company has business divisions structured by geography, some customers will buy products and services from more than one geographic unit. Think of a global retailer, like Tesco, buying from a geographically structured supplier, such as Mars. In order to ensure the customer gets similar levels of service and similar pricing, it is beneficial for Mars to coordinate all the business that is done with the Tesco. There are also opportunities to expand the amount of business with Tesco by introducing products or services Mars provides in one geography to new geographies.

A similar set of issues exists when the company has customers buying from more than one product division. CIW, the wire and equipment company, had people within group marketing who focused on these issues. Different individuals in group marketing had responsibility for different industrial sectors, such as oil and gas or shipping. These individuals developed strategies for how CIW could best serve companies in the sector. They also coordinated the business CIW did with selected global accounts in their sector.

P&G's largest customer is Walmart. Walmart buys products from all of P&G's six product divisions and from most of P&G's eight regional marketing and sales units. As a result, P&G has a team of more than 100 people at corporate headquarters, whose job is to help maximise P&G's sales to Walmart and to make sure Walmart gets priority treatment from all parts of P&G. Coordinating customers across business divisions is likely to add value if the customer values the coordination or if the customer is taking advantage of the different terms and conditions offered by different divisions. But it will not universally add value. Coordination costs money. If the coordination costs exceed the gains – additional sales or higher prices – the initiative will subtract value. Moreover, coordination can lengthen the chain of communication in a way that reduces the voice of the customer in the ears of individual divisions.

Cross-selling

The corporate level can encourage or force businesses to sell each other's products. This opportunity to add value is particularly relevant when a company is structured into product divisions that sell products to similar customers.

P&G is an example of this source of added value as well. Walmart is not the only customer that takes products from different P&G divisions. In fact, nearly all of P&G's retail customers buy from multiple divisions. As a result, P&G has combined its sales and marketing teams in each country. The teams sell all of P&G's products in that country. The benefit is higher sales from using the breadth of P&G's offerings to negotiate for additional shelf space. P&G also achieves lower costs from having one back office in each country, and often one salesperson selling products for multiple divisions.

Ashridge Business School is structured into divisions focused on tailored courses, open courses, distance learning, consulting and qualifications. For many years, each division was encouraged to cross-sell the services of the other divisions where appropriate. But, despite some successes, most managers felt that the opportunity was not being fully exploited. So Ashridge set up a central team sponsored by three of the divisions – tailored, open and distance learning. The purpose of the team was to ensure that customers of any one division are exposed to the services of the other divisions.

Audit firms, such as PricewaterhouseCoopers, used their audit relationships to successfully build consulting practices in tax, management consulting and corporate finance. The cross-selling was not orchestrated by a central function, and there were concerns among audit partners that poor service in new practice areas could undermine audit relationships. Nevertheless, by using a common brand and through selective introductions, the audit firms built significant additional lines of business.

While there have been concerns about the impact on the independence of audit opinions, to the point where PricewaterhouseCoopers sold its management and IT consulting business to IBM, the opportunity to cross-sell other services to audit clients is significant. As a result, PricewaterhouseCoopers is rebuilding a management consulting practice to replace the business it sold.

Cross-selling is a significant opportunity for added value in some companies. Where business divisions have multiple products or services that are bought by the same buyers in customer companies, there is often an opportunity to cross-sell.

Economies of scale

The corporate level can add value by providing a scale advantage to its businesses. The commonest source of scale advantage is in purchasing.

Travis Perkins Wickes is the largest builder's merchant in the UK. The company has depots and stores all over the country. They supply materials to building firms, from nails to tools and from washers to wood. Each depot and each retail store is a separate business unit.

One of the ways the corporate centre adds value is through purchasing power. By combining the purchasing needs of all of its business units, the corporate purchasing team can negotiate a price that is on average 5% lower than the price available to an individual depot.

To help achieve this bargaining power all depots are required to stock a core range of products. They are allowed to stock their own specialist products as well. But the core range typically accounts for 80% of sales. The discounts that the corporate team achieves are not passed on to the business units because corporate managers are afraid that they will be given away in lower prices. The discounts are retained at the centre and drop straight to the bottom line. This results in a near doubling of net profit margins.

Scale advantages are also common in activities that have high fixed costs, such as manufacturing. Mars, the confectionery and pet foods company, was structured into regional business units. However, the fixed costs involved in manufacturing, such as the set-up cost for a production run, made it more efficient not to manufacture all products in all regions. Hence the corporate parent helped the regional business divisions agree manufacturing schedules. This enabled some factories to specialise in a way that improved efficiency.

An alternative solution, chosen by Unilever, was to centralise manufacturing: putting one person in charge of all its factories worldwide. This manager was then able to reallocate manufacturing to the lower cost factories and consolidate specialist lines in special factories.

Some companies, like Nike or Dell, have developed a central skill at outsourcing. They can benefit from even larger economies of scale by subcontracting to external suppliers who are consolidating volumes across more than one company.

Economies of scale exist in many areas from payroll to manufacturing. But there can be a cost to centralisation: less flexibility and responsiveness at the business level. For this reason, companies typically focus on adding value in significant areas that have a big impact on performance, as in Travis Perkins, and in minor areas where the risk of negative side effects is low, such as payroll. Companies typically avoid looking for economies of scale where the benefits are small and the risk of harm to the business divisions is unclear or high.

Shared resources

The corporate level can add value by helping businesses share important scarce resources such as technical capabilities, locations, brands and distribution channels.

A common shared resource is the company website. At Ashridge Business School, for example, all the business divisions share one website. For example, one part of the website lists all the open courses that Ashridge runs. These pages include the courses run by the consulting business, the research units and the open programmes business. All the business units that share these pages expect to gain because the combined pages attract more attention in the market place than would be possible with separate pages for each unit.

Apple's app store is another example of a shared resource. The app store is an important source of advantage for the iPhone business. But it is also a source of advantage for the iPod business and the iPad business. As we will explore in Chapter 12, Apple has many shared resources – the app store, the iTunes store, the retail network and central design and technology teams – to the point where Apple can be viewed as a single business unit rather than a parent company with a number of business divisions. The more resources that are shared the more the concept of a business division disappears and the more the whole organisation becomes one integrated business.

Sharing resources is only likely to add value if the resource itself is scarce and hence a source of advantage for the business divisions. Apple is a good example of this. The app store, the iTunes store and the retail network are all scarce resources that provide advantage to each of Apple's product lines.

Multipoint competition

The corporate level can coordinate strategies across multiple divisions in order to gain advantage over a major competitor.

Before the acquisition by P&G, Gillette was a direct competitor to Energizer. The two companies had similar product ranges: wet shaving products and batteries (Gillette owned Duracell and Energizer owned Schick Wilkinson Sword). Each product category was a separate business division within each company. But, because the two companies dominated both product categories, they were locked in a global war, each trying to find a way to win market share from the other without undermining the profitability of their sectors.

In this situation, coordinating strategies across the product divisions can be important. Efforts to gain share in one product might bring a fierce response from the competitor in the other product. Moreover, actions in one area can be used to signal to the competitor what actions will get a strong response.

Another example is the competition between the snack divisions of United Biscuits and Pepsico for control of the snack market in continental Europe. In the 1990s, both companies were looking to expand their market share in continental Europe through acquisitions. KP Foods, the snacks division of United Biscuits, was structured by product type – potato chips, nuts and processed snacks – and by country – the UK, the

Netherlands, Belgium, etc. KP Foods had no presence in the USA, Pepsico's home base. Frito Lay, the snacks division of Pepsico, had a similar structure, and also had no presence in the UK, KP Foods' home base.

Initially, both companies focused on competing for acquisitions country by country. The competition seemed well balanced. Frito Lay had more financial strength, but KP Foods had better relationships with the owners of European businesses. Frito Lay then devised a multipoint strategy that left KP with no easy response. Frito Lay acquired a competitor of KP in the UK – Walkers. By investing in Walkers and attacking KP in its home market, Frito Lay was able to reduce the available cash and management time that KP had for acquisitions in continental Europe. Moreover, the Walkers strategy was so successful that KP soon had to abandon its European ambitions altogether.

Multipoint competition has been much discussed in the strategy literature.[1] In practice is it quite rare. However, when there is an opportunity to use the strategies of one division to advance the cause of another division, the added value can be significant.

Vertical integration

The corporate level can link business units that are at different points in the value chain to reduce stocks, limit wastage and gain other sources of advantage.

In the bulk chemical business, companies are typically structured into business units that create products at different points along the value chain. One unit will "crack" the crude oil or gas into component chemicals. Then, different business units will refine the different component chemicals in a secondary process, producing more complex chemicals and by-products.

Then, further business units will use a tertiary process to further refine the complex chemicals or convert the by-products into useful refined chemicals. At each stage in the value chain, chemicals are also sold to third parties.

Linking the strategies of these different business units is important. Each process can be designed to produce different percentages of the main chemical and its by-products. Unless the processes are designed with the downstream businesses in mind, it is easy to create an excess of some chemical or by-product that can be hard to sell to third parties. Moreover, without some coordination, downstream businesses would need to hold significant stocks of the materials they need. With coordination, it is possible to connect the businesses by pipes eliminating most of the stock holding.

Another example of added value from vertical integration is the oil industry. Since oil exploration can identify huge oil fields and since the value of the oil field is a function of how fast the oil is extracted, it important for oil companies to have sufficient oil refining capacity, within reasonable reach of the oil fields, to support fast extraction. As a result, most of the major oil companies have businesses involved in both exploration and refining. Of course, as the oil industry has matured and refining capacity has become available all round the world, this source of added value has diminished and in some regions disappeared altogether.

As with multipoint competition, added value from vertical integration is quite rare. The main reason is that the different stages of an industry value chain typically require different skills and cultures making them hard to manage under one roof. In other words, the subtracted value from managing them together is often greater than the gains from vertical integration. Nevertheless, as in the examples described, significant value can be added through vertical integration.

Sharing knowledge and good practice

The corporate level can help businesses share knowledge and good practice.

Unilever's Home and Personal Care businesses were, for many years, structured into regional business units. At the centre were category and brand managers whose main role was to add value by sharing knowledge and good practice across the regions. For example, there was a library of marketing advertisements so that regional managers could learn from successes in other regions. The category managers would spot successful new product ideas in one region, like Timotei shampoo in Finland or Axe deodorant in South Africa, and encourage other regions to copy them. Moreover, their efforts were supported by centralised training and career path management of Unilever's hundreds of country-based product managers. Product managers were deliberately moved to a different country every couple of years. One of the benefits was that they spread good practice and ideas as they moved. They also attended regular training courses at which good ideas were disseminated. The combination of central category coordinators and centralised career management added significant value.

Over the years, in order to maximise the sharing of knowledge, Unilever has centralised more decisions into the hands of global category and brand managers. As more marketing decisions are centralised, the regions lose autonomy and become less like business units and more like regional sales and merchandising teams. We will explore this middle ground, where companies are neither clearly separate business divisions nor a single unified business, in Chapter 12.

McKinsey & Co. is the world's top management consulting company. It is structured as a matrix of regional offices and industry sectors. But there is also a third dimension to the McKinsey structure – knowledge practices, such as strategy or organisation or operations. The partners who lead these knowledge practice areas are responsible for advancing the firm's intellectual property. They run projects to build on and document the best thinking and consulting tools. They maintain online knowledge platforms that can be used by consultants in their work. They nurture individuals who want to become experts in these areas. They organise knowledge sharing events and conferences. By ensuring that all consultants have access to the latest and best tools and ideas, they add considerable value.

Knowledge and good practice sharing is a much talked about source of added value. But it is important always to remember that the benchmark is the performance of an independent company. All companies are learning all the time from each other, from direct competitors, from consultants, from new hires and from customers. Money spent on knowledge sharing inside an organisation across business divisions will only add value if it results in faster and more useful learning than would have occurred if the business divisions had been independent. Often this is not the case. So, an assessment needs to be made of the opportunity – of why internal learning is likely to be faster or more relevant than external learning – before investing in a knowledge management effort.

New business development

The corporate level can lead the development of new businesses by combining resources from more than one existing business.

IBM's Emerging Businesses Opportunities (EBO) programme was an attempt to do this. By around 2000, IBM was concerned that it was failing to develop new businesses in an age when many of its competitors were being more successful. The problem, managers believed, was the complexity of the organisation, the suffocating requirements imposed on new initiatives by corporate functions and the difficulty of getting access to resources, not just financial resources, but engineers or selling and marketing capabilities.

The solution was the EBO programme. IBM decided to identify a handful of business opportunities with big potential and to provide each of these initiatives with special support to help them navigate the company's processes and complex organisation structure.

Since the EBO programme was IBM's attempt to catch up on its more nimble competitors, some of whom were start-up companies, it could be argued that the corporate initiative was about eliminating subtracted value rather than creating added value: it was designed to reduce the disadvantage of IBM's complex organisation structure. Most of the new businesses in the programme performed well. Therefore, the programme did appear to help IBM create more new business than it had before the programme. Whether it helped build more value than would have been created if the new businesses had been independent companies, able to freely contract with IBM or other companies for the resources they needed, is less clear.

A different example is that of American Express. The company owned a number of financial services businesses built up around its core card business. Each of the businesses was involved in large volumes of transactions. One opportunity to add value was to centralise these transactions activities into a corporate shared service. This gave significant economies of scale. Once established, the central service was then set up as a separate business division to win transactions business from other companies. Subsequently, Amex floated its transactions division as a separate independent company, making a substantial capital gain in the process.

New business development is a notoriously difficult way for corporate headquarters to add value. Many companies have attempted to add value by encouraging new business development, but few have succeeded. The failure rate of corporate venturing units, for example, is well over 90%. Nevertheless, like many of the types of horizontal added value, in the right circumstances, coordinated new business development can have a significant impact.

Risk management

The corporate level can assemble a set of businesses that together reduce the overall risks and hence the costs of protecting against the risks.

Banks and insurance companies trade in risk. By having a portfolio of loans in different countries and in different sectors, banks spread the risk of a downturn in one sector or one country. Insurance companies also benefit from spreading their risks across a range of businesses.

However, as secondary markets have evolved – reinsurance in the insurance industry and securitisation in the lending industry – it has become less necessary for insurance companies and banks to have a spread of risks.

Risk spreading often influences the thinking of managers in industrial companies as well. "I do not want to have all my eggs in one basket" is one thought. Another is the idea of "balance": greater stability from investing in multiple "legs". In markets that are highly cyclical, creating a real threat of bankruptcy during downturns, some form of balance or risk spreading through investment strategy is necessary. If risk cannot be spread through "reinsurance" or increasing the capital base, it may be necessary to seek counter-cyclical investments.

However, for most companies, especially in developed markets, risk spreading does not add value and balance is an unhelpful objective. Typically, in efficient markets, shareholders are in a better place to spread risks than management.

Shareholders can achieve balance without taking on the responsibilities of managing something they are less familiar with. Also, efficient markets usually provide alternative ways of reducing risk through financial instruments.

Horizontal added value mirages

The list of types of horizontal value is not complete. It is just illustrative. As we pointed out in the previous chapter, many ideas for added value are mirages: they sound good, but actually deliver no improvement in performance or cost more than they deliver. Moreover, added value initiatives that seem sensible, such as IBM's EBO programme, may be more about eliminating subtracted value than creating added value. So, if you have an idea for horizontal added value, how do you decide whether it makes sense or not?

Mirages are particularly common when managers are looking for horizontal value. This is partly due to a prejudgement that collaboration among business divisions is good in itself: the more the better. This mindset can foster initiatives that take up time and deliver little benefit.

The search for horizontal value is also due to a common belief that a portfolio of business divisions needs to be justified by synergies: the corporate glue. This mindset encourages managers to look for synergies even where they do not exist. In this environment, like the thirsty traveller, mirages are common.

We have pointed out that multipoint competition, coordinated business development, knowledge sharing and risk management can all suffer from mirages and subtracted value. The net is often negative. To reinforce this point, it may be useful to look more closely at a corporate-level activity that is common, presumed to add value and rarely questioned – leadership development.

Many managers argue that corporate headquarters can add value by providing leadership development and career paths for top managers, and by running a scheme for high potentials. People, they explain, are a company's greatest asset. So one way of adding value is for the corporate HR function to manage and develop a pool of talent for the company as a whole.

As with vertical value, we can unpick this logic by considering what would happen if the business divisions were independent companies. Independent companies have their own processes for developing talent, and if they are short of talent they will draw from the pool of people available in their industries.

So the talent pool run by a corporate parent will only add value if the parent is more successful at developing individuals than the processes used by independent businesses in the same industry. In other words, the talent pool that is created needs to be significantly better or significantly cheaper than that available to an independent company.

Clearly, there are situations where these conditions are met. If the businesses are all very similar and it is easy for managers to move between them and be effective, there is the potential to develop a rich skill pool. If the businesses are backward in their approaches to developing talent, there is the potential to raise standards. If there is an unusual shortage of talent, such as in China, there is an opportunity to gain an advantage by developing a proprietary pool of managers.

However, where these conditions do not exist, the net position is often subtracted value rather than added value. The policies that corporate headquarters puts in place to run a talent development programme – common pay grades, common bonus systems, common performance assessment forms, common management systems and common training programmes – often get in the way of employing the best talent and impose restrictions on businesses that reduce rather than improve their commercial success. For example, it is typical for a company with a strong talent development programme to appoint from within. Yet, as private equity firms have demonstrated, hiring tried and tested executives from the industry may be a lower risk option than promoting well-developed, yet untested, internal candidates.

So how should managers challenge their ideas for adding horizontal value to make sure that they are real? We repeat here the questions from the previous chapter. We make no apology for the repetition because we believe that vigilance is important. Managers need to have these questions at the front of their minds before they initiate activities at the corporate level.

1. Is there any reason to suppose that the business divisions would perform significantly less well in this area if they were independent companies? If so, why?
2. Is the proposed approach one that will help raise performance in the area of attention? Does it address the reason why?
3. Is there good reason to suppose that the people taking action on this topic at the corporate level know what they are doing and can set the right targets, give the right guidance or provide the right resources and support without significant subtracted value?
4. Is there any reason to suppose that corporate-level managers have an advantage that will enable them to create more value from this topic (and subtract less value) than other competing corporate groups?

We also explore the problem of mirages and the best way to select interventions for horizontal added value in a later chapter (Chapter 15).

Summary

This chapter and the previous one show that there are a large number of different ways in which corporate headquarters can add value to the operating units in the organisation. Moreover, there is no easy way of classifying the different types of added value. In an earlier edition of this book, Goold, Campbell and Alexander identified four categories – stand-alone influence, linkage influence, central functions and services and portfolio development.[2] A study by the consulting company BCG identified 19 types of added value (see more detail about this study in Chapter 9, p. 205). Other categorisations exist. But none is fully satisfactory.

The lack of easy categorisation is both frustrating and helpful. It is frustrating because managers would like to have a checklist of all of the different ways of adding value to make sure they have not missed anything important. It is helpful because it encourages managers to focus on the specific issues facing their specific businesses rather than on a generic checklist. In other words, managers need to figure out how to add value in their specific situation. In Chapter 10, we will describe how this can be done. The lack of a checklist also opens the door to creativity: managers can discover new sources of added value and build new strategies around them.

Notes

[1] Faye I. Smith and Rick L. Wilson, "The Predictive Validity of the Karnani and Wernerfelt Model of Multipoint Competition", *Strategic Management Journal*, Vol. 16, No. 2, 1995, 143–160; Lucio Fuentelsaz and Jaime Gómez, "Multipoint Competition, Strategic Similarity and

Entry into Geographic Markets", *Strategic Management Journal*, Vol. 27, No. 5, 2006, 477–499; Ming-Jer Chen and Kristin Stucker, "Multinational Management and Multimarket Rivalry: Toward a Theoretical Development of Global Competition", *Academy of Management Proceedings*, Vol. 1997, No. 1, Academy of Management, 1997.

[2] M. Goold, A. Campbell and M. Alexander, *Corporate Level Strategy* (John Wiley & Sons, 1994), 75–245.

CHAPTER NINE

EIGHT WAYS HEADQUARTERS CAN DESTROY VALUE

Corporate headquarters can as easily destroy or subtract value as add value: headquarters actions can cause business divisions to perform less well than they would as independent companies. Corporate-level actions and initiatives can result in less good decisions, delays in decision making, extra costs, distractions from commercial priorities, inefficient services and demotivation. It is for this reason that the Heartland matrix has "risk of subtracted value" on one of its axes.

While the existence of subtracted value has always been understood by managers – bosses can as easily hold you back as help you succeed – one of the first research projects to expose the size of the problem was carried out at Ashridge Strategic Management Centre.[1] The research focused on decision making in hierarchies.

The research involved studying major decisions in large companies. It showed that the corporate level has a significant influence on decisions. This was true whether the managers at the corporate level were trying to be influential or not. Because managers lower down want to avoid making proposals that are rejected by their bosses, they devote significant energy to second guessing what their bosses are thinking, even when their bosses are trying to be neutral.

One anecdote from the research serves to illustrate the issue. Managers from one product division of the US coatings company 3M wanted to enter the computer disk market. This was because 3M had excellent coating technologies, which made it possible to produce higher quality disks. However, 3M's previous applications of its coatings technologies had been on tape products, like masking tape. As a result, the senior executives had most of their business experience with tape products.

The product managers for the new disk were concerned that senior executives would feel uncomfortable with this diversification into a new industry and a new product category. As a result, when they made their presentation to gain approval for this new product, they positioned the product as a consumable accessory of the computer industry, in the same way that masking tape is a consumable accessory to industries like car manufacturing. They also avoided showing the product face on. "If they saw that the product was round, we thought it would scare them. We held it so they could only see the side, making it look more like something they were familiar with – a piece of tape."[2]

While this behaviour of the product managers proved to be helpful in the case of 3M's computer disk – the product launch was approved and 3M had some years of success in this product category – it illustrates the problem that hierarchies create. Corporate-level managers often reject good proposals because they are "unfamiliar", and business-level managers often change their behaviour or their proposals so as improve the chances of getting approval. While these changes can improve the chances of approval, they can also reduce the chances of success.

In another anecdote a business-level manager described a recent decision about an important negotiation. "My suggested approach was thoroughly discussed up and down the hierarchy.

My boss came and sat on the corner of my desk for an hour or more on at least three occasions. There is no doubt that all the dialogue caused us to come up with a better plan. But, there was a big cost in management time, and, frankly, I would rather have gone ahead with my original idea and been held to account for making it work."[3] This illustrates the fact that, even when the corporate level adds value, there is also often some subtracted value: in this case the management time and the loss of motivation at the business level.

The research concluded that the influence of higher levels of management can be highly positive or highly negative. It is rarely neutral, even when higher levels are trying to be neutral.

How much value can be subtracted?

Subtracted value can be large. Often it is greater than the added value. Sometimes it can reduce the total net value of a business by 50% or more.

In the 1980s, oil companies were concerned that the oil business would not offer sufficient growth, and they calculated that their oil industry skills could add value to the minerals industry. Oil companies had superior exploration skills, strong relationships with governments, financial strength and capabilities in managing major projects in remote locations: all capabilities that are also relevant in the minerals industry.

What the oil companies did not think about was the potential for subtracted value. Many of their engineering skills, while superior to those in the minerals industry, were expensive. This was appropriate in the high margin oil industry, but less appropriate in the low margin minerals industry. So the application of oil industry engineering standards to minerals businesses subtracted rather than added value.

While exploration is a driver of value in the oil industry, it is not so important in minerals. Being invested in low cost deposits is more important than finding new deposits. Hence, financing skills and relationships with other minerals companies, which together can enable a minerals company to exploit minerals that have already been found, creates more value than exploration skills. The oil companies encouraged their minerals divisions to spend more on exploration than was appropriate: subtracting rather than adding value in this area as well.

A third problem came from the long-standing strategy in oil of vertical integration. Without realising their own bias, oil executives, particularly in Shell, encouraged their minerals division managers to look for opportunities to integrate vertically. Since there are higher margins in downstream product areas, such as aluminium extrusions or copper piping, than in the basic mining or smelting activities, it seemed to oil executives that more vertical integration would drive up profits. But, managers skilled at mining or smelting proved to be less skilled at downstream products. So the influence of the oil executives again subtracted value rather than added value.

The net result of these and other sources of subtracted value swamped the added value. The minerals businesses owned by the major oil companies over a period of five years made average **losses** of more than 5% on sales, while minerals businesses not owned by oil companies made average **profits**, over the same period, of more than plus 5%. In other words, despite the sources of added value, the subtracted value caused the return on sales to fall from a positive 5% to a negative 5%. Not surprisingly, all of the oil companies sold their minerals divisions after a few years, taking significant write-downs on the money they had invested, on top of the losses they made.

First do no harm

Most of the evidence for subtracted value is anecdotal. However, a study by consultants at the Boston Consulting Group, titled First Do No Harm, went further.[4]

Matthias Kruhler, who led the research, defined 19 types of added value and 13 types of subtracted value. Together with Ulrich Pidun, he asked managers to rate the importance of each type of value within their company. They then defined six levels of added value ambition. At the highest level, corporate managers attempted to add value through almost all of the 19 types. At the lowest level, corporate managers limited their role to providing financial support.

Kruhler and Pidun found that the more ways in which a company attempted to add value, the higher were the recorded levels of subtracted value. In other words, like the anecdotes, as headquarters managers do more, they increase the risk of doing negative things.

Based on this analysis, the researchers identified an optimum added value ambition for any company depending on its industry and degree of diversification. Companies that attempted to add more value than the optimum, they argued, were likely to find that subtracted value began to offset their ambition: they would be likely to create less net value. While we are not suggesting that this finding points to added value limits, it does underline the significance of subtracted value.

The significance of subtracted value in this research is surprising, especially given the source of the data. Most of the managers who completed the questionnaires were from the corporate level, respondents who might have been biased in favour of believing more in the positive than the negative. So Kruhler and Pidun attempted to check their results against the valuations of the companies in their sample. The valuation data more than supported their questionnaire data. Companies with a management ambition beyond the optimum were valued, by the capital markets, less highly than companies closer to the optimum.

Another source of evidence for the existence and significance of subtracted value comes from spin-outs (divisions or businesses of larger companies that are set up as independent companies) and break-ups (companies that divide into two or three or four independent units). When separated, the combined value of the pieces is invariably greater than the whole. Data on the success of spin-outs suggests that their value on average increases by about 30% more than their sector over the following 18 months, and the value of the original parent company also performs better than average.[5]

To some degree this is not surprising. Managers are unlikely to spin out businesses or to break up an existing company unless there is strong evidence suggesting that the resulting total will be more valuable than the previous whole. But it provides hard evidence that, at least in some situations, subtracted value is significantly greater than added value.

Before we list the sources of subtracted value, it is worth just dwelling on the conclusion that subtracted value can be quite frequently greater than added value. It is not a conclusion that many business-level managers find surprising. They often experience this reality. However, given some of the easy ways in which a corporate headquarters can add value – lower cost of capital, lower cost of investor management, tax savings, cost savings from central services such as payroll – it is remarkable that the net impact can, in some cases, be so negative.

Sources of subtracted value

There are as many sources of subtracted value as there are sources of added value. This makes any categorisation dangerous because it can overlook some sources. The list that follows is based on nearly 30 years of exposure to corporate groups. But it is provided as much to illustrate the range of areas of subtracted value as to provide a checklist. We also provide the statements on subtracted value used by the Boston Consulting Group researchers (Figure 9.1). Respondents were asked to score their company against each statement.

Figure 9.1: Statements on subtracted value in BCG research

Negative influence
- HQ has insufficient expertise and skills with regard to the critical success factors of the SBUs
- Central decision-making is predominantly driven by political matters
- HQ prefers investing in SBUs that corporate-level management is familiar with
- HQ favours growth over value creation
- HQ favours corporate risk diversification over value creation
- As being part of the corporate portfolio, SBUs are excluded from beneficial capital market pressures
- Ongoing HQ interference decreases SBU managers' motivation

Overhead costs
- HQ offers services which are not needed by the SBUs
- Overhead charges are too high given the scope and quality of the services offered
- Some SBU resources are only needed to fulfil HQ's requirements
- HQ requirements prevent SBU managers from running their businesses effectively
- Complex HQ processes reduce flexibility and slow down decision making

Resource Competition
- Marginal SBUs are deprived of management attention
- Strong SBUs have to subsidise weak SBUs hence get less capital than they need
- SBUs have to play a portfolio role that prevents them from realising their value potential

Cost of Complexity
- SBUs are wasting resources on additional coordination effort for internal corporate processes
- Decision making processes are slowed down due to high coordination requirements
- Internal power struggles lead to wrong decisions and prevent SBUs from realising their value potential
- SBUs are wasting resources and time on tactical manoeuvres for influencing HQ decision making

In the chapter on added value, we gave examples, mostly named examples, to illustrate the material. Unfortunately, named examples of subtracted value are harder to get approved. Moreover, our objective is to convince you that subtracted value is a real problem in many areas of management. We believe it will be easier to do this by explaining, under each heading, why subtracted value is so common, rather than by providing many named examples.

Misleading strategic guidance

Corporate levels typically provide some strategic guidance to business divisions. This guidance may be the result of careful strategic planning work or it may be based on the biases and previous experience of senior executives. When the tobacco company BAT diversified into financial services by acquiring the insurance companies Farmers in the USA and Eagle Star in

Europe, managers expected to be able to add value. The idea was to take the marketing skills in the tobacco business and apply them to financial services. In consumer products, market share is the mantra. Unfortunately, it is different in financial services because large sections of the market are unprofitable. BAT encouraged its new businesses to gain market share, only to announce big losses a few years later as the risks that were taken to gain extra share were exposed.

Clearly, strategic guidance is more likely to be wise when corporate-level managers understand well the commercial challenges facing the businesses. It is more likely to subtract value when corporate-level managers have a less good understanding. A less good understanding is likely to occur when a company is moving into new areas, such as oil companies going into minerals; when the commercial environment in a market changes, such as when a new competitor enters or technology is changing; or when the top team comes mainly from one part of the company or one geography and has little experience of other parts.

When corporate managers have a less good understanding, one solution is to be less influential, especially in areas where the managers are less confident of their knowledge. Virgin Group, for example, does not have a corporate strategic planning process. This is because Richard Branson does not expect to give the businesses guidance on strategy. Of course, as we have pointed out, managers in businesses are likely to be influenced by the prejudices of their corporate bosses, even when their bosses do not want them to be. For this reason, Virgin likes the managers of its businesses to hold a significant equity stake, often as much as 50%. This causes them to do what they think is right regardless of the messages they think may be coming from Virgin Group.

The problem faced by corporate managers is not just about giving appropriate guidance. It is also about making sure that the managers in business divisions are hearing the message. In one major electronics company the long-standing leader launched a new growth and innovation strategy. This was in contrast to the previous 10 years, when he had focused on cost cutting and rationalisation. He complained to us that it was hard to get managers in his business divisions to change their orientation. Privately, some of his managers explained to us that, although the CEO was talking about growth, they knew that he was really more interested in margin improvements and cost cutting.

Inappropriate performance targets

What gets measured gets done. Hence, most corporate headquarters are keen to define performance targets for their businesses. The problem is that it is hard to define targets that add value.

If the targets are purely financial, business-level managers can become short term and may underinvest in future growth. If the targets are insufficiently stretching, business-level managers may hold back performance for the following year and deliver less than they could have done without the target. If the targets focus on growth, business-level managers may pursue growth at the expense of profit, resulting in profitless growth.

The Balanced Score Card is one solution to these problems,[6] but creates its own challenge: a loss of focus from using 10 or 20 performance measures. Moreover, any performance management tool is subject to gaming: managers in business units can work hard to convince their bosses to agree to "achievable" rather than "stretch" targets. In this game, corporate-level managers need to be exceptionally wise to win, because the business-level managers hold all the information. Not surprisingly, business-level managers often win, and the result is mediocre targets and mediocre performance. As one chief executive commented, "At budget time business managers always lie. The judgement you have to make is whether it is a big lie or a small lie."

Inappropriate capital constraints

One of the most powerful levers that corporate headquarters has over managers lower down is to grant or withhold capital. As a result, headquarters managers normally have elaborate capital approval processes, and they spend a considerable amount of time allocating capital across the portfolio of businesses.

The problem, as with performance targets, is that business-level managers have good reasons to want to game the system. They can see that they are in competition with other businesses to get capital. It is not just that they need to make a commercial case for the money. They often feel under pressure to make a better case than other businesses.

Typically, this competition causes them to ask for more capital than they need (because they anticipate that their bosses will scale back their requests) and to oversell their case (in order not to be outsold by others). The result is often too little investment in some businesses and too much investment in others – a double source of subtracted value.

The problem is made worse by a belief among most top teams, encouraged by most textbooks, that their main job is to allocate scarce capital. Yet, the presumption that capital is scarce is flawed. As we pointed out in Chapter 7, capital in any particular company is only scarce if it is trying to support more businesses than it can afford. Rather than short changing some or all of the businesses, the company would be better to sell some businesses to eliminate the shortage. The way to maximise performance is to ensure that every business has the optimum amount of capital. Anything more or less than the optimum subtracts value.

Of course, the tough bit is figuring out what is the optimum for each business, especially when the managers in the business are overselling their needs.

Inappropriate policies and constraints

Corporate headquarters sets policies that businesses are expected to follow. At one level, these are a necessary part of good governance, such as accounting policies and decision approval authorities. But there are also many other reasons for the existence of policies. They can exist as part of controls, such as policies about air travel or policies about talking with the press. They can exist to promote standardisation or fairness, such as common salary structures or standard IT applications. They can exist to aid economies of scale or purchasing power, such as rules about the choice of laptops. They can exist because they are expected to raise the quality of performance, such as policies on safety or technical standards.

Subtracted value occurs when a policy is inappropriate for one or more of the businesses. The policy can be generally misguided, such as a pay policy that is out of tune with the market place or an accounting policy that is poor practice. More normally, however, the policy is appropriate for some businesses but not for others. For example, a pay policy can suit the company's established businesses but not the needs of developing businesses or businesses in different markets.

As in other areas, the risk of subtracted value is greater if the company is entering less familiar businesses or the economic challenges in existing businesses are changing. This is because policies usually change more slowly than the environment and are likely to be applied across all businesses rather than selectively to those businesses where they are relevant.

Poor quality people decisions

Decisions about people are probably the decisions that have the biggest impact on the value of a business. Subtracted value occurs when corporate-level managers make less good people decisions than would have been made by the board of directors of an independent business. For example, they may be slower to remove poor performers or they may have employment policies that are more restrictive than those of an independent board.

Problems in this area are surprisingly common. Corporate-level managers can feel more loyalty and more attachment to business-level executives than independent boards, even though plenty of independent boards can suffer from this bias as well. This can make corporate-level managers slower to deal with underperformance.

Corporate-level managers can be more prone to look for solutions inside the company than an independent board, causing them to restrict the search for appropriate talent. Also, their pay structures, designed often to make it easier to move managers around the company, can make it hard to design a bespoke package to recruit the best external talent into senior jobs.

Finally, corporate-level managers can have a picture of the skills required that is influenced by the core businesses or the businesses in which they have previously worked. This picture may not fit other businesses in the portfolio that have different critical success factors.

Misguided synergy projects

Leaders of large companies are often looking for ways to create synergy (horizontal added value) from links across the businesses. In part this is because they believe that synergy is a significant way for them to add value. In part it is because they need to be able to justify the range of businesses that they own, and the easiest justification is that the businesses need to be together for reasons of synergy. Subtracted value occurs when the synergy initiatives have opportunity costs that are greater than the benefits of the initiative.

Research by Goold and Campbell suggests that subtracted value from synergy projects is a widespread problem.[7] Moreover, as Michael Porter has pointed out, synergies are frequently reluctant to appear.[8]

The reason why synergy projects often create more opportunity cost than benefit is because most synergies happen naturally between profit-seeking managers: they do not need corporate projects to drive the benefits. In other words, when the synergy benefits are greater than the opportunity costs, independent businesses can, and frequently do, work with each other for mutual benefit. It is only in limited situations that a shared owner can help release synergies that would not have been released between independent companies.

As we pointed out at the end of Chapter 8, synergy projects are often aimed at mirages: the opportunity costs are greater than the benefits. One example involved a CEO who was frustrated that his UK and US businesses were not cooperating over product development. After a few years of persuasion, he took a more directive approach. He insisted that the US business launch at least one product that was successful in the UK. His managers complied, but explained to us that the opportunity cost was greater than the benefit. In other words, they believed that they would have generated more incremental sales by launching one of their own products instead of one that had been developed in the UK.

Synergy projects redefine the priorities of the business-level managers. This can cause them to work on a less productive activity before a more productive activity. It is common, for example, to hear managers in business divisions complain that they are involved in too many coordination committees, best practice reviews, project teams and joint working parties. They feel that the burden of coordination projects is causing them to have less time to drive their business forward.

Inefficient central services

Companies frequently centralise some services. In fact, shared services divisions are becoming commonplace. These divisions provide accounting services, recruitment services, payroll services and IT services to the business divisions. The added value comes from economies of scale and from less duplication.

However, subtracted value also occurs. These central services can be slow, high cost and insufficiently tailored to the needs of individual businesses. Forced to take a one-size-fits-all service, a business division can be worse off than when it had its own staff doing the activity.

Despite benefiting from economies of scale and reduced duplication, central services are often inefficient because of the way they are governed. Often the service is a Cinderella activity inside a larger corporate function. Take an accounting services activity that reports to the group finance function. The leaders of the group finance function are typically busy with mergers and acquisitions or fund raising or capital allocation decisions. Hence, they give little attention to the operational efficiency issues in accounting services. Moreover, the group CFO is typically more of an expert than an operations manager.

Many companies have found that a shared services division can greatly improve the performance of the shared services activities. The division can be run by an operations manager, who can focus on cost per transaction and on service delivery. However, even this solution often underperforms. Because the shared services division is a monopoly supplier, it does not feel the normal pressures from customers when it underperforms. This can make it slow to adjust. Moreover, the head of shared services often has a direct line to the CEO of the group. This makes it possible for him or her to blame complaints on "unreasonable divisions" rather than face up to performance problems.

Delays and time wasting

Corporate-level managers take up the time of business managers. Typically, they use more of the time of business managers on corporate affairs and performance reporting than a typical board of an independent company does. Moreover, they create decision-making delays. Large decisions may have to pass through two layers of managers above the level of the business before being taken to the corporate board.

As with synergy initiatives, these delays and uses of time have opportunity costs. Unless the added value is greater than the opportunity cost, the net is subtracted value. One of the most frequent complaints by business-level managers in large companies is the slowness of decisions and the bureaucratic use of time, suggesting that this also is a major source of subtracted value.

Reducing the risk of subtracted value

Companies need to be alert to the risks of subtracted value and take active measures to reduce them. Just doing less, however, may not be enough.

Size the prize

The first defence against value destruction is to have a discipline of assessing and debating the size of the potential added value before initiating any corporate activity. Since subtracted value is hard to defend against, it is important that added value is large and hence likely to be greater than subtracted value.

If a company is considering creating a new corporate function, launching a strategic planning process or encouraging synergy between the North American and Asian divisions, an estimate should be made of the size of the likely added value. If the benefit to the businesses is significant (say greater than 10% increase in profits), it is worth taking the risk of subtracted value. If the benefit is small, the new activity should only go ahead if the risk of subtracted value is small or manageable.

The hurdle of 10% improvement is high. But it is not meant as a firm line. The hurdle serves to alert managers to the challenge of subtracted value. If a company is considering entering or acquiring a new business, it is appropriate to set an even higher hurdle, such as 20%. In a new business situation, the risk that subtracted value will be greater than added value is even higher, so the hurdle needs to be raised.

Encourage pushback

Managers in the businesses can more easily identify subtracted value than managers at the corporate level. So it is important to listen to their concerns and encourage them to explain their thinking when they are uncomfortable with something.

Of course, business-level managers are not always right. If they were, there would be little opportunity to add value. So their arguments need to be challenged. Frequently, corporate managers will still act, even when business managers are unhappy. But in these circumstances, corporate managers need to take extra care to ensure they are right, and may want to prove their case in part of the organisation before imposing a change more widely.

Encouraging pushback is the opposite of the culture in many companies. "One company" campaigns, phrases like "not invented here" or "not a team player" and the natural reluctance of subordinates to tell their bosses that their ideas are misguided often dominate the culture. Reluctant agreement is more common than rigorous debate.

Strong performance measures for business units are helpful. They give business managers the incentive to resist inappropriate corporate interference. Some companies go even further. As mentioned earlier, Richard Branson prefers the management teams of Virgin's businesses to own as much as half of the business giving them plenty of incentive to push back any negative corporate influence.

Focus

As the BCG research shows, less is often more: less ambition for corporate integration and corporate functional influence can generate more net added value. If the corporate managers are focused on driving a few sources of added value, they are less likely to be subtracting value.

Based on our experience, three to seven areas of focus seem to be a reasonable number for a corporate team. Each area of focus should offer considerable potential for added value: hence the 10% rule.

Of course, a corporate team will not completely limit its activities to the main areas of focus. There will be some compliance activities that do not add value but are required by law or by normal practice. There will also be some less important activities, such as central payroll, that are expected to add some value. These less important activities should be frequently challenged because of the risk that they subtract value. Do we really need this compliance activity? Are we convinced that central payroll has no negative side effects?

Research on the link between strategy and execution further suggests that, at any point in time, the corporate team should have a "main effort": an added value focus that is the most important for that period.[9] General Electric under Jack Welch is probably most famous for the clarity of its main effort. Each year in January, the top 400 managers would meet in Boca Raton in Florida to review the previous year's performance and agree targets for the following year. At the same time, Jack Welch would announce the corporate initiative that would be the main focus for the year. It varied. Early in his tenure it was "No. 1 or No. 2". For three or four years running it was "six sigma". In the late 1990s, it was "destroyyourbusiness.com". While there were many other initiatives going on, all managers were clear about the main focus for the coming year.

Summary

One of the major insights from our early work on large companies was the realisation that corporate headquarters can make things worse as well as better. This is no surprise to any manager working within a business division and, as a result, we have the joke "I am from headquarters and I am here to help you". However, the full implication of this risk of subtracted value is, in our experience, not given enough attention.

As we have tried to show in this chapter, subtracted value is an ever-present problem for good and obvious reasons. Managers considering new businesses or new corporate initiatives need to assess the risks of subtracted value before they make decisions.

Notes

[1] Michael Goold and Andrew Campbell, *Strategies and Styles* (Basil Blackwell, 1987).

[2] From interviews carried out at 3M.

[3] From interviews in a chemical company.

[4] Matthias Kruhler, Ulrich Pidun and Harald Rubner, "First Do No Harm: How to Be a Good Corporate Parent", Boston Consulting Group, March 2012.

[5] David Sadtler, Andrew Campbell and Richard Koch, *Breakup: When Large Companies are Worth More Dead Than Alive* (Capstone, 1997), 34–35.

[6] Kaplan and Norton, "The Balanced Scorecard", *Harvard Business Review*, 1992.

[7] Andrew Campbell and Michael Goold, *The Collaborative Enterprise* (Perseus Books, 2000).

[8] Michael Porter, *Competitive Advantage*, (The Free Press, 1985), chapter 11, 383.

[9] Stephen Bungay, *The Art of Action* (Nicholas Brearley Publishing, 2010).

CHAPTER TEN

HOW TO IDENTIFY SOURCES OF ADDED VALUE FOR YOUR COMPANY

The last three chapters have described sources of added value and sources of subtracted value. We also provided, at the end of the added value chapters, some questions managers can ask themselves to challenge ideas they have for adding value. In this chapter, we will describe some analytical tools that managers can use to help identify sources of added value in their own companies. We devote a chapter to this topic because managers are often looking for additional sources of added value, or wish to confirm that they are not overlooking opportunities to help their businesses improve. We will also provide some tools for summarising sources of added value so that they get appropriate attention from headquarters.

We start by looking at analyses that can be done bottom-up: focusing on the needs of the business units and business divisions. We then describe ways of addressing the same issues from the top down: focusing on the insights and capabilities of the managers at the corporate level. This double perspective helps identify all the opportunities (which we will refer to as opportunities-to-add-value) that fit with the skills of managers in headquarters and are likely to make a real difference to overall performance.

We recognise that in many companies, particularly integrated companies that involve significant shared activities and central functions, the main opportunities-to-add-value may be obvious. In CIW, for example, technology, product development and global branding were all centralised functions and major sources of added value for the regional divisions. The analysis that follows will seem less important in these companies, where the issues are likely to be more about how to maximise added value and minimise subtracted value rather than which sources of added value to focus on. These issues are addressed in Part IV.

However, even for integrated companies, careful analysis of the opportunities to add value can be helpful. In CIW, which was structured into regional divisions, there was tension between the equipment product line and the European region over the management of sales staff. Sales of equipment frequently involved bespoke engineering that was best provided from a global team. Hence, there were issues about the how the global team of equipment salespeople and the European region should work together, and which sales staff should report centrally and which locally. Clarity about the opportunity-to-add-value is essential for helping resolve these kinds of internal issues.

Opportunity-to-add-value analysis – bottom up

Each business division has strengths and weaknesses. Each business also has some business opportunities that it will find difficult to exploit on its own. Opportunities-to-add-value come from identifying those areas of weakness that can be addressed by corporate headquarters and those business opportunities that will be accessed more easily with help from headquarters or from a sister company.

Bottom-up analysis (see Figure 10.1) can be carried out for each business division one at a time. It can also be applied to

Figure 10.1: Opportunities to add value – bottom-up analysis

For each business unit or business division:

• What are the main decisions, changes and improvements facing this business over the next 3–5 years: the main tasks?

• Is the business likely to find any of these difficult to execute: is it likely to underperform in any of these areas without help?

• Could any of these areas of likely underperformance be corrected by a skilled parent company? If so, they are opportunities-to-add-value.

• Identify more opportunities-to-add-value by listing the things that go wrong in this industry. What mistakes do even good managers typically make? What mistakes have competitors made? Each area of typical mistake is an additional opportunity-to-add-value.

• Consider what the parent companies of competitors to this business do to add value to these competitors. Anything these parent companies do is an additional opportunity-to-add-value.

• Finally, consider the check list (see Figure 10.3) to see if there are any other opportunities-to-add-value that you have missed.

a potential new business. It starts with a list of the major tasks that the management team of the business will need to carry out over the next two or three years to optimise the performance of the business. For example, in a business that manufactures products for a global market, the task list might be:

• Expand in China
• Develop and launch a new range of products utilising a new technology
• Reduce costs by consolidating the manufacturing footprint
• Improve technical selling skills
• Improve the software used in the enterprise operating system
• Hire a supply chain manager with good global sourcing skills

Typically, there will be 5–12 tasks that will have a significant impact on the performance of the business over the next two or three years. Mostly, these are tasks to improve things or do something new or different. The list of tasks should not include the business-as-usual tasks, such as continue to satisfy core customers or operate manufacturing within tolerances, unless these are areas that need significant improvement. If the business is already performing these activities well, they are unlikely to be areas where the business managers need help. Nor should the list focus on financial targets, such as raise profit by 10% per year or double the size of the business. These are the outcomes of things the managers need to do. So the list should focus on the operating tasks that will deliver the desired financial performance and market position.

Often it is useful to do this analysis at an organisational level below that of the division, especially if the divisions are made up of business units or profit centres. The objective with this bottom-up analysis is to understand the tasks facing managers at the lowest level at which a multi-functional view of the business is being taken.

Do the managers need help?

With a list of tasks, the first way to identify opportunities-to-add-value is to examine each task to assess whether the management team concerned is likely to do the task well or not. Where the managers in the business are expected to perform below optimum or where it is clear that the managers will need help, there is an opportunity-to-add-value.

Some items on the task list will be easy to judge. The business will have a track record of doing it well or less well. For example, if global sourcing is a current area of weakness, the business could benefit from help, and it is easy to judge that this is an opportunity-to-add-value. Of course, the ability to help depends on the skills of managers in headquarters. If managers in headquarters have a lot of experience hiring supply chain managers with global sourcing skills, it is likely that headquarters will be able to add a lot of value to this operating task. Also, if corporate headquarters owns another business division with excellent global sourcing skills and capacity to do global sourcing for both divisions, it is likely that headquarters can rearrange global sourcing across the two divisions and add a lot of value. But if headquarters does not have these skills or relevant other divisions, it may not be able to provide the help needed: the opportunity-to-add-value still exists, but headquarters may not be able to do anything about it.

Other items on the task list will be harder to judge whether there is an opportunity-to-add-value. Normally, these are new challenges where managers in headquarters are unlikely to have more experience than the business managers. For example, expanding in China is difficult for most companies. It may not be obvious whether the business division has a weakness in this area or not. In these cases, the analysis involves assessing whether an opportunity-to-add-value could exist if corporate headquarters had certain skills or resources. For example, one of the difficulties in China comes from the shortage of managerial talent. If headquarters owned other business divisions in China, and headquarters was able to move management talent from these sister divisions to the division that wants to grow in China, then headquarters could add significant value. In other words, there is an opportunity-to-add-value if headquarters has the right combination of skills and resources.

The bottom-up analysis nearly always identifies opportunities-to-add-value. This is partly because the analysis imagines that headquarters has the appropriate combination of skills and resources. Care, however, should be taken to avoid fantasy. It is important to keep the list of opportunities-to-add-value realistic. For example, if headquarters knew which products would succeed and which would fail, it could help businesses reduce the cost of new product development. Or, if headquarters knew how fast the market would grow, it could help businesses invest the right amount in capacity. But it is unrealistic to expect that headquarters will know these things. Hence, an opportunity-to-add-value based on prescience by managers in headquarters is fantasy.

Distinguishing between fantasy and reality requires judgement. What is fantasy in one company may be reality in another. If a company owns multiple business divisions in China, all of which are growing, it is fantasy to suppose that headquarters will be able help one division by moving managers from another division: all divisions are likely to be short of managers. But, if some businesses are growing and others are declining, then helping one division by moving managers is quite easy.

The judgement can be improved by debating it with the managers involved: they often recognise when they need help, and they may have good arguments why they do not need help. Surprisingly, there is often easy agreement between headquarters managers and managers in the business divisions about the list of opportunities-to-add-value. Managers in the divisions are able to see the help that they need and often welcome the analysis.

Occasionally, however, managers in the divisions disagree: they argue that they will not underperform. When this happens it is important to lay out the logic clearly. Why is it likely that this business will need help or why is it likely that headquarters could add something that is helpful? When the logic is explicit, both sides can discuss the validity of the logic rather than focusing on the more threatening issues of underperformance and possible interference from headquarters. If agreement cannot be reached, it is the judgement of the managers at corporate headquarters that should take primacy, but only after allowing the logic of their thinking to be challenged and tested.

What are typical mistakes?

The second way of identifying opportunities-to-add-value from the bottom up involves making a list of the mistakes that managers in competitor companies in the same sector typically make. For example, in cyclical businesses, managers typically overinvest at the top of the cycle. In product businesses, managers are typically slow to cannibalise existing products. In highly profitable businesses, managers typically allow overheads costs to grow too high. Each of these mistakes is a potential source of added value. If corporate managers are alert to the mistakes and know how to steer the business away from these errors, significant value can be added.

When focusing on competitor companies it is important to look primarily at similar businesses. If the division concerned is selling luxury products to China, then the analysis should focus primarily on the business divisions of competitors that sell luxury products in China. A typical mistake of these competitors might be to be slow in expanding into provincial cities. Managers may presume that most luxury business is in the main cities – Beijing and Shanghai. Another mistake might be to rely too heavily on expatriate managers rather than building up a talent pool of Chinese managers. If these are typical mistakes made by competitors, then they are mistakes that may also be made by the business division being analysed. Hence, with the right skills and processes, headquarters may be able to help the business division avoid both mistakes.

When thinking about opportunities-to-add-value that arise from avoiding mistakes, it is important to have in mind a base case performance. This involves defining an overall performance measure such as profit or customer satisfaction. Any performance improvement above this base case is added value.

What are rival parent companies doing?

The third way of identifying opportunities-to-add-value is by looking at what rival parent companies are doing. First, focus on a business division. Then list the market place competitors of this division. Then define the parent companies, if any, of these market place competitors. Then try to find out how the parent companies of these competitors are helping them. If most of the competitors are focused businesses without a parent company, this might signal that it is hard for parent companies to add value.

Where the competitors have parent companies, the analysis aims to understand what benefits these businesses are getting from their parent companies. Without direct access to these companies it is hard to know how they operate. However, there are ex-employees of the company and other sources, such as articles or speeches by managers of the company or published case studies, that provide useful information about what is going on in rival parent companies. Anything that another company is doing to add value is an opportunity-to-add-value your company should also consider.

Sometimes opportunity-to-add-value analysis produces a long list of ways in which corporate headquarters could help each business: it can be 10 or more opportunities-to-add-value for each business. Sometimes the list is quite short, just two or three items. It is rare that there are no opportunities to add value.

Opportunity-to-add-value analysis – top down

Top-down analysis involves talking with managers at the headquarters level to find out whether the bottom-up analysis has overlooked any significant opportunities-to-add-value. Sometimes managers with experience can see significant areas for improvement that do not get identified in the bottom-up analysis. For example, a head of corporate IT or HR may be able to spot that the functional experts in the businesses have significant weaknesses that need correcting. The chief financial officer may spot an opportunity to reduce working capital. The chief executive may know that operating ratios in some businesses are out of line with good practice or that the businesses are focused on local customers when the future lies in globalisation.

Figure 10.2: Sources of horizontal added value

- One face to the customer
- Cross-selling
- Economies of scale
- Shared resources
- Multipoint competition
- Vertical integration
- Sharing knowledge and good practice
- New business development
- Risk management

These top-down opportunities-to-add-value may have already been included in the list generated from the bottom-up analysis. Hence, the top-down analysis may not produce any significant new opportunities-to-add-value. However, in most cases the top-down analysis does identify some additional opportunities-to-add-value.

An area of particular interest in top-down analysis is synergy across business divisions (horizontal added value). Opportunities for good practice sharing, cross-selling, cost sharing or eliminating duplication do not always surface from the bottom-up analysis. Hence, it is useful to check against the list of types of horizontal added value given in Chapter 9 (see Figure 10.2).

Another area of particular interest in top-down analysis is performance management. A CEO or CFO, who knows what ratios and what profit levels constitute excellent performance for each business division, can add a lot of value by ensuring that the business divisions set themselves high enough targets and commit to the changes needed to deliver the targets.

A third area of particular interest in top-down analysis is people quality. The appointment of the top team of a business is the one decision that has the biggest impact on performance. If headquarters managers know how to find, assess and motivate high quality managers for each of its business divisions,

Figure 10.3: Common opportunities-to-add-value

1. Size and age. Old, large, successful businesses often build up bureaucracies and overheads that are hard to eliminate from the inside. Small, young businesses may have insufficient functional skills, managerial succession problems and lack of financial resources to ride a recession. Are these factors relevant to the business?

2. Management. Does the business have top quality managers relative to its competitors? Are its managers focused on the right objectives/ambitions? Is the business dependent on attracting and retaining unusual sorts of people?

3. Temptations. Does the nature of the business encourage managers to make mistakes (e.g., maturity often leads to excessive diversification, long product cycles can lead to excessive reliance on old products, cyclical swings can lead to too much investment during the upswing)?

4. Linkages. Could this business effectively link with other businesses to improve efficiency or market position? Are the linkages complex or difficult to establish between the units concerned?

5. Common capabilities. Does this business have capabilities in common with other businesses that could be built, shared and transferred between the businesses?

6. Special expertise. Could this business benefit from specialist or rare expertise that the parent possesses or could possess?

7. External relations. Does this business have difficult to manage external stakeholders (shareholders, government, unions, suppliers, etc.) that could be better managed by the parent company?

8. Major decisions. Does the business face difficult and infrequent decisions in which it lacks expertise (entering China, major acquisitions, major capacity extensions)? Would it be difficult to get funding for major investments from external capital providers?

9. Major change. Is the business facing a need to make major changes that its management have insufficient experience of?

10. Business definition. Appropriate business definitions may change over time. As a result, the current definition of the business may have too narrow or too broad a product market scope, and too much or too little vertical integration. The trend to outsourcing and alliances is changing the definitions of many businesses, creating new parenting opportunities. Is each business defined so as to maximise its sources of competitive advantage?

they are likely to be able to add significant value. This opportunity-to-add-value is one that has been exploited by some private equity companies. By strengthening the management team of the businesses that they buy and by giving the managers substantial incentives, these private equity firms have found that they can often double profits or growth rates.

Before drawing a line under the search for opportunities-to-add-value, it is helpful to review the checklist in Figure 10.3. This list can often stimulate further thoughts about opportunities-to-add-value that may have been overlooked.

One warning: the top-down analysis can easily become self-serving. Since headquarters managers are keen to justify their existence, the top-down analysis can often generate many opportunities-to-add-value that were not identified in the bottom-up work. Care needs to be taken to check each additional top-down item to make sure that it is addressing something important to the success of the businesses. The list of tasks for each business is helpful in this regard. If the opportunity-to-add-value is focused on one of the major tasks, then it is likely to be relevant to the performance of the business. But, if the opportunity-to-add-value is about something not on the task list, it may well involve distraction costs that are greater than the benefits.

The opinions of business managers are also helpful in identifying top-down initiatives that are likely to distract more than they contribute. One particular area where the top-down appetite is often greater than the real benefits is in best practice sharing and other forms of synergy. In their desire to create the "glue" that justifies owning a range of businesses, headquarters managers often push for synergy initiatives that look good on paper, but end up generating more work than benefits. We say more about synergy initiatives in Chapter 15.

Sorting and challenging opportunities-to-add-value

When the bottom-up and top-down analyses are complete, there will be a long list of opportunities-to-add-value. Typically, the list will include big items, such as "help business units expand in China" or "reduce cost of sales by 5% through purchasing synergies" and smaller items such as "lower the cost of debt" and "share best practice in leadership training". Moreover, there will be opportunities that exist in only one or two business divisions, for example "help win contract A with the Department of Defence" or "help the business find a new office to rent in Shanghai" or "help the business appoint a new supply chain manager".

A useful first step is to identify the big opportunities-to-add-value that are relevant to at least half of the businesses in the group. A good test of significance is the 10% rule. Will the efforts of corporate headquarters result in improvements that increase overall corporate performance by 10% or more? This can be done by looking at last year's profit before tax for the whole company (let's say $100 million). Then use 10% of this (say $10 million) as the hurdle. Is headquarters likely to raise profits by at least $10 million per annum by focusing on this opportunity-to-add-value? In the main, these will be opportunities-to-add-value that are relevant to most of the business divisions. But some may be opportunities-to-add-value that make a big difference to only one or two large divisions. Typically, there are less than seven of these "10% opportunities". Sometimes there are only one or two. In our experience, there are very few situations where there are no 10% opportunities.

We say more about the 10% hurdle in Chapter 13. There is nothing magical about the 10% number. It is just an opportunity-to-add-value that is large enough to warrant attention from all managers concerned. It is also large enough that the net is still likely to be positive even if some subtracted value occurs as part of the effort to create the added value.

The next step in sorting opportunities is to decide which of these 10% opportunities will be targeted by headquarters. Ideally, all will be targeted. But often there are reasons for excluding some opportunities. Reasons for excluding opportunities are:

- the current headquarters team is unlikely to be capable of developing the skills or resources needed to address the opportunity
- the headquarters team has limited resources and will achieve more, at least in the short term, with a tight focus on fewer sources of added value
- the divisions concerned have more important things to focus on
- the divisions concerned have been earmarked for sale

Companies often find that there is a poor match between the 10% opportunities and the skills of the headquarters team.

For example, the businesses may need help expanding in China or developing their digital commerce channel, but the headquarters team typically does not have anything special to offer in these areas: it does not have special knowledge or resources that will help with expansion in China or digital commerce. Or the businesses need help cutting costs and rationalising global manufacturing, but the headquarters team consists mainly of marketing people with growth rather than rationalisation skills. When this happens it is easy to presume that the headquarters team will be able to quickly build the required skills. This is rarely possible. A significant change in headquarters skills normally requires significant changes in people including often changing the CEO or COO or CFO. Even when significant changes are made, headquarters teams often still fail to build the relevant skills (see Chapter 14 for more on building "parenting skills").

The final step in sorting and challenging opportunities-to-add-value is to decide how many of the smaller opportunities to address. If the analysis defines only five 10% opportunities, it is likely to define 20 or more smaller opportunities.

The default position with regard to smaller opportunities is none. This is because the time of senior managers in headquarters is the scarcest resource in the company. Anything that distracts them from the 10% opportunities is likely to have opportunity costs that are greater than value added. Moreover, when the opportunity-to-add-value is small, unintentional subtracted value can easily exceed the added value.

In practice, however, there are often quite a large number of smaller opportunities that can be addressed without distracting senior managers and without the risk of significant subtracted value: for example, central purchasing of laptops, standard forms for expenses claims, combined outsourcing of facilities management and central processing or outsourcing of payroll work.

Each of these smaller opportunities-to-add-value should be challenged to confirm that the added value is hard to dispute, that the opportunity cost is low and that the risk of subtracted value is low. The following challenge questions are helpful:

1. Does everyone agree that this activity will add value?
2. Is there agreement about the size of the likely cash flow benefit this activity will create compared to the alternative of letting the businesses do what they want?
3. Could this activity distract senior managers in headquarters from more important priorities? What is the likely opportunity cost?
4. Is there any chance that this activity will be done badly, for example, at higher cost or with time delays or with less good decisions/results?
5. Is there any chance that this activity will constrain the commercial freedom of any of the businesses?
6. Is there any chance that this activity will reduce the motivation of senior managers in the businesses or distract them from more important priorities?

Smaller opportunities need a good outcome on all of these questions. Because the upside is small, there is no reason to take risks. As BCG, the consultants, so eloquently put it, "first do no harm".[1]

Summarising opportunities in a value staircase

A value staircase (Figure 10.4) is a helpful tool for linking opportunities-to-add-value to the main tasks faced by each business. A value staircase can be developed for each business. The steps of the staircase represent the major tasks for the managers in the business unit. The height of the step represents the impact each task is expected to have on the value of the business (the incremental discounted cash flow that will accrue if

Figure 10.4: The value staircase

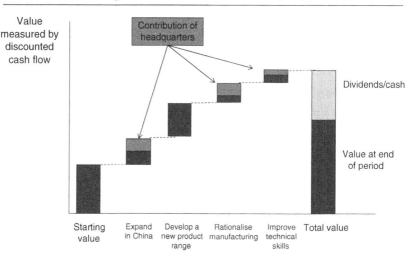

the task is executed well). The value staircase starts with the estimated net present value of the current business: the base case. Each step increases the value above the base case.

The staircase is most useful if it is looking three or more years ahead. The size of the steps can then be significant, especially if the objective is to double the value of the business over the period. Cash taken out of the business and dividend payments during the period should be included as part of the value generated over the period. Hence, the final column in the staircase is the value of the business at the end of the period plus the cash and dividends released by the business during the period (all, of course, discounted to make the numbers comparable).

The staircase helps managers in the business focus on those things that deliver the most increase in value. Hence, it is a useful visual tool for summarising the plans. What is more, the added value of the corporate levels can be represented on the value staircase in the form of shading on some of the steps in the staircase.

The shading represents the contribution of corporate headquarters to the achievement of the value in the step. It is that part of the step that might not happen without support and influence from headquarters: it represents the opportunities-to-add-value. Deciding how much shading to give each step is difficult – and it may seem inappropriate for headquarters to try to claim credit for the achievement of the business. But, the discussion is normally helpful. It provides a vehicle for aligning the thinking of the corporate-level managers with that of the managers in the business.

The value staircase can be used as a value budget or a value contract between the business unit and headquarters. Together with shading that represents the contribution of headquarters, the value contract can become a commitment by all concerned to do certain things and achieve certain targets.

Summarising opportunities in a value added table

It can be useful also to draw up a table with the major opportunities-to-add-value (the 10% opportunities) on one side and the main headquarters functions along the top. In the boxes of the table, write down what each headquarters function needs to do to help ensure that the value is created (see Figure 10.5). We discuss the value added table in more detail in Chapter 13.

Most major opportunities will involve contributions from more than one headquarters function. This table helps to ensure that the actions of the functions are coordinated. It also helps the managers in the businesses see the links between different headquarters functions. Each box in the table can be filled out with text explaining the role of the function or, as in the figure, it can be used to show more visually the relative effort from each function.

A further benefit comes from exposing activities within the headquarters functions that do not have a place in the table. These activities are candidates for elimination because they may

Figure 10.5: Value added table

Major sources of group-wide added value	CEO	Legal	IS	Finance	Technology	HR	Marketing	Lean	Risk
Continuous improvement using Lean methodologies	*			*		**		** *	
Acquisitions	***	**	*	**	*	**	*	**	*
Market development especially in the chemical industries	*	*				*			
Performance stretch and incentives	***		*	**	**	*		** *	
Help restructure/integrate/rationalise footprint/and rationalise product range	***	**	**	**	***	**	**	**	*

Key: Three stars = major role. No stars = no role.

distract from the main focus. Of course, they may also point to areas of added value that have been overlooked.

A final benefit of the table is that it exposes empty boxes: functions that are not involved in one or more of the opportunities-to-add-value. This is healthy. Not all corporate functions should be involved in all opportunities. It helps managers at headquarters and in the businesses see the different roles and different contributions of different functions.

Summary

Most companies are comfortable asking the question "What value does headquarters add?" But few are able to give a crisp answer, and even fewer have done any structured analysis of their own opportunities-to-add-value or thought deeply about which opportunities to address and which to leave unaddressed.

This chapter described the analytical steps that can be taken by any company. They involve bottom-up analysis of the needs of the business divisions and top-down analysis of the ideas and capabilities of managers in corporate headquarters. The chapter also suggests ways of structuring the analysis using value added tables and value staircases to help clarify, communicate and integrate the different opportunities-to-add-value.

Since subtracted value is an ever-present risk, the chapter also suggests some challenges that managers can use to limit the activities of headquarters and so reduce the risk of subtracted value.

Note

[1]"First Do No Harm" Report 2012, Boston Consulting Group.

PART IV

MANAGEMENT STRATEGY: HOW TO STRUCTURE, HOW MUCH TO CENTRALISE AND HOW TO GROW THE BUSINESS DIVISIONS

CHAPTER ELEVEN

STRUCTURING THE ORGANISATION INTO BUSINESSES AND DIVISIONS

Throughout the first two parts of this book, we have used the terms business division, business unit or operating unit to describe a part of the organisation that is semi-autonomous, performance accountable and largely self-managing. It has been important to make a distinction between these semi-autonomous divisions and the corporate headquarters because

- if business divisions are semi-autonomous and self-managing, there is a need to justify the existence of corporate head-quarters: an alternative would be for the business divisions to be independent organisations
- without the existence of "something above the level of the business division", there would be no need to develop sepa-rate strategy concepts for corporate groups: large organisa-tions could just use the normal tools of business strategy
- a corporate headquarters is the organisational unit to which business divisions report: headquarters, therefore, needs a strategy just in the same way that business divisions need strategies

However, in practice the distinction between business divi-sion and corporate headquarters can be complex. Often there are layers between the business division and the corporate headquarters, such as sectors or regions. In addition, in some companies, significant activities, such as product development or sales or supply chain have been centralised and form part of headquarters. The "business divisions" are then not complete competitive entities: they could not be independent companies. In this case, the corporate headquarters is less of a parent organisation and more the centre of a large single business that has multiple product lines.

In this chapter we consider how to define business divisions, how to structure the organisation and how to distinguish between business divisions and corporate headquarters.

What is a business unit or business division?

The concept of business unit or business division has been evolving over the last 50 years. Alfred Chandler first recorded the existence of a separated and largely self-managing part of the organisation in his famous book *Strategy and Structure*.[1] He noted that some large American companies – Dupont, General Motors and General Electric – were organised into business divisions.

The reason for this structural innovation, known in academic circles as the M-form or divisional structure, was that managers did not have the time or knowledge to make all the decisions that were rising to the top of the organisation. The top of the organisation was becoming a bottleneck. By setting up business divisions, work could be decentralised to management teams lower down, who could be held to account for the decisions they made. Also, because the decisions were being taken closer to the market and the operational challenges, the quality of decisions improved. Companies using the divisional structure were more successful and grew even larger.

The divisional structure quickly gained acceptance among most large companies. It was also a way of organising that made diversification easy, contributing to the rise of the conglomerates of the 1960s and 1970s. Companies like LTV, Litton and ITT in the USA, and Slater Walker and Grand Metropolitan in the UK expanded by acquiring a diverse range of businesses. These companies created a separate business division for each company they acquired.

At this stage the business unit, in the form of the "business division", was a convenient way of decentralising decision making so that the work load at the top of the organisation could be reduced, and managers lower down could be held accountable for performance – mainly profit performance.

Strategic business units

It was not until the invention of the term strategic business unit (SBU) that the phrase "business unit" began to have a more precise meaning. The term SBU emerged as a result of consulting work done at General Electric (GE). Reginald Jones, GE's CEO in the 1970s, encouraged managers to spend more time on planning and strategy. This raised important questions both about how to do strategy work and about how to structure the organisation for planning purposes.

As managers developed strategic plans they found that the existing organisation structure was getting in the way. Some divisions had overlapping strategic issues. This made it hard to produce a plan for one division without also producing a plan for others. Also, in some divisions, the activities were only partially, if at all, related to each other. In these divisions it appeared to be better to develop a separate strategy for each separate activity, rather than for the whole division as a collective.

This lack of alignment between the organisational unit (division) and the unit for which a separate strategy was needed spawned the concept of the SBU. The SBU became the organisational unit that is sufficiently integrated to need a dedicated strategy and sufficiently separate from other units that its strategy is largely independent of what the other units are doing. In other words, an SBU is a part of the organisation that could be treated as an independent company and set up as a self-managing and accountable business. At the extreme, an SBU is a part of the organisation that could be floated in an IPO (initial public offering).

Using the insights gained from the SBU concept, GE and many other companies defined their organisation divisions so that they better aligned to their SBUs: each business division could have its own strategy, which could be defined without much coordination with other divisions. This made it possible to do strategic planning from the bottom upwards. The corporate headquarters would give some broad guidelines, and the SBUs would then develop, with only limited coordination, separate strategies for their separate businesses.

Despite the power and practical usefulness of the SBU concept, consultants and academics have not be able to develop a tool that determines precisely how to define the boundaries of an SBU or how to decide where one SBU stops and another starts. In part this is because the commercial environment is in flux, making stable definitions in any particular situation unhelpful. But it is also because the definition of an SBU is one of the outputs of business strategy work: the definition is a choice that managers need to make as a result of their analysis. It is a choice they make about their field of focus. It is not an input to their strategy analysis because it would constrain many of the core questions that need to be asked in a strategy process about the scope and focus of the business.

Strategic Groups

Academics, grappling with the same definitional issues, developed another concept – the Strategic Group.[2] Rather than focusing on the organisational structure, academics looked at the competitive market place. A strategic group is a group of competitors

- producing a similar range of products
- with a similar value chain of activities
- using similar channels to market
- selling to similar customers
- presenting their products in similar ways

In other words, a strategic group is a group of competitors each of which has a similar business model and strategy.

In most industries, it is possible to distinguish clear strategic groups. In the car assembly industry, for example, there are strategic groups for "luxury sports" cars like Porsche and Lamborghini, "super luxury" cars like Rolls-Royce and Bentley, "luxury" cars like Mercedes, Cadillac and Lexus, "mass market" cars like Ford, VW and Toyota, and other groups. For example, there is a strategic group for "London taxis". Each group has a product range and target customer that differs from other groups. Each group has a centre of focus that is different from other groups. There can be considerable overlap at the boundaries between groups (see Figure 11.1). But most important, each group has some competitors in the form of focused companies or SBUs of larger companies that only compete in that strategic group.

Strategic groups exist because companies in the industry focus on different sources of competitive advantage. These different sources of advantage require different and partly incompatible skills or resources, making it hard for competitors in one group to win business from competitors in another group. It is like tennis players and squash players. Being good at one of these sports makes you less good at the other, so no players play both sports at the top competitive levels. For example,

Figure 11.1: Map of strategic groups in car assembly

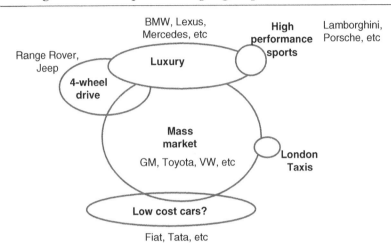

having a mass-market brand like VW makes it harder to compete successfully in the luxury and super luxury markets. To compete in these parts of the market, VW, like Toyota with Lexus, acquired a separate luxury brand – Audi – and set it up as a separate SBU. Because success in the luxury market requires skills and resources that are partly incompatible with those needed to succeed in the mass market, VW (and Toyota) have found that it is better to set up their luxury business in a separate organisational division. In other words, companies need a separate business division (SBU) for each separate strategic group in which they choose to compete. To be a successful competitor in a strategic group, a company needs an SBU focused on that strategic group.

A completely separate SBU will control all the elements of its business model. Often, however, there are significant synergies from combining some functions across SBUs. When this happens, an SBU becomes a BU: a profit centre that is not completely separate because it is operationally linked to other BUs. In the car assembly industry, research and development are often combined in a central function because there are significant economies of scope (shared technology and basic research) and some economies of scale. So a division such as Audi, for example, is not in full control of all of its technology. Technology is centralised at the Volkswagen level. Central technology also serves other Volkswagen business divisions including Lamborghini, Bugatti, Ducati, Man, Scania, Volkswagen, Porsche, Seat and Skoda. Audi, nevertheless, has sufficient autonomy over important decisions and sufficient control of the projects it is sponsoring within central research, to be able to compete successfully in the luxury sector. Audi is a separate profit centre and has significant decentralised powers. But it is not a full SBU. The implication is that a BU, with sufficient control over its sources of advantage, can also be a successful competitor in a strategic group.

Of course, the art of good strategy is to be different from and superior to competitors. Hence, many successful strategies break the rules of the existing strategic group structure in a way that gives the company advantage over two or more sets of competitors. Apple, for example, competes across four industries – computers, music players, personal consoles and telephones – without setting up four separate business divisions. Apple competes in at least four strategic groups, but does not have an organisation structure with four SBUs. This works because Apple is exploiting some sources of advantage that the existing competitors are overlooking (see Chapter 12). Frequently, however, companies that try to redefine the rules of the game find that the rules, which have evolved over time from the actions of their competitors, are wiser than they are. In other words, they are not successful.

In conclusion, at one extreme, a business division or business unit is an SBU: a part of the organisation that has full control over all important elements of its business model, and is held accountable for profit performance. At the other extreme, a business division or business unit is little more than an operating unit that can serve its customers without significant coordination with other similar operating units, but also without full delegated authority for all parts of the business model needed to deliver value to its customers. Audi falls somewhere in the middle of this range but closer to the SBU end. Apple's iPad division is more at the operating unit end. GE's aero engines business is more at the SBU end.

Three ways to structure

A large multi-activity company can be structured in three basic ways – as a value chain of operating functions, as a group of business units or as a matrix of business units (see Figure 11.2).

If the company is structured as a value chain, which is close to the structure of Apple in 2011, the leaders of the company are viewing the whole organisation as a single business. The heads of the main operating functions, such as technology,

Figure 11.2: Three ways to structure operating activities

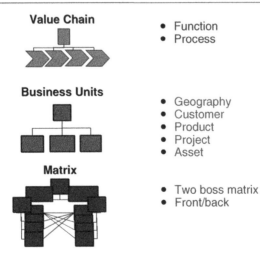

Value Chain
- Function
- Process

Business Units
- Geography
- Customer
- Product
- Project
- Asset

Matrix
- Two boss matrix
- Front/back

operations, marketing, sales and service, will report to the CEO. Net profit will be a meaningful calculation only at one point, that of the whole company because many costs are shared. As a result, many decisions need to be centralised. The tools of business-level strategy are normally sufficient. With only one business, the issues of corporate-level strategy do not need attention.

If the company is structured into units, each of which can succeed or fail without close coordination with other units, the leaders of the company are viewing the organisation as a portfolio of business units or business divisions. Net profit can be calculated for each business division. As a result, many decisions can be decentralised to the managers leading the business divisions. Clearly, with this structure, each division will develop a business-level strategy. In addition, a separate corporate-level strategy – what divisions to invest in and how to manage the portfolio – is needed for the company as a whole.

If the company is structured into some form of matrix, the leaders are viewing the organisation as an integrated company, but one that is too large or too complex to run as a single business unit. For example, international companies typically have a product/geography matrix. They have product divisions with global responsibility for their products and geographic divisions with responsibility for all products sold in a region or country (see Appendix for more discussion of international strategy). The matrix forces the two dimensions, product and geography, to work together, while allowing the corporate level to decentralise many decisions. To help the different sides of the matrix to work together, the structure typically also involves transfer pricing systems and coordinating mechanisms.

In the matrix, both sets of divisions (product and geography) are typically set up as profit centres (even though this may involve double counting some costs and revenues). But, and this is a defining feature of matrix structures, despite the transfer pricing systems and coordinating mechanisms, head-quarters will still be closely involved in arbitrating over disputes and checking that managers are coordinating in ways that achieve the best overall performance.

Each division will develop its own business-level strategy based on its performance measures, but the strategies will need to be coordinated. Corporate-level strategy is therefore critical for helping leaders decide what range of divisions to invest in and how best to coordinate and integrate them.

The three types of structure described are rarely seen in their pure form. Most companies employ a mix of these struc-tures: centralising some functions and decentralising others to business divisions; as well as giving profit responsibility to one dimension, such as global product units, while reserving sig-nificant powers and responsibilities for other dimensions such as geography. Companies also have different structures at dif-ferent levels. If the parent company is structured into three divisions, each division may have a different structure. One may be a value chain, one a business unit structure and one a matrix structure.

The same three basic structures also exist in not-for-profit organisations. They can be structured into a value chain of functions, a set of separable operating divisions or a matrix of operating divisions. The main difference is the lack of a simple performance measure, such as profit. Nevertheless, the prin-ciples are the same, even though the performance measures may be a combination of metrics relating to the organisation's mission.

Choosing the right structure

So how do managers decide which of the three basic types is appropriate for their company? The appropriate structure is dependent on the strategy. If the sources of advantage that underpin the strategy come from global functional excellence, then a functional or value chain structure is best. If the sources of advantage come from product, then a divisional structure based on products is best. If the sources of advantage come from intimacy with and tailored solutions for different market segments, then a divisional structure based on markets is best. If the sources of advantage come from a combination of product technology, market intimacy and functional excellence then a three-dimensional matrix consisting of product divisions, market divisions and central functions is the best structure.

Having made this vital point about structure following strategy, it is also important to recognise that the simple divisional structure has many advantages. It is the structure that provides the most accountability. It is the structure that promotes the most initiative, and often the highest levels of motivation. It is the structure with the lowest management cost, because it requires the least amount of coordination and dialogue. As a result, when in doubt, the default choice is a simple divisional structure.

Even when there are sources of competitive advantage that cross the structure, it is often still possible to retain a simple divisional structure and capture some of the cross structure advantages through central functions or coordinating mechanisms.

Customising the divisional structure

In 2011, CIW was an example of a customised divisional structure. The wire and equipment company had a strategy underpinned by sources of advantage that were both local to a region and global. Local sources of advantage came from close customer relationships, control of local distributors and responsive service both for its products and for technical support. These sources of advantage were best delivered through regional structures responsible for manufacturing, logistics, marketing, sales and service.

Global sources of advantage came from technology and from standardising components across the global product range. These sources of advantage were best delivered through global product structures with responsibility for technology and product management. There were also some sources of advantage to be gained from developing intimate relationships with a few global customers, especially in particular market sectors such as construction.

So CIW, like many international companies, could gain advantage from three dimensions: the regional dimension, the product dimension and the customer or market segment dimension.

Recognising that their managerial skills were not highly sophisticated, CIW's leaders rejected a matrix solution. Instead they chose a structure of regional divisions. This gave priority to the regional sources of advantage. The global product and global customer sources of advantage were addressed by headquarters functions. In other words, CIW's headquarters aimed to add value to the regional divisions by coordinating technology, product range and global customers across the regional divisions.

The CIW example is interesting because the company had three structures over a five-year period (see Figure 11.3). In 2008, the company was dominated by its European operations, with a functional structure for managers looking after Europe and related regions and a divisional structure for India, South America and the USA. The reason for this odd structure was that the Indian, South American and US businesses had been acquired, and had been left relatively independent during a period when managers were focused on other commercial issues. The European business acted as headquarters for these divisions.

Figure 11.3: CIW's organisation changes (simplified)

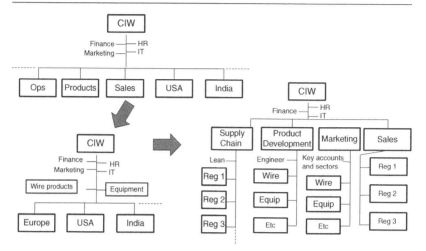

The South American and other regional divisions were each structured as a value chain with functions involved in product technology, manufacturing, marketing, sales and service. There was some coordination of technology and product development orchestrated from Europe, but this was limited.

When the leaders decided to focus on the synergies available from a more global approach to technology and product management, the structure was changed: technology and product management were centralised. The people in these functions mostly remained in the same locations, Sweden or Brazil or the USA, but they reported to or were controlled by central functions. At the same time, Europe was set up as a regional division, alongside India and the other divisions.

This structure helped deliver some synergies and accelerate some technology development, but it was probably always a staging post on the way to even closer global integration.

When Molsand acquired CIW in 2012, the Molsand managers decided to move from a regional divisional structure to a global value chain. This meant centralising manufacturing, marketing and sales alongside products and technology. The regional organisations were no longer business divisions. They became sales teams.

The value chain (or functional) structure is normally the best alternative to a simple divisional structure. It ensures close coordination and reduces the risk of silos. It makes functional excellence easier, and it reduces duplication. Its main disadvantage is the strain it places on the top team. All cross-functional decisions rise to the top. Unless this team functions well, it can easily become a bottleneck. Another disadvantage is the reduced ability to tailor solutions for different markets and the reduced influence of managers in these markets.

The CIW example illustrates the structural choices. Even though there are only three basic structures there are many different ways of combining them and customising them to suit the situation the company is in.

Matrix structures

The matrix structure aims to get the best of both worlds: high accountability in each division and close collaboration across divisions where needed. However, experience suggests that a matrix structure should be the least preferred organisational choice. It is complex. It can double the amount of time managers spend on decision making. It requires leaders who have good skills at coordinating and influencing. It often leads to confusion and demotivation.

Nevertheless, some kinds of coordination are too complex to be solved with either of the other two forms. Procter & Gamble, for example, had a matrix of product divisions and geographic markets, supported by a global business services division.[3] Each side of the matrix had some responsibility for profits and had considerable delegated authority for its area of responsibility. The product units (global business units) had prime responsibility for profit. The geographic units (market

Figure 11.4: The four parts of P&G's structure in 2009

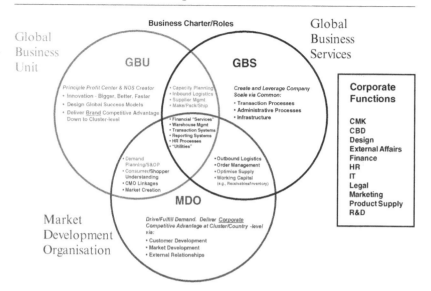

development organisations) were focused on revenues and gross margins. But neither could succeed without the other, and the profit and margin calculations were dependent on transfer prices. In addition, there was a global services division providing efficient services as well as strong central functions in areas like marketing and logistics, to make sure that the matrix did not overlook synergies in these areas (see Figures 11.4 and 11.5).

While P&G's matrix is extreme because of the company's size, a product/geographic matrix with strong central functions is typical of many global companies that have a spread of related products. Often, the product divisions and regional divisions are linked by transfer pricing. This means that both the back-end product divisions and the front-end regional divisions are fully profit accountable. These front/back matrix structures can be closed structures: the regional divisions only sell products provided by the product divisions and the product divisions only supply the regions. But they can also be open

Figure 11.5: The management layers in P&G's matrix in 2009

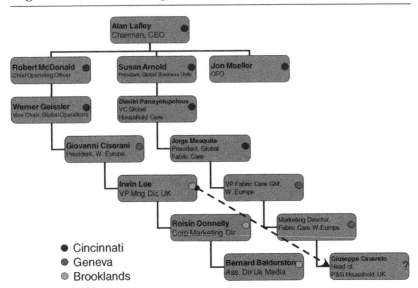

structures: the regions can buy products from third parties and the product divisions can sell to third parties. At IBM, the front/ back structure is "open". The Global Services Division (GSD) can buy hardware and other services from competitors of IBM, if the managers in GSD believe this will do a better job of meeting the needs of their clients. The Hardware and Software divisions can also sell to competitors of GSD.

Despite their problems, matrix structures are common. The complexity of the coordination needed in many large global companies means that simple divisional structures or simple value chain structures are not enough.

Distinguishing headquarters from divisions

Corporate headquarters consists of all the managers that do not report to one of the business divisions.

In a simple divisional structure, this definition provides clarity. When CIW was structured into regional divisions, the technology staff, the product management teams and the central marketing teams were all part of headquarters. In addition, there were finance, HR and IT staff in headquarters, who did not report to divisions.

However, even in simple divisional structures, the lines can be blurred. In South America, the technology staff working on product development continued to report, for the purposes of pay and day-to-day management, to the South American region; but their work was directed by the central technology team. In other words, it was possible to argue both ways, that they reported to the regional division and that they reported to the central function.

In a matrix structure, the situation is often even more blurred. Managers located in product divisions or in market divisions may also have corporate-wide responsibilities. Part of the time they are working for the division and part of the time they are working for corporate headquarters. For example, a finance manager in a product division may also be leading a global initiative to reduce working capital across all product divisions. A sales person in one geographic market may have responsibility for a global customer that is headquartered in that market but buys many of its supplies in other markets. This dual hat problem can be particularly severe for the heads of the divisions, who are expected to be both champions of their divisions and members of a corporate team making decisions about the whole.

In a functional structure, the picture is a little clearer: there is no corporate headquarters because there are no business divisions.

So how should we distinguish between headquarters and divisions for the purpose of corporate-level strategy analysis? Fortunately, the ability to draw precise lines is not critical. The simple rule of "all managers that do not report to one of the divisions" is a sufficient rough guide. Beyond this distinction, finer grained distinctions are made around individual areas of added value. So managers working on a cross-divisional project to reduce working capital are adding value to the performance of the divisions and hence are, at least conceptually, part of headquarters for the time they put into the project. The CIW technology team in South America only worked on developments for South America: they were not adding value across divisions. So they would be best thought of as part of the South American division rather than part of headquarters.

At the margin, distinctions become complex. Take, for example, the HR professional who reports to group HR, takes most of her instructions from group HR, but spends all of her time as the business partner for one division. Is this person part of headquarters adding value to a division or part of the division with added value coming to her from her relationship with group HR? Rather than wrestle with this dilemma, it is often helpful to view the person through both lenses: as a member of the division and as a member of headquarters. Sometimes some additional insight is gained from one lens or the other.

Summary

In this chapter, we have explored what we mean by business divisions and we have looked at different structural forms. How a company is structured is an important managerial decision. If the chosen structure is a value chain of operating functions, the issues of corporate-level strategy fade into the background. The company is being run as a single business unit.

In all other situations, the company will have some form of headquarters above the level of the business divisions. This raises the issue of what headquarters should do and how it will add value to the business divisions. It also raises the issue of how much autonomy business divisions will have. Both these topics are addressed in Chapter 13.

Any precise definition of what is contained in headquarters will fail to cover all situations. The rough guide of "those managers who do not report to business divisions" is a useful starting point. If more fine-grained judgements are needed, they should be built round an understanding of how value is being added.

Notes

[1] Alfred Chandler Jr, *Strategy and Structure* (MIT Press, 1962).

[2] M. Hunt, "Competition in the Major Home Appliance Industry", doctoral dissertation (Harvard University, 1972); M. Porter, *Competitive Strategy* (Free Press, New York, 1980).

[3] Mikolaj Piskorski and Alessandro Spadini, "Procter & Gamble: Organisation 2005 (A)", Harvard Business School Case 9-707-519, revised 2007.

CHAPTER TWELVE

CORPORATE-LEVEL STRATEGY IN INTEGRATED COMPANIES – THE APPLE EXAMPLE

In Chapter 11 we explained that the distinction between head-quarters and business divisions can be blurred, especially when important operating activities have been centralised. We also showed that there can be many variations of the three basic organisation structures – value chain, simple divisions and matrix of divisions.

LVMH, the global fashion company, had, in 2012, a simple divisional structure. However, within the divisions, the structures were all different. Some were almost single businesses. Others consisted of separate "maisons": independent brands, each set up as a global business with its own global strategy.

The fashion division was a portfolio of "maison", such as Fendi and Guerlain, each of which was a separate "division within a division". But the wines and spirits division was more integrated. It had a value chain structure. The brands, such as Moët et Chandon and Hennessey, were not separate business units. They were product lines within a larger business. The watches and jewellery division was half and half: most of the division consisted of large brands such as TAG Heuer, which operated as independent business units; but there was also a single unit that looked after all the smaller brands. This unit had a value chain organisation structure – product development, supply chain, marketing, sales – and acted as one business. These smaller brands were managed together as if each brand was a different product line within one integrated business.

LVMH has greater or lesser integration within its different divisions. But, even within a global "maison" like Louis Vuitton, there is also a question of how much integration to require across geographic regions. Each geography is a profit centre and some geographies have special products or services that are only available in that location. So, at least in part, Louis Vuitton is a multi-divisional organisation, even though it is managed, as far as possible, as if it were a single global business. For those interested primarily in international strategies in global businesses, we discuss the links and overlaps between corporate-level strategy and international strategy in the Appendix.

In this chapter we will address the grey area of integrated organisations, such as Apple or CIW or Nokia or LVMH's wines and spirits division or Louis Vuitton. In these integrated organisations, important operating activities have been centralised, so that the business units do not control significant parts of their business model. Integrated organisations are a grey area between single businesses and multi-divisional organisations.

Many organisations, possibly even the majority of organisations, are in this grey area. In the last 20 years, many companies have become more focused and more integrated. Moreover, any multi-national company will have profit units in different countries that act, at least in part, as business divisions. In addition, even in diversified companies like LVMH or GE, some divisions will be integrated. So, in this chapter, we will show, using Apple as an example, how these organisations can benefit from the corporate strategy frameworks of this book.

Integrated organisations

In Unilever, the hair care business unit in Japan is typical of many international companies. It was an organisational unit that developed its own strategy and was held accountable for profits. However, it did not control many parts of its business model. The brands that it used were mainly international brands that were controlled at Unilever's corporate headquarters. The products that it sold and the technologies these products were built from were controlled by Unilever's central research function and central supply chain function. The prices at which it sold these products and the way they were positioned in the market were partly determined by headquarters. The unit in Japan did have delegated authority, but only for the sales and marketing strategy within Japan and for some local brands that only sold in Japan.

Was the hair care unit in Japan a separate business division or was it just the marketing and selling arm of some larger business? Using one perspective, the Japan unit was just a geographic part of a larger global business unit – international hair care or international personal products. From this perspective the Japan unit is part of a larger Unilever business division competing in the "strategic group" (see Chapter 11) "global personal products" against companies such as the personal products division of Procter & Gamble, the hair care division of L'Oréal and other international personal product companies. From this perspective, the Japan unit was part of Unilever because it was an essential element of Unilever's global hair care business.

Using another perspective, the Japan unit was a separate business division that was benefiting from a significant amount of added value from its corporate headquarters, the global personal products division. This perspective has substance to it, because the Japan unit could have been an independent sales and marketing agency that sold Unilever's hair care brands in Japan. With this perspective, the Japan unit was competing in the strategic group – "marketing and distributing hair care products in Japan". No doubt there were other organisations, most of them independent companies that focused on this strategic group. With this view, the hair care unit in Japan was part of Unilever because Unilever could add value to it in ways that could not happen if the unit had been an independent company.

Both of these perspectives have some validity. Yet the two perspectives lead to a slightly different approach to strategy development. One perspective causes the strategist to use the tools of business strategy and international strategy, and focus analysis at the level of the global personal care market or global hair care market. The strategy for Japan would be mainly determined by this global strategy analysis. While the other perspective causes the strategist to use the tools of business strategy at the level of "hair care in Japan", and the tools of corporate-level strategy at the level of "international hair care" or "international personal products". Both approaches cannot be right – or can they?[1]

In highly integrated companies, like Unilever's personal care business, LVMH's wines and spirits business or Apple, this dilemma about what is the business unit is common. In these grey area situations, there is no objective right answer. The only right answer is the answer that managers choose and structure around. Do leaders want to manage the different parts of the organisation as semi-autonomous business divisions, where most of the entrepreneurial thinking and accountability is at the business division? In this case, functions outside the business divisions should consider themselves to be support functions to the business divisions. Alternatively, do leaders want to manage the different parts of the organisation as one team, where the business divisions are not the main focus for entrepreneurial activity and accountability? In this case, functions outside the business divisions are equal members of the team for the purpose of power and decision making?

In the former, the company is a corporate group that consists of a portfolio of business divisions reporting to a corporate headquarters. The tools of corporate-level strategy will be vital to help the leaders decide which business divisions to invest in and how to manage the collective.

In the latter, where leaders are treating the organisation as one entity, the company is a single business. Here the tools of business-level strategy will be the most useful to help the leadership team decide which products and markets to focus on and how to gain advantage over competitors.

In many cases, however, top managers take a position in between these two extremes. This is often the case in global companies with one product line, like Louis Vuitton. Managers say that they would like the business divisions to feel autonomous and take responsibility for some entrepreneurial activity. But they would also like the central functions to be entrepreneurial and lead some of the major business decisions. They would like the central functions to support the business divisions, but they would also like the business divisions to act as part of a larger team and support the central functions. In cases such as these, it is possible to view the company in two ways. It could be a corporate group consisting of multiple business divisions or it could be a single large business. Top managers have not fully decided.

In these cases and in cases where top managers have decided but there is doubt about whether the decision is the right one, our recommendation to strategists is to do the analysis both ways. First, assume that the company is a single business and focus on business strategy tools. Then, assume that the company is a corporate group, and do the extra analysis that is required.

Fortunately, the two sets of analyses overlap. The business logic analysis is the same for both corporate strategy and for business strategy: both approaches to strategy require an analysis of market attractiveness and relative competitive advantage. Hence, the additional analysis required for corporate strategy is mainly about added value and capital market conditions. In other words, the burden of doing both sets of analysis is not great, while the extra insights gained can be significant.

Apple

Apple has been one of the most successful companies of all time, and has also been, at some points in time, the most valuable company in the world.

Apple was founded on April Fool's Day in 1976 by two college dropouts Steve Wozniak and Steve Jobs.[2] The first two products, Apple I and Apple II, were instant successes, and the company went public in 1980 making the founders multi-millionaires. The vision was to make computers accessible to ordinary people: "a computer in the hands of every person in the world". One of the unique features was a user interface that involved normal typeface and other friendly features, as opposed to the computer languages that most users were required to learn at that time.

In 1981, IBM entered the personal computer market and the PC was born. The global standards of the PC threatened Apple's position as leader in the personal computer market. Sales grew, but market share fell. By 1984, Apple was in crisis. Disagreements between John Scully, hired from Pepsico, and Steve Jobs led Jobs to resign in 1985.

Between 1985 and 1990 Apple grew successfully around its core Mackintosh (Mac) computer. It had an interface based on graphical icons, software that was proprietary and integrated with the hardware and better peripherals than equivalent PCs. But it had lost the race to become the industry standard.

Between 1990 and 1997, the company struggled. There were two new chief executives and many twists in its strategy. There were attempts to make Apple more open by forming industry partnerships, and by licensing other companies to make Apple clones. There were attempts to broaden the product range into PDAs (personal digital assistants), TV set-top boxes and portals. There were attempts to compete on price through cost cutting and outsourcing. There were attempts to create a new and superior operating system.

The failure to succeed in developing a new operating system led to the acquisition of NeXt, a software company led by Steve Jobs. Along with the acquisition, Jobs became an adviser to Apple, and then, as problems deepened, he was appointed CEO.

Jobs took Apple back to its roots. He focused on creating a superior computer product that could run Microsoft software as well as Apple software. To fund this, he persuaded Microsoft to make a significant investment in Apple. He cut out PDAs and many other new developments; reduced outsourcing; terminated cloning; and recommitted to premium pricing.

The iMac, Jobs' first product, was a huge success and started Apple's journey from failing personal computer company to the most successful company in four industries – personal computers, digital music players, music retailing and mobile telephones.

In 2011, Apple was structured functionally. Reporting to Steve Jobs were:

- Timothy Cooke, responsible for sales (channel sales, education sales, online sales, iPhone sales) and Japan
- Jeffery Williams, responsible for supply chain and manufacturing

- Bob Mansfield, responsible for hardware engineering, divided into architecture, engineering, iPhone/iPod design and iPad design
- Craig Fredrighi, responsible for Mac software engineering
- Scott Forstall, responsible for operating system software
- Jonathan Ive, responsible for industrial design
- Philip Schiller, responsible for marketing, divided by product (iPhone, iPad, Mac hardware and Mac software)
- Eddy Cue, responsible for consumer apps and internet services
- Ronald Johnson, responsible for retailing

as well as people representing finance, HR, communications, general counsel and mobile advertising.

Was Apple a single business unit or a corporate group? The closest thing to a business unit in the Apple top structure was Ronald Johnson's area (retailing). This unit was competing in the strategic group "computer retailing", and, with appropriate transfer prices could be set up as a largely self-managing, profit accountable, business unit. Other parts of the organisation could also be set up as business units: the app store reporting to Eddy Cue, and possibly parts of Timothy Cooke's responsibilities, such as iPhone sales or Japan. However, most of the organisation appeared to be structured as a single value chain: software, hardware, supply chain, marketing and sales. The structure suggested that Steve Jobs viewed Apple as a single business unit rather than a corporate group.

But Apple competed against companies as different as Dell, Nokia, EMI, Amazon and Samsung, and had a diverse range of products from software to hardware to peripherals and from mobile phones to music to desktop computers. So Apple was clearly competing in more than one strategic group. Following the rules of business unit definition (see Chapter 11), we could conclude that Apple should have multiple SBUs, one for each strategic group. This would suggest that Apple might be more successful if it was structured as a corporate group, with five or six business divisions, for example computers, music, apps, phones, iPads and retailing.

Let us, therefore, do the analysis of Apple both ways: as a single business and as a corporate group.

Apple as a single business

Steve Jobs appeared to view Apple as a single business; so we will start with this perspective. Business strategy analysis involves understanding the markets Apple is competing in and the sources of advantage that Apple is exploiting. The Business Attractiveness matrix is a helpful way of getting perspective (see Figure 12.1).

The Business Attractiveness matrix suggests that Apple's success is not a result of choosing attractive markets. Certainly, the markets Apple is in were growing. But, in most of the markets, the average profitability of competitors was low. As a result, Apple's high profitability must come from exploiting

Figure 12.1: Business Attractiveness – Apple

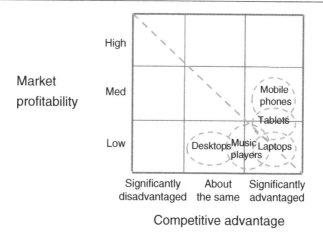

Competitive advantage

some sources of competitive advantage that other companies were not exploiting.

Detailed analysis of Apple's value chain in each market against the value chains of its main competitors could help us understand these sources of advantage. Since we do not have the data to do these detailed analyses, we are reduced to speculating what the analyses might reveal. Let's take four probable conclusions.

First, we might discover that Apple's higher profitability was partly due to its ability to charge a significant price premium over most of its competitors. This premium was possible because Apple's customers perceived that the products delivered significantly higher value. This perception was due in part to the design and functionality of the products, in part to the ease of interconnectivity across products, in part to the music and applications stores that supported the products and in part to the brand.

Second, we might discover that Apple's technology and product development costs were lower as a percentage of sales than those of its competitors. This may have been partly due to the premium pricing, which increases sales values relative to development costs; partly due to the small number product development projects at any point in time, which reduces development costs; and partly due to the way that Apple ran product development projects, with simultaneous development, significant CEO involvement and ambitious time lines.

Third, we might discover that Apple had higher than normal marketing and selling costs. This may have been partly because it had lower volumes against which to cover its branding costs, partly because it spent highly on its brand and partly because it had its own retail outlets to ensure that users were properly exposed to the experiences its products could create.

Fourth, we might discover that Apple's supply chain costs were higher than those of equivalent competitors. This may have been partly due to low levels of outsourcing and partly due to higher specifications for some inputs, such as glass.

If these conclusions were right, Apple's sources of advantage were:

- integrating hardware and software design in a way that creates superior user experiences
- focusing development effort only on those product ideas that have the potential of becoming a market leader, which results in better products and lower development costs
- running development efforts with an uncompromising commitment to producing a product/service combination that can be a market leader
- controlling the supporting services and peripherals to ensure that the user experience is superior
- demonstrating the unique experience to users through Apple stores
- ensuring quality through investing in higher than average costs of components, production and operations

This analysis has implications for Apple's future product and market strategy and for its organisation and management approach. With regard to future products and markets, Apple would be likely to succeed in any product area where the above list of behaviours and principles would lead to advantage. These behaviours and principles worked in personal computers, music players and mobile telephones. They might also work in gaming, in home entertainment or in a market like domestic robots. The market would need to be one where user experience and brand were important, where integrated software and hardware was critical to user experience, where supporting services and products were needed and where technology was advancing so that, at particular moments in time, it would be possible to produce breakthrough products.

Apple's management model would be unlikely to work in B2B markets like servers or telephone exchanges because users have little influence on the purchase decision and brand is less critical than technical specification.

With regard to organisation and management, the analysis suggests that Apple would need a chief executive or powerful chief designer able to select the few projects with real potential, lead the product development process and ensure that the core functions involved in product development (software, hardware, design and marketing) are tightly integrated. Also, some activities would need to be driven by the central team rather than decentralised around products or markets. These central activities include brand management, shared sales channels, such as the retail outlets and shared services, like the online stores, that support more than one product line.

Apple as a corporate group

Let us now imagine that, following the death of Steve Jobs, Tim Cooke, the new CEO, was considering whether to treat Apple as a corporate group rather than as a single business. How would he decide to make this change? What different strategic analyses would he need to do? And what implications might this analysis have for his choice of businesses to invest in or management strategy to pursue?

Steve Jobs was able to run Apple as a single integrated business, because all the products were part of one business model that was built around product development, shared online sales, shared distribution and the Apple brand; because Jobs had some unique skills; and because he was supported by a special team of individuals who also had unique skills. Tim Cooke might decide to change this approach and view Apple as a corporate group if:

- the decision-making load at the top of the organisation was becoming too great or too far removed from the technologies

and markets involved – as Apple increased its number of products, this would be a distinct possibility
- the business models required in different product areas were diverging – for example, in computers, a model based on unique, interconnected products might no longer succeed against business models based on lower cost or higher reliability or better service support
- it was not possible to find people capable of filling the demanding senior roles, such as selecting the few new products to develop or managing software development across a broad range of products or working across software, hardware and design at executive level

If Tim Cooke chose to view Apple as a corporate group, he might create business divisions for computers (laptops and desktops), music (iPods and iTunes), mobile phones and iPads (including the app store). He might also have a business unit for retailing. He would then do the three sets of analysis that are part of good corporate-level strategy – business attractiveness analysis, parenting value added analysis and capital markets analysis.

The business attractiveness analysis would show that his business divisions were in low margin sectors (very few consumer electronics companies make high returns). The business divisions will succeed only if they have significant advantage over competitors. In other words, they will need to have the sort of advantages described in the previous section. So one of Tim Cooke's tasks would be to ensure that each business division was clear about its sources of advantage and was able to deliver these advantages. Any business division without clear sources of advantage should be considered for radical change, closing or selling.

Tim Cooke could then turn to parenting value added analysis. He would probably define the following major sources of group added value:

- the Apple brand
- centralised control of product development. One of Apple's unique advantages appeared to be the ability to select a few development projects where there is breakthrough potential. This was unlikely to be a skill that could be easily decentralised to business divisions. Another feature of Apple's approach was the simultaneous development of software, hardware and design as an integrated package. The corporate headquarters would need to control this either by having all three functions report into headquarters or by imposing on the business divisions a model of how to do product development
- shared distribution channels, such as retailing. These channels might not be shared for all products. But, there would be opportunities to share sales channels for some of the products
- shared supporting services and peripherals, such as the iTunes and apps stores
- shared supply chain. Since cost is important and manufacturing volumes are important to cost, there is likely to be significant value added from sharing at least parts of the supply chain across business divisions

Finally, Tim Cooke would need to do capital markets analysis. From this he would be likely to conclude that the capital markets often create booms in new hot sectors. When this happens, companies in these sectors become overpriced. The booms are often followed by slumps in which shares become underpriced. As the technology continues to advance, slumps are likely to be followed by further booms, until the sector matures and share prices settle down to a more predictable path. Hence, any acquisitions should be timed carefully to exploit the inevitable share price slumps (or should be paid for with equity not cash) and any disposals should be timed to exploit the share price booms. While this is interesting analysis, it is likely to be less useful to Tim Cooke because Apple's advantage appears to be in green fields development, rather than in clever acquisitions and disposals.

So what implications do these three analyses have for Tim Cooke's decisions about the markets and products to focus on and how to manage Apple? The analysis suggests that Apple should focus on markets where Apple's ability to add value is high:

- where the Apple brand is an advantage
- where Apple's approach to product development is an advantage
- where shared distribution channels are possible
- where shared supporting activities, like online stores and peripherals, are significant
- where there are common elements in the supply chain

Heartland businesses will be those that tick all these criteria. Edge-of-heartland businesses, like domestic robots, might tick only some of these criteria. They may have significantly fewer opportunities for shared supporting activities and/or fewer opportunities for shared sales channels or supply chain. Any business that could not use the Apple brand or where the approach to product development needed to be significantly different would probably be outside edge-of-heartland.

Ballast businesses, as computers or music players could become, should only remain part of the company for capital market reasons: if the exit value is lower than the hold value. Value trap businesses, as TV might be, should be considered only if the market is unusually profitable, which is unlikely to be the case in TV. Alien territory businesses, such as animated movies (one of Steve Jobs' businesses when he was not with Apple), should be considered only for exceptional reasons.

Exceptional reasons might include a special personal relationship with a major player in the industry, like Pixar, that would
give Apple some privileged position with customers or suppliers; or it might be an imperfection in the capital market that
caused an acquisition to be unusually cheap.

The corporate strategy analysis also has implications for
how Apple should be managed. Product decisions and product
marketing decisions should be decentralised to the divisions.
Headquarters should keep central control over the brand, the
product development process, shared distribution channels,
shared peripherals, online stores and shared elements of the
supply chain. These headquarters activities would be the main
sources of corporate added value.

Product divisions such as computers might need more separation and autonomy as their business models diverged from
the heartland model. A new, edge-of-heartland product, such
as domestic robots, would also need more separation and
autonomy. If Apple acquired a business or set up a venture in
a less related industry, such as movies, this division would need
to be given much more autonomy and separate status.

Does corporate-level strategy analysis contribute any insights that would be unlikely to surface from business strategy analysis?

The main purpose of this chapter has been to explore integrated organisations where the distinction between corporate
headquarters and business divisions is not clear. We try to show
that corporate-level strategy can contribute to strategic thinking
even in these highly integrated companies that might otherwise
only use business strategy analysis.

Apple is a perfect example of a company that, in 2011,
seemed to be in multiple industries with multiple products, yet
had no clear business divisions. So what could corporate-level
strategy analysis contribute to strategic thinking at Apple?

The first message is that both business-level analysis and corporate-level analysis, not surprisingly, come to a similar understanding of Apple's past success and implications for future strategy. This is reassuring. It demonstrates that the principles of strategy are broadly the same whichever way you look at the problem.

The second message is that viewing Apple as a group is likely to cause managers to give more attention to some issues. For example, the group perspective will be likely to cause managers to think more about:

- whether to retain a significant presence in a product area like computers. Positioning computers as a potential ballast business, could cause some different discussions about its long-term place in Apple's future
- how far to diversify into a product area, like domestic robots, that does not benefit from shared peripherals, online stores and shared distribution channels. The need to debate the dimensions of heartland and edge-of-heartland encourages managers to think in different ways about new product ideas
- how far to decentralise product management and marketing into product-focused divisions. Viewing Apple as a group of divisions inevitably raises the issue of what activities to decentralise to the divisions and what to centralise to corporate headquarters

Viewing Apple as a single business makes it less likely that a decision would be made to exit any existing product category. The loss of a product category would be likely to be seen as giving a point of attack to a competitor.

Viewing Apple as a single business makes it less likely that new products would be launched that do not share sales channels, peripherals and online stores. Managers are likely to see the business as having one business model that includes sharing these elements. In other words, viewing Apple as a single business is likely to constrain somewhat the portfolio options that managers seriously consider. Viewing Apple as a corporate group would encourage managers to ask some broader questions about portfolio strategy.

The area where corporate-level strategy is most likely to influence managers is in making decisions about the degree of centralisation and decentralisation. Business strategy tools do not provide much help to managers with these decisions. Viewing Apple as a single business would make it less likely that divisions would be set up with decentralised responsibilities. A single business is normally structured by function. Viewing Apple as a corporate group immediately raises the question of how to define the divisions and what powers to decentralise to divisions. Moreover, the tools of corporate-level analysis are well designed for helping with these decisions. By focusing on the question of added value, corporate-level strategy provides a logic for centralisation and decentralisation decisions.

Many chief executives in more integrated companies wish to generate more initiative among their operating units. They do this by decentralising some decisions and some activities to operating units. This allows them to set all-encompassing performance targets, such as profit rather than more focused targets for sales or volume. Corporate strategy analysis, especially the analysis of value added by corporate levels, helps managers get the right balance between centralisation and decentralisation when they are making these decisions.

Of course, in single businesses, managers still need to make decisions about centralisation. But getting the balance right is less important to success, because there is less emphasis on decentralised profit responsibility and because the top team meet regularly and are involved in most major decisions. As a company becomes a corporate group, business divisions are given more accountability for profit, and connections between divisions are often loosened. As a result, the top team meets less regularly, because it has less to coordinate. In these circumstances, getting the balance between centralisation and decentralisation right is more important.

While business-level strategy analysis addresses most issues. The different perspective of corporate-level strategy, particularly the added value logic, helps with decisions both about the range of products and markets to enter and about the management approach. In particular, it is likely to spark different discussions about the degree of centralisation and decentralisation.

Tim Cooke would be unwise to make changes to the level of centralisation at Apple, without considering both sets of analyses. If he decided to increase centralisation, he would be affirming Apple as a single business. If he decided to decentralise a bit further, he would be exploring the alternative of managing Apple as a corporate group.

Summary

This chapter has explored integrated organisations. They are common. Companies, like Apple, or divisions of larger companies, like the wines and spirits division of LVMH, where integration is important to success, are common. For example, most international products have a mix of central integration of product and branding and decentralised local marketing and sales (see more about international strategy in the Appendix). In fact, most readers will be from organisations with some level of integration.

In these organisations the distinction between corporate headquarters and business divisions is blurred. It is possible to view the organisation as a single business, but it is also possible to view the organisation as a group of business divisions.

> In these circumstances, it is useful to do strategy analysis in two ways. The tools of business strategy analysis can be used as if the organisation is a single business. In addition, the tools of corporate-level strategy can be used as if the organisation is a corporate group. Fortunately, there is a good deal of overlap between the two sets of tools. Also, normally, the two sets of tools will lead to similar conclusions. However, it is also normal to find that the corporate-level analysis provides some different perspectives and generates some additional discussions, especially on the issue of centralisation and decentralisation.
>
> Ultimately, the leaders need to decide where on the sliding scale between a corporate group and an integrated business they want to locate their company. Without doing both sets of analyses, they will find it hard to see both alternatives with enough clarity to make a wise choice.

Notes

[1] For a discussion of international strategy and how it overlaps with corporate strategy, see the Appendix.

[2] Much of the material on Apple is drawn from an award-winning teaching case by Loizos Heraculeous and Angel Papachroni, "Strategic Leadership and Innovation at Apple Inc.", Warwick Business School, 2012. There is also an extensive Harvard Business School case series on Apple Inc. by David Yoffie.

CHAPTER THIRTEEN

HOW MUCH TO CENTRALISE: DESIGNING CORPORATE HEADQUARTERS

This chapter focuses on how to design the activities and functions at corporate headquarters: what to centralise and what to leave in the business divisions. This is probably not a chapter for the casual reader. It is aimed at the manager or adviser who needs practical tips and a guiding framework for this difficult work. A well-designed corporate headquarters is essential to implement the corporate-level strategy; but it is also corporate overhead. Getting the balance right between cost, added value and avoiding the risk of subtracted value is important. It is not work that should be done lightly. We suggest a process with four steps.

The first step is to define the activities, functions, processes and personnel needed for good governance and compliance. These include things such as filing tax returns, maintaining a risk register and setting policies in support of health and safety legislation. These activities are necessary to ensure that the company fulfils its legal, regulatory, fiduciary and stakeholder obligations.

The second step is to define the additional activities, functions, processes and personnel needed to add value. The emphasis will be on the sources of added value that are central to the corporate strategy and the role that each function and each senior executive plays in creating this added value. There will also be other, smaller sources of added value that are not critical to the corporate-level strategy, such as centralised payroll. These should only be included in the design if there is little risk that the activity will subtract value.

The third step involves thinking through and laying out the relationships that the functions will have with the business divisions. We distinguish between four different functional roles, each of which is associated with a different relationship. These roles are policy, shared service, championing and core resource. It is important for all individuals at corporate headquarters to be clear about their role. High added value and low subtracted value depend not only on the skills of the people in corporate headquarters, but also on the effectiveness of the relationships between these people and the business divisions.

The fourth step is to summarise and communicate the new design. There are three techniques for doing this: produce an organisation chart in the form of an organisation model; get each headquarters function to develop a functional plan; lay out the implications for the decentralisation contract for each division.

In too many companies, the corporate headquarters is a legacy organisation, assembled and added to, like an old house, by different architects for different purposes. A clean slate review often injects new energy and clarity, increasing added value, reducing overhead and reducing the risk of subtracted value.

Step 1 – Governance and compliance

Many corporate-level policies and the activities that support these policies exist for compliance and governance reasons. It is helpful to define these activities first. By compliance and governance, we mean policies and activities that are required by the law, by significant stakeholders or by normal good practice. In other words, if policies, such as accounting policies or policies about safety or policies about decision authorities, did not exist, the managers leading the organisation would be breaking the law or could be accused of negligence.

Policies are not the only form of governance and compliance activity. The work of teams involved in funding the balance sheet, managing relationships with bankers, producing the annual statements of account, liaising with shareholders, administering board meetings, making tax returns and executing standard budgeting processes and controls are all examples of governance and compliance activities. These teams exist primarily because the activity they perform is non-discretionary: the organisation has to do it whether it adds value or not. The primary purpose is to make sure that the organisation is well governed and there is no basis for an accusation of negligence.

Some jobs fall into governance and compliance. An organisation must have a CEO. Public limited companies must have a finance director and a company secretary. In financial services, a head of Risk is necessary. In some countries, other positions are required.

Research carried out by Michael Goold and David Young in 1998 provided a list of functions and typical staffing levels for governance and compliance activities.[1] Figure 13.1 lists the typical functions.

In 1999, companies with 10,000 employees had on average between 20 and 30 staff in governance and compliance functions. Companies with 50,000 employees had between 50 and 80 governance and compliance staff. For those interested in how their company compares, we provide a ready reckoner tool in Figure 13.2.

In a design project, there are often debates about particular activities. Managers seeking to defend their jobs or the activities they are involved in will often argue that the activity is necessary as part of governance and compliance. For example,

Figure 13.1: Typical governance and compliance functions*

Function	Average Number of staff**
General Corporate Management	5.5
Treasury	2.2
Taxation	2.7
Financial Reporting and Control	8.1
Company Secretarial and Legal	3.7

* Based on UK companies in 1998
** Assuming a company with 10,000 employees that is not in financial services or government control

Figure 13.2: Ready reckoner for compliance and governance staff

Baseline: Median staff numbers			26

How to adjust baseline for:

1. Companies of different sizes:

Employees	2,000	multiply by	0.37
	5,000		0.65
	10,000		1.00
	20,000		1.54
	50,000		2.71
	100,000		4.17

2. Different types of businesses:

Turnover per employee	£50,000	multiply by	0.68
	£100,000		1.00
	£200,000		1.46

3. Different parenting strategies:

Degree of synergy between businesses (scored 0–10) added to degree of influence from corporate functions (scored 0–20)

Score	0	multiply by	0.63
	5		0.79
	10		1.00
	15		1.26
	20		1.59
	25		2.01

Lower quartile		19
Upper quartile		36

the head of talent may argue that it is a necessary part of good governance to maintain files on the top 100 managers. The head of internal audit may argue that frequent checks are needed on accounting processes.

There are no right and wrong answers to these debates. The best starting place is to be clear about the legal requirements. Is there a risk that the board will be considered legally negligent if it runs the company without the activity, policy or process? But leaders will often want to go considerably beyond what is legally required. Hence, the exact list of activities and the exact number of people that are needed for compliance and governance is an executive decision.

Of course, a company can suffer under too much governance and compliance. It is easy for governance and compliance activities to expand in ways that involve excessive reporting, checking up and meetings, adding unnecessary costs and slowing down decisions. Hence, when the decision is to go for extra governance above what is legally required, the reasons need to be clear.

The governance and compliance step should define a minimum size, in terms of number of personnel, and a minimum set of policies, activities, processes and functions for corporate headquarters. Once the initial top-down judgements have been made, there should be an opportunity for business divisions to challenge, especially if they think that the approach to governance and compliance may interfere with commercial success. Subtracted value is always close to the surface. Challenge by business divisions can help keep it to a minimum.

Step 2 – Added value

Once the compliance and governance activities are clear, the next step is to determine what additional staff and activity is needed to execute the parenting strategy. As we explained in

Chapter 10, the corporate-level strategy will have identified a handful of major sources of added value, typically three to seven, and a longer list of minor sources of added value that are part of the parenting strategy. These lists are the starting point for step 2.

If the corporate-level strategy does not include such lists, for example if the strategy addresses only the size and shape of the portfolio of business divisions, some work will be needed to produce these lists. Chapter 10 describes the analyses that will be needed. In addition, it will be necessary to facilitate two or three meetings of the executive team to agree the lists that emerge from the analysis.

Once the lists have been agreed, focus first on the **major sources of added value**. Against each major source, identify the corporate-level activities that are needed to create the added value. An added value table (see Table 13.1 and Chapter 10) can help lay this out. Along the top of the table list the major sources of corporate added value. Down the side of the table list four types of corporate management:

- the main corporate-level managers, such as the CEO, CFO and general council
- the main corporate-level committees that are likely to be needed, such as the board, board subcommittees and the executive committee
- the main functions that are part of headquarters, such as finance, HR, and legal
- the main processes that are part of the management approach, such as budgeting, capital expenditure approval and strategic planning

Table 13.1 is an added value table based on a company providing services to the US Department of Defense and the UK Ministry of Defence in different parts of the world. Added value from headquarters to the business divisions comes from

Table 13.1 Table showing headquarters role against added value

HQ functions, roles and processes	1. Give guidance on business models, operating challenges and major decisions	2. Coordinate relationships with main customers, such as DoD, MOD, UN, ...	3. Coordinate operations in selected countries	Etc
CEO	• Lead the process of developing and delivering guidance	• Be available for interactions with any major customer • Be the lead contact for DoD	• Be available to act to resolve conflicts between divisions	...
CFO and Finance Function	• Ensure that BUs provide accurate information on the profitability of contracts and lines of business	Limited	Limited	...
IT	• Give guidance on IT operating issues	• Ensure systems are compliant with customer requirements	Limited	...

(Continued)

Table 13.1 (*Continued*)

HQ functions, roles and processes	1. Give guidance on business models, operating challenges and major decisions	2. Coordinate relationships with main customers, such as DoD, MOD, UN, ...	3. Coordinate operations in selected countries	Etc
HR	• Give guidance on HR operating issues	Limited	• Lead the coordination of recruiting and compensation issues • Facilitate movements	...
Other functions	...	...	...	
Executive Meeting	• Individuals expected to volunteer advice base on their experience	• Each major customer to be discussed at each Executive	• Coordination issues **not** addressed in Executive Meetings	...
Business Review Process	• Major challenges, decisions and changes to business model should be flagged at these Reviews	Limited	• Help identify businesses that need special support	...
Etc	...	...	...	

a number of sources, such as the experience the headquarters team has in these businesses and their knowledge of and relationships with the main customers.

Each box in the table describes the work the manager, committee, function or process will need to do to help deliver the added value. Some of the boxes record a limited role. Some of the boxes can contain a long list of things to be done. It is also useful to estimate, within each box, the number of staff needed over and above the number of staff that has already been identified for governance and compliance activities.

Frequently, the staff needed for governance and compliance can also do the added value work. For example, the CEO is required for governance purposes, so no extra person is needed for the CEO to "lead the process of developing and giving of guidance".

As the work needed for each source of added value becomes clear, additional managers, committees, functions or processes can be added down the side of the table. Also, some managers, committees, functions or processes may be eliminated if they have no contribution to make to the major sources of added value and no governance or compliance role.

Once the added value table is complete, turn to the list of **minor sources of added** value. Typical items on the list are things like central payroll, economic forecasting, diversity training or central property management. They are likely to save some cost or improve some element of performance. But, if they are not part of a major source of added value, if they do not meet the 10% test (see page 229), they are minor sources of added value.

Caution is needed before any additional activities are added to corporate headquarters in support of these minor sources of added value. Activities in support of minor sources of added value are often major sources of subtracted value. As a result, they need to be strongly challenged:

- Does everyone agree that this activity adds value? If there is significant doubt, it may be better to focus attention elsewhere.
- Are there any risks that this activity could subtract value? If there are risks, the added value is unlikely to be large enough to warrant taking the risks.

To explore the risks of subtracted value, managers can ask:

- Is it likely that the activity will be done badly – at high cost or low quality or in a way that is insensitive to the needs of business divisions?
- Will the activity take up the time of any senior managers in headquarters or in the business divisions, and hence create an opportunity cost?
- Might the activity reduce the commercial flexibility of the business divisions?
- Might the activity reduce the motivation and initiative of managers in the business divisions?

If there are concerns about the added value or risks of subtracted value, the activity should be rejected: corporate strategy should be focused on activities that will deliver significant added value rather than on dubious or risky activities. The message here is not that smaller headquarters are better than larger headquarters (see sidebar "Small headquarters or large headquarters"), it is that it is dangerous to include activities within corporate headquarters unless the added value is clear and the risk of subtracted value is low.

In a review of an existing corporate headquarters, there is frequently a long list of current activities that do not pass the challenge. Managers at headquarters may seek to protect these minor activities partly because jobs are at stake and partly because they believe there is some net benefit. It is important, therefore, to be rigorous in the challenge process. Cutting out activities can make a significant positive contribution.

It is worth just explaining here why we do not challenge as rigorously the major sources of added value. The reason is that the prize – the added value – is so large (10%) that it is worth risking subtracted value. Moreover, it is also worth devoting time to ensure that the risks are managed. When the prize is small, we find that senior headquarters managers will often not devote sufficient time to manage the risks effectively. As a result, it is better not to take the risk.

Small headquarters or large headquarters

Is a small headquarters better than a large one? The answer depends.

Michael Goold, David Young and David Collis did a major research project in six countries to explore the size of corporate centres ("Corporate Headquarters: An international analysis of their roles and staffing", David Young, Michael Goold et al., FT Pearson, 2000). They demonstrated that there is a wide spread of sizes in terms of number of people in headquarters (see figure). Some companies had only a handful of people in headquarters. Others had thousands.

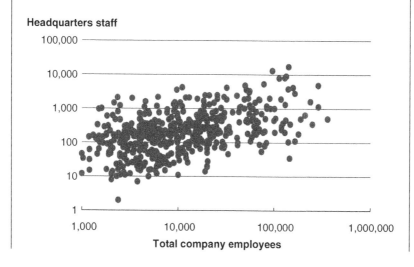

> The size of headquarters depended in part on the size of the company and its complexity. But, by far the largest influence was the parenting strategy: the leaders' views about how headquarters should be adding value to the business divisions.
>
> On average companies with larger headquarters tended to be more profitable than companies with smaller headquarters. The difference was not marked, and it was not clear whether the difference was because large headquarters were adding more value and hence contributing to superior performance or because superior performance enabled companies to afford larger headquarters.
>
> The wide variation in the size of corporate headquarters makes benchmarking hard and of dubious benefit, except in governance and compliance activities which are more common across companies and geographies.

Step 3 – Clarifying relationships

High added value and low subtracted value are dependent on the quality of the relationships between managers in headquarters and managers in the business divisions. Hence, the third step is to clarify the nature of the relationship that is needed to maximise the effectiveness of each activity.

Each headquarters activity should be allocated one of four types of headquarters role. The four roles each involve a different relationship between headquarters managers and business divisions. Unless these relationships are clear, it is hard for headquarters to be effective.

The first role is the **policy and guidance role**. A corporate function that has a policy role develops policy and guidance to which other parts of the organisation must adhere, or at least they are expected to support. For example, the finance function determines the accounting rules; the HR function defines the incentive structure for top managers; and the IT function provides guidance on the use of standard software. Policies and guidance are typically approved by the executive committee. This gives authority for functions to impose the policies on business divisions.

Many of these policies exist for compliance and governance reasons. For example, it is common for the central legal team to review all major contracts entered into by a company. A board that did not require this legal review could be considered negligent.

Other policies exist for added value reasons rather than for compliance reasons. The policy is imposed on the business divisions because headquarters managers believe it will help raise performance or promote synergy. For example, a pay and incentives policy often exists to facilitate the movement of managers between divisions. A policy to limit divisions to one supplier for laptops or logistics services helps gain economies of scale in purchasing.

Guidance, rather than policy, often comes from the CEO or from senior line executives. The guidance may be about strategy or people decisions or cost levels or a range of other issues. Guidance can also come from corporate functions. Guidance falls within "policy and guidance" if the person giving the guidance has power. The business divisions then know it is something they need to implement, even if they are not fully convinced of its value. So the policy and guidance role involves a power relationship: it covers things that are mandatory.

The second role is the **coordinating and championing role**. This is guidance without power. Managers in this role are expected to encourage coordination across divisions or champion some cause. A typical example is the lean unit. Managers in this unit are experts in lean methodologies. They are expected to champion lean ideas and motivate the business divisions to implement them; but they do not have the power to impose their ideas on the divisions.

Another example might be a manager with responsibility for coordinating three businesses with operations in China. While the manager may have no power to impose decisions on these businesses, she may be expected to persuade them to work together to help each other succeed in China.

A third example might be a global account manager or industry sector manager, who is expected to champion the interests of his account or sector so that the separate product divisions each succeed. But he has no power to tell them what to do.

The relationship between a championing unit and the business divisions is a sales relationship. The championing unit seeks to persuade the business divisions of the wisdom of its guidance.

The third role is the **shared service role**. In contrast to the policy role, a shared service unit exists to serve the businesses, not to tell them what to do. The service may be centralised for skill or scale reasons; but the relationship between the central service and the business divisions is one of a supplier to a customer. The power should be with the business divisions. Of course, a central service should explain the limits of its skills and mandate, and it should offer advice to a business division if it believes the division is about to make a mistake. But the final choice should be that of the business division not the central service.

Frequently, policy and shared service roles are integrated within one corporate function. The finance function, for example, sets accounting policies, but it also runs the accounting services that generate the numbers for each business division. The IT function sets the IT security policies and also provides desktop services for business divisions.

Normally, combining these two roles does not work well. Because the nature of the relationship with the business divisions is so different and because the skills needed to be effective are so different, the policy and service roles require different types of people, with different personalities. Many companies have found that performance improves if the "kick arse" policy functions are separated from the "kiss arse" service functions. Typically, this is achieved by putting all shared service functions into a central services unit, reporting to a manager whose main skill is running operations and whose main focus is the satisfaction of managers in business divisions.

The fourth role is the **core resource role**. In this role the central function is responsible for some resource or capability that is critical to an area of competitive advantage. The resource might be a shared brand. It might be a team of technical service engineers. It might be a central research lab.

Leaders of core resources have a tricky task. They are normally in charge of something important that has been centralised: the business divisions would rather have full control of the resource themselves. Moreover, because the resource is scarce, the leader of the function must decide how it is to be allocated. Typically, there are more demands from the business divisions than capacity, particularly for the rarest skills. This brings the leader of the function into conflict with the business divisions. Yet the ideal relationship is one of partnership. The function and the business divisions should together resolve their differences. Maintaining a partnership mindset despite conflict is hard.

Core resource functions will set some policies. But, because they control most of the resources they need to execute their role, their policies are mostly internal to the function. Core resources may also provide services to business divisions. But, because their resources are scarce, the prime focus is not the satisfaction of the business divisions. The prime focus is the optimum use of the resources across the organisation and the building of additional competitive advantage.

When the four roles are clear and are separated from each other, the relationships between corporate functions and business divisions normally work well. This allows the amount of added value to increase and the amount of subtracted value to reduce. When the different roles are combined in one department or function, it can be hard for the department to execute the different roles with equal competence. It can also be hard for the business divisions to distinguish the different roles. This can cause relationship confusion, loss of added value and increases in subtracted value.

Clarity also simplifies the job of the CEO. If the business divisions and the corporate functions are squabbling, as is very common, it is relatively easy for the CEO to decide how to respond. If the squabble is with a policy function, the CEO should back the policy function or get a new policy head. If the squabble is with a shared service or with a championing unit, the CEO should back the business division: the power should lie with the business divisions. It is only when the CEO is confronted with a squabble between a core resource unit and a business division that he or she needs to get closely involved, understand the issues and try to find a mutually beneficial solution.

Step 4 – Document and communicate the design

Once the first three steps are complete, the remaining task is to document and communicate the design. Managers need to make the design as clear as possible for all functions and operating units, so that there can be as little room for dispute and empire building as possible. Too often, CEOs allow their headquarters to evolve and grow. Too often, there are disputes about territory and powers between functions and operating units. Too often, a natural desire to empire build means that headquarters numbers, costs and activities creep up over time without justification. A clearly documented and communicated design helps with all of these problems.

There are three outputs of this step that are helpful – an organisation chart in the form of an organisation model, a strategic plan for each function and a statement defining the decentralisation contract for each division.

An **organisation model** makes clear where the power lies, who is part of headquarters and what the relationships should be between each headquarters function and the business divisions. This is achieved visually by drawing the business divisions as the base of the organisation and the headquarters functions and shared services as supporting activities (see Figure 13.3).

The business divisions are positioned as reporting to the CEO (or COO if there is an intermediate layer) and all on the same level in the chart. A long vertical line is drawn from the CEO down to the divisions. Headquarters functions are placed either side of this line depending on their role. It is helpful to place the more powerful headquarters functions

Figure 13.3: A way of drawing organisation models

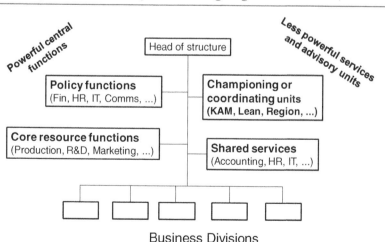

(policy and core resource) on one side (normally the left side) and the less powerful functions (championing and shared service) on the other side of the vertical line (normally the right side). Where one function has multiple roles (a design we suggest is often suboptimal), it is positioned with regard to its dominant role.

This organisation model shows the distinction between divisions and headquarters functions. It also shows the relationships that are needed between headquarters functions and business divisions. The relationships among business divisions is either an arm's length relationship based on mutual self-interest (a simple divisional structure as in the chart) or a more complex interdependent relationship (a matrix structure).

Figure 13.4 is the organisation model of CIW prior to the acquisition by Molsand.

Figure 13.5 is the organisation model for a European retailer. It looks different from the model for CIW, but it is achieving the same objective: clarifying the relationships between the business divisions and the headquarters functions.

The organisation model provides a lot of information about the headquarters design. However, more detail is needed to

Figure 13.4: CIW organisation model

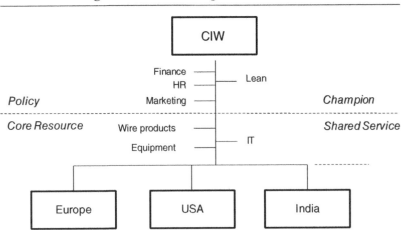

Figure 13.5: European retailer – group structure

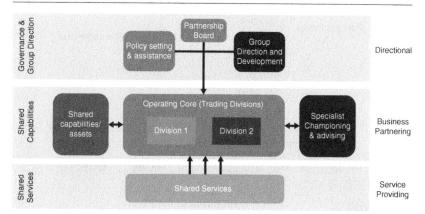

Each box adds value in a different way, involves different types of work and as such requires different capabilities, different ways of working and different types of relationship with the Divisions

help the headquarters functions perform as designed. One helpful tool for achieving this is to get each headquarters function to produce a functional plan. It is also often helpful to get the leader of each corporate process, particularly those that involve more than one headquarters function, to produce a plan for the process.

The **functional plans** define the activities to be carried out by the function, distinguishing between

- compliance and governance activities
- activities that support the major sources of added value
- activities that support minor sources of added value that have been passed by the challenge process described on page 232

The functional plan also distinguishes between policy activities, championing activities, shared service activities, and core resource activities, and provides an organisation chart for the function in organisation model format (see Figure 13.6 for an example HR function).

Figure 13.6: HR function

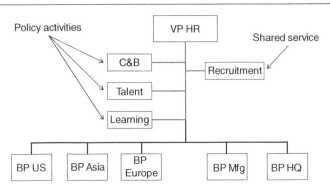

HR Business Partners

In our experience, good functional plans are rare. But examples do exist. When Unilever created a category management function at corporate headquarters, the company produced a 20-page booklet that defined the powers of this new function giving illustrations of how it would get involved in a variety of decisions that had previously been the responsibility of business divisions. The illustrations helped distinguish situations where the function had a policy role, a championing role and a service role.

The functional plan should also define metrics. How will the function measure its performance: how should the rest of the organisation judge whether the function is doing a good job or not? One important metric that is often overlooked is the satisfaction levels of managers in business divisions. If the main objective of the function is added value, the business divisions are often best positioned to judge whether the function is effective. Even if the main objective of the function is governance and compliance, the business divisions are often also well placed to judge the function's effectiveness.

The final part of functional planning is to encourage challenge both from managers in headquarters and from managers in business divisions. This challenge is helpful both to get agreement between headquarters functions and business divisions and to reduce the potential for subtracted value. The functional plans are the point at which the headquarters design is converted into planned actions. It is easy for functional leaders to interpret the added value table or the analysis of minor sources of added value or the organisation model in a way that gives the function more status or more activities than intended in the design. It is human nature to see one's own team in an enhanced light. The challenge process is an opportunity to correct any of these misinterpretations.

The third output that is helpful in communicating the way the organisation will work is the **decentralisation contract**. A decentralisation contract can be prepared for each division, especially where divisions have differing degrees of autonomy. The decentralisation contract is like a franchise agreement between headquarters and the management team running the business division. Divisions are not much interested in the design of headquarters. They want to know what effect the design has on them. The decentralisation contract is one way of communicating the design to the divisions and clarifying what authority the division has.

The decentralisation contract defines

- the broad objective for the division (which will have come from the portfolio strategy work)
- the powers that have been delegated to the division (the reverse of the powers that have been retained by headquarters)
- the processes for decisions that require headquarters involvement
- the relationship between the division and each corporate function in terms of "policy", "shared service", etc.
- the relationship between the division and other divisions in terms of overlapping issues, transfer prices and such like

The decentralisation contract is the "job description" for the division. It is not just about the relationship between the division and headquarters: it also covers the relationship with other divisions. Hence, it provides some extra information about how the organisation will work together.

Where all business divisions have an equal degree of autonomy, it can be rather repetitive to develop decentralisation contracts for each division. The alternative is to define the powers that have been retained and reserved for headquarters. The implication being that all other powers have been delegated to the divisions. This is the path the oil company BP chose when redesigning its corporate headquarters in the 1990s. One of the outputs was a booklet defining the "reserve powers". The implication of a statement of reserved powers is that all other powers have been decentralised to the business divisions.

AECI, a South African chemicals company, used the phrase "freedom supported by a framework". The framework defined the limits on the freedom of business divisions. It consisted of four elements, the first three of which were mainly governance and compliance:

• policy controls in areas such as cultural norms, health, safety and the environment
• financial controls and reporting
• legal controls and decision authorities
• influences from the company's five sources of added value

The reserve powers or framework approach implies a uniform model for all business divisions.

Once a new design has been agreed and put in place, it is important to keep testing its effectiveness. Metrics and performance measures are helpful, but so are anecdotes and informal comments from managers in the business divisions. More formally, an annual or six-monthly survey of managers in business divisions is often a helpful signal that headquarters is working as hard on its own efficiency and effectiveness as it expects business divisions to be on theirs. It is also helpful to have annual reviews of the plans of headquarters functions to match the annual reviews of plans for business divisions.

Summary

This chapter has focused on the design of corporate headquarters. Headquarters activities should be designed to achieve two objectives: good governance and added value. Headquarters needs to comply with the law and stakeholder requirements. But the most important task of headquarters is to add value to the business divisions. Hence, most of the important design decisions are about how best to add value at low overhead costs and with low risk of subtracted value.

In many companies, too little attention is given to the design of corporate headquarters. Functions gradually extend their influence. Business divisions make decisions without following the rules. Powerful individuals mould the relationships and activities to their preferences. The results are often unsatisfactory. In our experience, few corporate headquarters get high marks from their business divisions.

To some extent, the tension between headquarters and business divisions is natural; but, more often than not, it is because headquarters is underperforming. Most companies could add more value and subtract less value if they devoted more time to headquarters design. In fact, this ought to be a priority for the CEO. The headquarters team is the personal team of the CEO. If he or she is not setting up and running his or her personal team with care and attention, how can he or she demand high performance from the executives running the business divisions?

Note

[1] David Young and Kay Dirk Ullmann, "Benchmarking Corporate Headquarters Staff", Ashridge Business School Report, 1998; David Young, Michael Goold et al., *Corporate Headquarters: An International Analysis of Their Roles and Staffing* (FT Pearson, 2000).

CHAPTER FOURTEEN

DEVELOPING NEW CAPABILITIES AT CORPORATE HEADQUARTERS

One of the central points of this book is that the best corporate headquarters are able to add more value to their businesses than other corporate headquarters. These corporate headquarters have some advantage over their rivals in capabilities, such as performance management or choosing people or marketing, or in resources, such as brand or money or patents.

Another central point is that companies should try to align their portfolio of businesses with the capabilities and resources that they have at headquarters or vice versa. By aligning the two, companies can achieve their longer-term objective of becoming the best owner of their businesses.

Why headquarters capabilities can be misaligned

At many points in time the portfolio of businesses and the skills of headquarters managers may not be aligned. This can happen for a variety of reasons. For example, a company looking for growth may invest in a new business that is closely linked to the company's existing business. For example, oil companies owned refineries that produced different grades of fuel. It was relatively easy for them to add equipment to these refineries to crack the fuel into chemical subcomponents. This took oil companies into the chemical industry. Initially, oil companies were not the best owners of these new chemical assets. But they invested heavily to develop the headquarters skills needed. In less than 10 years, the oil companies developed large and profitable shares of the bulk chemicals market.

Encouraged by this success, oil companies tried to diversify further: into speciality chemicals and fine chemicals. From an asset perspective, this diversification only involved adding further equipment to do further refining. However, speciality chemicals involve different selling skills and require a different business model. So oil companies found themselves struggling to be good owners of these new speciality chemicals businesses. As before, they invested in the headquarters skills needed. However, on this occasion, like nearly all bulk chemical companies, they failed to become good owners of these businesses. It proved too difficult for them to develop the appropriate headquarters skills. As a result, the oil companies mostly sold or closed their fine and speciality chemicals businesses.

A second reason why a company may invest in a business for which it does not have the appropriate headquarters skills is because of the growth and profit potential in this market. This is what the German engineering company Mannesmann did when it entered the mobile telephone business in Germany. When a company does this, it needs to develop new headquarters skills unless it intends to quickly sell the business to a rival that already has the appropriate skills. Mannesmann chose the latter option, and sold to Vodafone after only a few years.

A third reason that may cause a company to own a business for which it does not have appropriate headquarters skills comes from imperfections in the capital markets. The business may be cheap, allowing the company to enter at a discount. Low acquisition prices enabled Associated British Foods (ABF) to enter the beat sugar business by acquiring British Sugar and to enter the low cost clothing market by acquiring the retailer Primark. Initially, ABF was not the best owner of these new businesses: ABF was originally a bakery. But, over time, ABF learnt how to "parent" these businesses, so that they became two of the most successful divisions in the company.

A fourth reason comes from changes in the market place or industry that a company is already in. A famous example is Intel. The company was built on memory products. Using this success, managers entered related markets such as microprocessors. Over time the sources of advantage in the memory market changed from technical leadership to large-scale manufacturing. Companies in Asia, with large-scale manufacturing skills and with access to cheaper capital than Intel, were able to add more value to their memory businesses than Intel. Despite attempts to match these parenting skills, Intel ultimately withdrew from the memory market.

This chapter focuses on the challenge of developing new headquarters skills so that a company can be better aligned with its existing businesses or so that it can enter new businesses with promising growth prospects.

We will start by explaining why the success rate is low: why companies that try to develop new headquarters skills, like Intel or the oil companies, often fail. We will then provide some advice about how companies should set about the task of developing new headquarters skills. We will close with some advice on when companies should invest in developing new headquarters skills and when they should choose the alternative route, like Mannesmann or Intel, of selling the businesses concerned.

Why is it so difficult?

In our research and consulting work we have frequently been close to companies trying to develop new headquarters skills. More often than not, their efforts have failed. In other words, the headquarters has failed to develop the skills needed to add significant value in the way intended. Some examples will help illustrate the problem.

A major oil company had been managed with a focus on strategic objectives and loyalty to the company values. Because of benchmark comparisons with a major competitor, the company concluded that its businesses could and probably should produce higher profit margins. This successful competitor had lower operating costs and higher margins on similar assets. So the company decided that there was an opportunity-to-add-value through setting higher performance targets, tightening controls and instituting a tougher budgeting process.

The company hired consultants, changed its budgeting and target setting processes and instituted formal review sessions focused on financial performance. Performance improved a little. But the company did not get close to the benchmarks.

The problem was that the same managers were sitting across the table in these budgeting and performance review sessions. They knew each other well. As a result, although the headquarters managers mouthed a tougher approach asking for stretch targets and threatening consequences for missed budgets, managers in business divisions knew they did not really mean it: they knew that, so long as they remained loyal to the company values and to the agreed strategy, their jobs would be safe.

A company with a portfolio of food businesses providing products for retailer brands decided that there were opportunities to expand these private-label businesses by launching its own brands. The businesses had good technologies and strong operations, but they lacked the management skills needed to develop and build their own brands. So there was a significant opportunity-to-add-value.

Unfortunately, the headquarters managers did not have strong brand marketing skills. To help the businesses build new brands, headquarters needed to build new skills itself. As a result, a new executive was hired at board level. The executive had significant experience in Procter & Gamble. She also brought with her some other managers with brand experience.

The new marketing and branding team at headquarters defined new marketing and branding processes for the businesses to follow, helped the businesses hire additional branding skills, evaluated all existing brands, searched for opportunities for new brands and became closely involved in approving and developing the marketing campaigns for those brands selected for investment.

The result was a significant increase in the costs of marketing and branding, but little increase in the percentage of business coming from brands or in the profitability of the few existing brands. The reasons for lack of progress can only be surmised. Managers in the businesses complained that she never fully understood their businesses, and tried to impose on them processes and investment policies that did not fit their skills or opportunities. Also, the brands that she was trying to improve may have had limited potential: one was a niche sausage with a loyal but limited following. Finally, launching new brands in a crowded food market, especially in a sector dominated by retailer brands, has a low probability of success, however well the projects are executed. After three years the new marketing director left, and an internal appointment was made. The company has still made little progress with its branded ambitions.

A company with a portfolio of retail businesses decided that there was an opportunity to add value by developing better skills in warehousing. The businesses all had large numbers of stock-keeping units. This made warehousing and stock keeping a particularly important part of the value chain. Efficient warehousing with short delivery times could reduce the supply chain costs and significantly reduce stocks. Some businesses seemed to be more successful at this than others.

The company decided to try to help its businesses with warehousing challenges. The first step was to ask the head of one of the more successful businesses to lead a project to explore the opportunity. The project confirmed the opportunity. The next step was to appoint a warehouse coordination manager at the headquarters level. The manager chosen was the warehouse manager who already reported to the project leader. This warehouse manager kept his business-level job and took on the headquarters role in addition.

The new warehouse coordination manager set up a warehouse coordination committee consisting of the warehouse managers from each of the business units. One of the first agenda items for this committee was a major warehouse investment in one of the businesses. The warehouse coordination manager wanted to make sure that this new investment took advantage of best practice from around the group. As a result the investment was discussed at each coordination committee meeting.

The discussions generated a long list of extra work items for the manager leading the major warehouse investment: for example, he was advised to visit other warehouses in the group and meet other equipment suppliers. It turned out that these extra work items served only to delay the project and increase costs. The new warehouse was serving a business that required same-day delivery, a performance level not required in the other businesses. Hence, there proved to be little opportunity for this project to learn from other businesses in the group.

After a year, the warehouse coordination committee was disbanded. The warehouse managers found that they were not learning enough from each other to justify the time they were spending together; and the warehouse coordination manager was finding the extra work difficult to handle.

So what makes it difficult to develop new headquarters skills? The prime reason that new "parenting skills" are hard to develop is that they are difficult skills. These skills are unlikely to be available in the open market. In order for a manager in a headquarters role to be able to add value in some new area, he or she must

1. understand the politics and culture of the company to be able to function effectively
2. understand some important aspect of the businesses better than the managers running the businesses
3. be respected enough that managers in the businesses will pay attention
4. know the managers in the businesses well enough to know what sort of interventions are likely to be helpful to them
5. understand enough about the business models of each business to know what interventions might subtract value
6. understand enough about other interventions by headquarters managers to be able to avoid opportunity costs or conflicts
7. have the power, leadership skills, technical skills and access to resources to be able to execute the chosen interventions without any significant negative side effects

Not surprisingly this combination of knowledge and skills is rare.

Take the warehousing example. The warehousing coordination manager probably had sufficient knowledge and skill for conditions 1, 3 and 6. But probably failed conditions 2, 4, 5 and 7. To be successful, he would have needed to know how to improve each business, to understand the strengths and weaknesses of the different warehouse managers, to understand the priorities facing each manager to be able to spot interventions that might subtract value and to have the authority, persuasion skills and the technical knowledge to give the appropriate help. When this list of requirements is laid out, it is not surprising that the warehouse coordination manager fell short in a number of dimensions.

We can make a similar assessment of the food company. The manager hired from Procter & Gamble will have been highly skilled in branding and in launching new brands. But she probably only met three or four (2, 3, 6 and possibly 7) of the seven conditions. Coming from the outside, she will have known little about the politics and culture of the company. Also, she will have known little about the managers in these businesses. Finally, she had significantly less experience of working in fresh foods and with private label products, and hence may not have known what interventions might subtract value in these businesses.

In the oil company, the leaders met most of the conditions (1, 2, 3, 4, 5), but still failed to have the skills to make the intervention successful. They assumed that "performance management" was a commodity skill that could be easily trained into managers by consultants. They observed that there are plenty of companies with strong performance management skills. Hence, they hired consultants and set about copying processes that were successfully used by others.

But they underestimated the changes they would personally need to make to implement performance management (condition 7), and they did not see the conflict between performance management and their historic commitment to strategy and loyalty to company values (condition 6). Realising that their leaders still put strategy and values ahead of performance, managers in the businesses quickly judged where the real priority lay.

Many opportunities to add value exist because of the strengths and weaknesses of existing managers and because of the existing habits, processes, politics and culture of the organisation. For example, companies typically have less focus on short-term margins because they are committed to longer-term objectives; or companies have weak marketing because managers believe that technology is the main source of advantage. To make changes that add value, headquarters managers need skill, determination, understanding and a strong power base. Changes that add value cannot easily be brought into the organisation by consultants or new hires.

But some companies do develop new headquarters skills

BP, the British oil company, was known in the 1980s as a technically competent but not commercially aggressive company. It was a member of the oil elite, but it was not anyone's benchmark of excellence.

In 1990, two managers rose to the top of the company – Bob Horton and John Browne. They had been working together in the chemicals division of BP, and then in the core business – BP Exploration. They had a different way of managing, with much greater focus on costs and on accountability for profit.

Initially, this new way of managing was resisted by many managers at BP. Moreover, when Bob Horton made a public gaff saying that he thought he was cleverer than the average manager at BP, he was quickly removed. But, the process of change had started. Bob Horton's replacement was a better politician and he continued most of the changes. By the time John Browne was made chief executive, some five years later, the old management model had been broken.

Browne decentralised the organisation. He set up 90 business units around 90 major assets. Browne set targets for each unit and expected managers to deliver against them or suffer as a result. Browne drove down costs. In the process, he found that large oil companies had large amounts of unnecessary costs, and that engineers could become as enthusiastic about optimising profit as they had previously been about optimising engineering excellence. In fact, Browne had discovered this when he was working in BP Chemicals and then again when running BP Exploration. So, applying these same ideas to the whole of BP was a small extra step.

Armed with these insights Browne began acquiring other oil companies, applying the same management medicine and dramatically pushing up profits. The headquarters at BP had learnt some very important knew skills. These were skills that added billions of dollars to the market capitalisation of BP, which, at one point, became the most respected of the major oil companies. With the possible exception of Exxon, BP was thought to be the best managed oil company.[1]

Many companies have developed significant headquarters skills in managing safety or total quality. GE, for example, committed to total quality through its six sigma campaign in the mid-1980s. By making the initiative top priority for four or five years in a row, by showing commitment from the top and by demonstrating the benefits, companies like GE have developed new headquarters skills, significantly raising performance in their business divisions.

How should companies develop new headquarters skills?

Given the difficulty of developing new headquarters skills, it is reasonable to ask how companies do it. There are two basic paths. New skills can emerge from managers, like John Browne, who gain experiences when inside a business division and then progress to the headquarters level. Alternatively, new skills can be crafted by the top team as a result of a deliberate attempt to change the focus of managers at headquarters.

The first path is more successful. If a manager emerges from the business divisions having developed some skills that can be used more widely across the portfolio of businesses, there is a greater chance that this individual will have the needed capabilities. Consider the seven conditions. The manager will understand the culture (condition 1). The manager has some superior business knowledge (condition 2). The manager is likely to have respect based on his or her track record in the company (condition 3). The manager is likely to know the other managers well (condition 4). The manager is likely to know about other corporate interventions and their impact on business managers (condition 6). The manager is likely to have the power and skills to intervene effectively (condition 7). The manager's main weakness may be an insufficiently nuanced understanding of the other businesses (condition 5).

Of course, not all insiders meet all these conditions, as shown by the warehouse example. But the odds are better for this path of development than for the alternative.

GE provides a good model of the alternative approach. When Jack Welch wanted to increase the headquarters skills in a particular area he went through the following steps:

1. Identify the area, such as six sigma or sales force effectiveness, and do some analysis to confirm that it is an opportunity. The analysis often involves consultants and pilot projects.
2. Define the skill and appoint a leader. Welch would find someone inside the company who could be a credible champion of the new skill. It would be an insider because the person must understand GE. The person also had to be a credible champion so that others would pay attention. To some degree, this is about deliberately looking for the John

Browne or someone equivalent. Six months or a year might then be devoted to developing the tools and methods of the new headquarters skill. Often this work was also done with the help of outsiders. The work also would involve trials and pilot projects.

3. Announce the new initiative. The announcements were always made at Boca Raton during the January conference of the top 400 people. The announcement would define the opportunity. It would be supported by Welch and other members of the board. It would be the only significant new initiative that involved all of those present. The presentations would demonstrate the skills, processes and methods, and would explain to managers how they could contribute. The presentations would include a dramatic success story: a pilot that had been spectacularly successful. Managers would be given time to debate the initiative and give feedback, but not to slow down progress.

4. Three months later an email survey would be sent to 10,000 or so managers across the group to find out whether the new initiative had started to touch them and change their behaviour. Where managers reported that little was happening, the business or function would be visited by the leader of the initiative or Jack Welch himself. The determination to make change around the initiative would be evident. As the main initiative of the year, it was not discretionary.

5. Throughout the year, the leader of the initiative would collect stories of efforts made and lessons learnt. The central team would share this knowledge, orchestrate training, support efforts in the field and document the best processes and approaches.

6. Successes would be celebrated and shared inside GE and outside. The objective would be to help those making progress feel like pioneers and heroes. Those who did not engage should feel left out.

7. Finally, at the next Boca Raton conference, a report would be given on what had been achieved over the previous year. Welch would not be willing to give himself a bad report.

But the GE example also shows us that, even when all of these steps are followed, the effort can still fail to deliver the result required. Jeff Immelt followed most of these steps in his campaign to add more organic growth to GE's businesses. There were some small differences. Immelt hired Beth Comstock, from the outside, as the new head of marketing to help him drive the growth initiative. He also went public with his approach to growth (the growth wheel[2]) before he had fully proved that it was working. In his favour, though, he kept focused on growth for four or five years, and he was himself evidently the leader of the effort.

So why did Immelt's initiative fail? Maybe it was the economy. But more likely, it was that Immelt failed condition 2: he did not "understand some important aspect of the businesses better than the managers running them". Managers are natural seekers of new opportunities and growth. They are highly motivated to beat their competitors and build their empires. They understand their markets. They understand their technologies. They are in the best place to propose and drive growth for their businesses. In this situation, it is hard to see how a team of growth experts at corporate headquarters or a CEO with a personal desire for growth are likely to add value.

Unless there is some specific reason that is causing managers to grow more slowly than they should, such as too much focus on North America (a problem Jack Welch tackled with his "No. 1 or No. 2" campaign) or slow reaction to the rise of the Internet and online competitors (a problem Jack Welch addressed with his "destroyyourbusiness.com" campaign) or too much focus on products rather than services (a problem Jack Welch approached with an "add services" campaign) it is likely to be hard for corporate headquarters to make any positive contribution. The normal entrepreneurial challenge of finding growth in slow growing markets may not be something to which headquarters can add value.

This brings us to the last section of this chapter – when should managers consider selling a business rather than trying to develop the relevant new headquarters skills?

When it is best to sell rather than develop new skills

In Part II of this book, we gave three logics for selling a business. Managers should sell when the market price for this kind of business is higher than the discounted value of future cash flows. In other words, when the market for this kind of business is overvalued (capital markets logic). Managers should sell when the business is in an unattractive market and has a weak competitive position. These businesses are normally such trouble and such absorbers of management time that it is better to give them away than keep them (business logic). Managers should sell when the business lies in the alien territory or value trap sections of the Heartland matrix. This is when the risk of subtracted value is greater than the potential for adding value, and there is likely to be a better owner for the business (added value logic).

In this section, we will focus on the latter reason: when the business is a value trap. In value trap businesses there is a significant opportunity to add value, but the risk of subtracted value is high (see Figure 14.1).

In value trap businesses, headquarters managers not only need to develop the skills to avoid subtracting value, but they often also need to develop additional skills at adding value: the potential to add value is likely to be greater than their current capabilities.

Figure 14.1: Heartland matrix

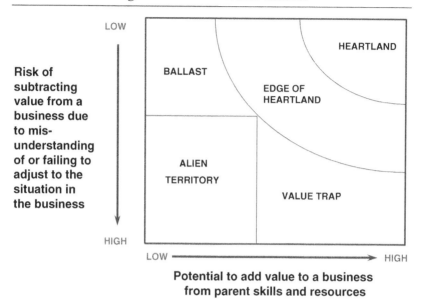

Potential to add value to a business
from parent skills and resources

Since the positioning of businesses on the Heartland matrix is based on judgement, some tests are needed to help decide whether the company is likely to be better selling or holding on and building the needed skills.

The best tests focus on people. Is there an individual who can be a natural champion for this business in corporate headquarters? This individual will be someone who understands the business, usually because he or she has worked in it. He or she will also have enough influence to stop interference by headquarters that is likely to subtract value. This individual, or it may be more than one, is the main reason for believing that subtracted value will be low. The existence of this individual may be enough to push the business out of the value trap space and into edge-of-heartland.

In addition, is there an individual or team who can be a natural champion for the new headquarters skills needed to add value to the business? Because there is potential to add value, it does not mean that the value will be added. What we are looking for is someone or some team that has enough track record at adding this sort of value to this kind of business to be confident that the potential will be realised. The person who can defend the business from subtracted value may also be the person who can champion the added value. But often they are different. In combination, they will meet most of the conditions listed on page 309.

To be confident that keeping the business and building the appropriate skills is the right decision, headquarters managers should believe that they can limit subtracted value and maximise added value. This is most likely when it is linked to capable, trusted people. Without these people, confidence is little more than hope: the company would do better to sell than to hold on.

Summary

This chapter is about headquarters capabilities: the skills needed to add value to businesses without subtracting value. The main message is that these skills are not commodity skills that can be hired easily through head-hunters. If they were readily available, most companies would have them and they would not be a source of advantage. By definition, therefore, these capabilities depend on unusual individuals who have had unusual experiences. As academics describe it, these are path-dependent skills. It is hard for others to gain the skills without following the same path of experience.

As a result, building new headquarters skills is closely linked with people. Skills can be built from a zero starting point. But this is a tough road that requires leadership with the determination of Jack Welch. The easier path is to build round people: to add headquarters skills when people with the needed unique skills emerge or are found. When the appropriate skills cannot be found, headquarters managers should consider selling the businesses affected or at least keep these businesses at arm's length until the new skills are found.

It is also important not to overreach. We were taught a lasting lesson by an executive in Hanson Trust. Hanson Trust was one of the most successful conglomerates of the 1980s. The executive described a situation where the managers of one of his businesses had come to him explaining that the technology was changing and the business would need a significant cash injection to invest in the new technology. "I knew that we at headquarters did not have the skills to understand the technology. I also knew that this was the sort of decision we were not good at making. We were better at controlling working capital and containing costs. So we sold the business."

Notes

[1] Some years later, the focus on costs and on performance at all costs was taken too far. BP's engineers began to cut too many corners. There were problems in Alaska and in Texas, then with the Deepwater Horizon drilling rig in the Gulf of Mexico. The fall of BP, which happened after John Browne had been fired for lying in court about where he met his boyfriend, demonstrates that every initiative to add value also contains some risk of subtracted value, and that it can be hard to keep the balance favourable.

[2] Christopher Bartlett, "GE's Growth Strategy: The Immelt Initiative", Harvard Business School, Case No. 9-306-087; Thomas Stewart, "Growth as a Process: An Interview with Jeffrey R. Immelt", *Harvard Business Review*, June 2006.

CHAPTER FIFTEEN

ENCOURAGING SYNERGY AND COOPERATION ACROSS BUSINESS DIVISIONS

In Chapter 8, we described ways in which headquarters can generate synergy by promoting certain types of horizontal coordination. This chapter is about the difficult task of getting the coordination to work: getting managers in different business divisions to work together rather than avoid each other.

We devote a chapter especially to the management of synergy because it is something that many companies feel they do badly. When we researched this topic, we found very few management teams who responded "Ah yes, synergy. We do this quite well in our company. We get a lot of collaboration between our business divisions without much tension or negative consequences." The more normal response was "We find this rather difficult. We can probably tell you more about how not to do it rather than how to do it."

Synergy is the extra value that arises when business units work together in ways that would not have happened if the units were independent companies. Of course, the vast majority of collaboration between business divisions could happen and does happen between independent companies. Buying and selling services happens between independent companies. Benchmarking happens between independent companies.

Hiring talent happens between independent companies. Many of the areas of typical interaction between business divisions within a group also happen between independent companies. In other words, most interactions are not synergy: there is no added value in the way we have been using the term in this book. The value would typically be created even if the business divisions were independent companies.

However, some forms of interaction are difficult to create between independent companies. This may be for legal reasons. For example, if two businesses addressing the same market want to have discussions about pricing strategy, this is only legally possible if they are owned by one entity. It may be because of competing objectives. For example, if there is excess capacity in a market and one factory needs to close, independent companies are unlikely to volunteer their own factory. It may be because of communication difficulties. For example, managers in independent companies might not naturally form relationships with or exchange data with similar managers in other countries.

Whatever the reason, an important aspect of synergy is that it is value that would not normally emerge without the businesses being part of the same corporate group. Hence, it is a small subset of the broader collaboration value that is an essential part of our economic system.[1]

Why is synergy so difficult?

In his book *Competitive Advantage*, Michael Porter opens a chapter on the benefits of horizontal synergy with the following words: "Achieving interrelationships in practice has proven to be extraordinarily difficult for many firms."[2] He then provides eight pages of "impediments to achieving interrelationships".

Competitive Advantage was written in 1985, but little has changed. Any manager with experience of a corporate group can attest to the wisdom of Porter's words. Moreover, even when synergy is the main focus of managerial attention, as happens following an acquisition that is justified by synergies, the results are often disappointing. Despite creating a programme office, despite setting up 10 or 20 work streams aimed at different types of synergy, the net result is often less than expected.

Yet, value is created by interrelationships between independent companies in the market economy every day. Moreover, some of these relationships are remarkable in their complexity and ingenuity. One example involved the chemical operations of the Dutch company DSM. Part of the chemical plant produced PVC, a plastic chemical used to make products. The PVC plant had originally been installed because one output from the main plant was suitable for conversion into PVC.

DSM, however, was a small competitor in the PVC market and found it difficult to make a profit from this plant. It decided, therefore, to sell the plant to a French company that specialised in PVC. But, because the plant was on a DSM site and connected to DSM's other plant, complex interrelationships had to be devised.

DSM was contracted to manage the plant for the French company. The agreement covered the management costs and provided incentives for DSM to improve productivity. Planning for the plant, performance management, accounting and commercial activities were done by the French company. A complex formula was agreed for the price DSM would charge for the input chemicals. Also, a line was painted on a pipe leading into the plant. The French company owned the chemicals on one side of the line. DSM owned the chemicals on the other side.

This example demonstrates that managers are capable of creating highly sophisticated interrelationships, even between competitors in the same industry. So why is it common for leaders of corporate groups to be frustrated by the lack of interrelationships between business divisions? Why do companies find it difficult to get their business divisions to work together?

This question was the subject of a major research project by Andrew Campbell and Michael Goold.[3] The conclusion was that much of the frustration was due to four biases that caused managers to mismanage synergy:

1. Managers are biased towards believing that synergy exists. Because managers are looking for an explanation for the range of businesses in their company, they presume that synergies must exist, when often they do not. This causes them to engage in many "interrelationships" that are doomed. The authors referred to these presumptions as "mirages": managers are thirsty for synergy, and hence are liable to see synergy when it does not exist. Part of the reason for Michael Porter's comment that interrelationships are "extraordinarily difficult" is that interrelationships are often attempted when there is little or no potential to create value. Not surprisingly they fail.

2. Managers are biased towards believing that some managerial intervention is needed to release synergies. When a synergy opportunity is identified, managers set up coordinating committees or transfer pricing systems or best practice sharing conferences. They ignore the fact that managers in business units freely interact with suppliers, customers and business partners without having their bosses set up coordinating committees and knowledge-sharing events. In other words, most value from collaboration, if it exists, will be released by normal interactions between "consenting managers". If the interrelationship is not happening, it is probably because the managers concerned have more important things to do. Managerial intervention to encourage synergy is only needed if there is some blockage getting in the way of normal commercial behaviour.

3. Managers at corporate levels are biased towards believing that they have the skills needed to solve synergy blockages. When something is getting in the way of normal commercial behaviour, such as personality clashes or self-interest or lack of operating skills, managers at the corporate centre assume that, by getting involved, they are likely to solve the problem. Unfortunately, their involvement often serves to make things worse. Clearly, if the manager does know how to remove the blockage, intervention makes sense. But, if not, leaving well alone may be better.

4. Managers are biased towards believing that collaboration is a good thing. This causes them to be cavalier about setting up sharing processes, coordination committees and cross business project teams. These activities all have significant opportunity costs. Also, businesses that are working closely together, particularly when encouraged by the corporate centre, are harder to hold to account: each can use the other as an excuse for low performance. Finally, some relationships can have a negative impact. When two businesses are working together, one can "contaminate" the ideas of the other. Different businesses often depend on having different business models. When one business copies the business model of another, it can reduce performance as well as increase it.

How to be sensible about synergy

If the biases that managers have are the main reasons that cause interrelationships to be "extraordinarily difficult", then the solution is to improve the way managers think about synergy: to eliminate the biases in their minds. Campbell and Goold suggest four disciplines that will help managers be sensible about synergy.

The first discipline is to **size the prize**. Before encouraging any interrelationship or collaboration, managers should assess the size of the likely net benefit in financial terms. How much extra profit is the collaboration likely to create, net of any costs? Clearly, the prize is difficult to calculate with any accuracy. But it is normally possible to give an order of magnitude estimate. Is it €1 million, €10 million or €100 million?

Once the prize is clear and the participants have reviewed the calculations, there is little chance of pursuing a mirage. Also, it may not be necessary to do anything else. If the prize is significant, the participants may well collaborate without further stimulus.

The second discipline is to **identify the blockage**. If the prize is significant and the participants are not voluntarily working together, there will be a blockage. Often the blockage is about priorities. One or more of the participants has other more important tasks. While it may be possible to overcome this blockage by finding additional resources, frequently the competing priorities need to be identified as an opportunity cost and the prize recalculated.

Other blockages include:

- insufficient information – one or more participants do not see the potential
- inaccurate evaluation – one or more participants are sizing the prize inaccurately
- lack of motivation – one or more participants do not have the incentive to engage in this collaboration, for example because most of the prize is captured elsewhere or because of personality conflicts
- lack of skills, resources or processes – one or more participants do not have the skills needed or believe that other participants do not have the skills needed to make the collaboration work

Once the blockages have been identified, an intervention should be targeted at removing the blockage rather than on some general appeal for collaborative behaviour. If the blockage is about incentives, then the solution is to change the incentives. If the blockage is about skills, there may be little that can be done unless new skills can be developed or found. If the blockage is about erroneous calculations, then providing additional information may solve the problem. If the blockage is due to managerial bias, then changing the manager may be the only solution. If no blockage is identified, no action is needed: consenting managers will address the synergy when their other priorities allow.

The third discipline is **build on existing skills**. Interventions, such as coordinating committees or central functions or best practice forums, frequently cost more than they achieve, even when they have been carefully selected as the appropriate intervention for addressing a particular blockage. The reason is that the skills of the people leading the intervention – chairing the committee, leading the central function or designing the forum – are insufficient. Almost by definition, existing managers will not have much experience of similar interventions and they may not have the skills to intervene wisely.

Hence, managers need to be humble about what is doable and what should just be left on the table for another day. The concept of a "natural champion" is helpful here. If the intervention requires deciding between difficult alternatives or persuading reluctant divisional managers, it is only likely to be successful if led by someone who is recognised in the company as a natural champion of the subject area. This means that the person is recognised as the leading expert in the company and trusted to play straight. Without a natural champion, most interventions achieve little.

Another concept that is helpful is that of "well-grooved mechanisms". The companies that are most successful at releasing synergy benefits often have particular mechanisms that they have used many times before. Managers understand the mechanism and know how to get the best from it. Examples are technology centres at 3M, coordinating committees at Unilever or peer groups at BP.

The fourth discipline is **look for downsides**. Any intervention has both upsides and downsides. A common downside is opportunity cost: the actions managers could be taking if they were not spending time on this intervention. Opportunity costs should be considered when sizing the prize and when looking for blockages, but it is also helpful to reconsider the opportunity costs once an intervention has been selected.

Other downsides include loss of accountability, loss of motivation, loss of influence in other areas, contamination across business models and confusion among managers about the direction of organisational change. Each situation will be unique. Hence, a checklist of sources of downside is not as helpful as listening to those who are uncomfortable with the proposed intervention. In other words, managers need to look for downsides that are particular to the intervention being considered.

These four disciplines – size the prize, identify the blockage, be humble about skills and look for downsides – can be combined in a **process for choosing interventions** (see Figure 15.1). The process starts with an estimate of the size of the prize. If it is small, no further work is needed. If it is unclear, some further exploration is needed. If it is large and clear, the process moves to the next step, identify the blockage.

If there is no identifiable blockage, no further work is necessary. Managers should be left to collaborate as they want. If the blockage is unclear, some further exploration is needed. If the blockage is clear, the process moves to the next step, identifying a few ways of intervening that will address the blockage. A good discipline is to identify three ways of intervening to ensure a range of options is considered.

Once three possible interventions have been identified, the final step in the process is to evaluate the options to find out which is best. The criteria for evaluation are:

Figure 15.1: Framework for choosing interventions

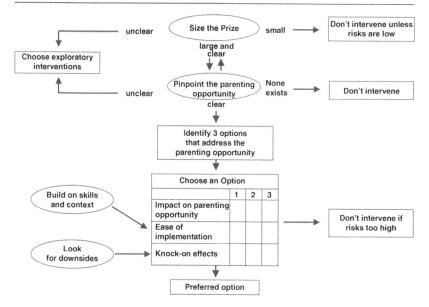

- the effectiveness of the intervention at removing the blockage
- the ease of implementing the intervention
- the risk of downsides from the intervention

If the risk of downsides is high for all interventions, it will be better to do nothing rather than choose the best of those available. Of course, it may be possible to design a fourth intervention that avoids the risks. In fact, it is normal that the process of evaluating three options results in choosing a fourth option that includes some of the strong points of the other three and avoids some of the weak points.

An important part of this process is the number of points at which the conclusion is "do nothing". Being sensible about synergy is often to do nothing rather than to launch some initiative that costs a lot, achieves little and causes managers to resist future initiatives. Being sensible about synergy is like building a dry stone wall. Each new initiative, like each new stone on the wall, needs to be positioned carefully so that it does not wobble, before another initiative/stone is added. In this way, trust builds and enthusiasm for synergy rises. The alternative is a growing frustration as each new project destabilises the organisation, draining away the trust needed for successful collaboration.

Summary

This chapter has explained why leaders often complain that the managers in charge of their business divisions are reluctant to work together. It also explained why efforts to create synergies across a portfolio of businesses frequently deliver less than expected.

The solution is for managers to be more thoughtful about both when and how to encourage coordination. Managers need to know the size of the benefits that will be delivered, and they need to understand why sensible managers lower down the organisation are not already working together to get the benefits. They also need to be ready to do nothing. If they cannot find a way of intervening that has good chances of success, a synergy project is likely to do more harm than good.

Notes

[1] Felix Barber, "Strategy, Partners and Agreements: How to Set Things Up so People and Companies Will Do What You Want", forthcoming.

[2] Michael Porter, *Competitive Advantage* (Free Press, 1985), Chapter 11, 383.

[3] Andrew Campbell and Michael Goold, "Desperately Seeking Synergy", *Harvard Business Review*, 1998; Andrew Campbell and Michael Goold, *The Collaborative Enterprise* (Perseus Books, 2000).

PART V

RETROSPECTIVE

CHAPTER SIXTEEN

LESSONS FROM 20 YEARS OF CONSULTING EXPERIENCE

We have found that the three logics described in this book have been invaluable in guiding our clients about which businesses to expand, shrink, launch, buy or sell. The added value logic, in addition, guides decisions about corporate structures, headquarters functions and management processes that are needed to make the group of businesses successful. In the last 20 years, we have encountered very few senior managers who disagree at an intellectual level with these ideas.

Yet we have also encountered a large number of companies where the senior team does not follow this approach in its day-to-day work. Portfolio decisions fail to take account of one or more of the three logics. Headquarters managers take actions that are not primarily guided by added value principles. The corporate strategy is not clearly articulated and communicated, or else seems to be at odds with our principles. We have been puzzled and concerned by this failure to convert intellectual acceptance into practical application.

The main issue is with the thinking linked to added value logic. Managers often acknowledge that corporate headquarters should add value, but they do not invest enough time in clarifying and sizing the main sources of value; they do not build them prominently enough into their portfolio decisions; and they do not drive their headquarters managers to focus on them. Typically, they spend more effort looking for attractive businesses than for businesses to which they can add value. They also tolerate too many central initiatives, projects and functions, and do not think through the costs and subtracted value that can accompany these well-intentioned initiatives.

In this closing chapter, we reflect on the reasons for short-comings in what managers do and on what might rectify the situation. Our observations are based on our consulting experience since we published *Corporate-Level Strategy* in 1994. Over this period, our clients have been grappling with corporate strategy issues and have been, to a greater or lesser degree, attempting to follow our principles.

We divide the chapter into three sections:

- Thoughts that get in the way of our approach to corporate strategy: watch out for these.
- Tricky situations where it is tempting to do the wrong thing: beware the temptations.
- Simple tips to help bring the right thinking to the fore: try them.

Thoughts that get in the way

There are several common ways of thinking about corporate strategy which seem superficially attractive, but can conflict with our approach.

Corporate strategy is about investing in attractive businesses

Summaries of a company's corporate strategy, of the sort found in the chairman's statement in the annual report, are very often phrased in terms of an aspiration to shift the portfolio into businesses with higher margins and/or higher returns, and with faster growth prospects. This laudable and widely held objective is expected to appeal to investors and is, of course, fully consistent with business logic, as we have described it in this book.

But business logic should not be the only driver of corporate strategy. It is also important to ask whether the parent is able to add any value to the more attractive businesses into which the company wishes to move (added value logic) and whether it expects to be able to buy into or develop these businesses at a discount to their true value (capital markets logic). If the new, more attractive businesses are not in the company's current heartland, there is a serious danger of subtracted value, and if the new businesses are widely seen as attractive, the price of entry to them may well be too high to justify the move. Business logic alone can lead to corporate strategy moves that end up destroying value.

Our antidote: make sure you get all three logics onto the table and do not overemphasise business logic to the exclusion of added value logic and capital markets logic.

Portfolio balance is critical

Many executives believe that corporate portfolios need to be "balanced". They need to include a mix of fast growth and slow growth businesses, of cash-generating and cash-using businesses, of businesses with a presence in different regions of the world, of businesses from cyclical and less cyclical sectors. Portfolios of this sort will be more robust, more insulated from problems that may arise in particular sectors or geographies, more self-sustaining and more consistent in the returns they deliver. We recognise that this line of thinking is appealing.

However, while there is some value in all of these ideas, the thinking is usually muddled. Investors are perfectly capable of diversifying and balancing their own portfolios if they wish to do so. It is rarely the job of corporate managers, except in special circumstances such as closely held family companies, to perform this function. Hence, initiatives to balance the portfolio are rarely justified, unless they are also supported by one or more of the three logics, which they very often are not. Often, attempts to balance the portfolio have more to do with the preservation of management jobs and careers than with sound corporate strategy.

Our antidote: Be alert when anyone uses the word balance. It is seductive and can cover up sloppy thinking.

"Best practices" should drive the design of headquarters

We have often been asked to advise companies on how to ensure that their planning process or HR function or process for post-merger integration is "World Class" or "Best Practice". Managers understandably want to know that their activities are not out of date or at a significant disadvantage. Yet, this thought shows a misunderstanding of the challenge of leading a good corporate headquarters.

Each company's headquarters needs to be designed to support its own specific strategy and sources of added value. Because companies differ greatly in the sources of added value on which they focus, their headquarters are likely to differ in size, composition, skills and processes. There is no best way to do things, no template of best practices to follow. In fact, for most headquarters activities, best practice is a positively dangerous thought. It motivates companies to establish departments and processes by reference to what successful but very different companies do and without regard to whether these practices will add any value to the businesses in this particular group. It is a thought that leads to an administrative mindset, which is more concerned with sophistication and comprehensiveness than with the needs of the businesses.

This is not to say that best practice thinking has no place. There are some governance activities common to most companies, such as producing the annual report. Here, benchmarking can be helpful. But only for activities that exist mainly for governance reasons.

Also, rival parent analysis is an important part of good strategic thinking. Leaders need to know how their rivals are adding value to check whether their own company has parenting advantage. Rival parent analysis can also show a company new ways of adding value. But even here, leaders should be cautious. They need to understand whether the activities of one of their rivals can be copied or whether they rely on cultural or historical factors that cannot be replicated.

Our antidote: Be vigilant in focusing on added value logic rather than best practice thinking. Avoid "corporate excellence" programmes and prefer "fit for purpose" programmes. Look out for headquarters managers who justify initiatives with reference to what other companies do.

Lean is best

Many efforts to redesign a headquarters are, explicitly or implicitly, driven by cost. The CEO decides that he or she wants to cut overheads and launches a programme to do so, even if it is announced under the more neutral banner of "redesigning" the headquarters.

It is certainly true that corporate function heads, driven by the quest for best practices or simply by an enthusiasm to do more, often expand the size, cost and powers of their functions beyond what is needed. So, periodic projects to cut corporate costs are needed. But an emphasis on cost or an implication that a lean headquarters is better can distract managers from the real purposes of headquarters, to add value. The best corporate strategies are not founded on the leanest headquarters. Rather, the headquarters should be right-sized to deliver the added value and governance tasks that are needed. A focus on cost reduction risks throwing the added value baby out with the bureaucratic bath water.

Our antidote: Regularly use a challenge process, such as the three tests (page 180), to make sure that all initiatives and activities have an added value or governance rationale that can be justified. Use the opinions of managers in business divisions to root out inefficiencies and bureaucracy. Even have regular cost cutting initiatives, just make sure that the focus is on added value and not cost.

"What can they do for us?"

There is a whole way of thinking about the relationship between the corporate parent and the businesses that begins with the question: "What can they (the businesses) do for us (the parent)?" Because the parent owns the businesses, it feels justified in expecting things of them, whether it is growth, cash flow, profitability or whatever. The parent's performance is then a reflection of how well the businesses have been doing.

Although an understandable perspective, it is exactly the wrong way to think about corporate strategy. The fundamental question is the reverse: "What can we (the parent) do for them (the businesses)?" Unless the parent has some added value contribution to make, it will be difficult to justify owning the businesses. Unless the parent is doing something that helps the businesses, the corporate strategy is no more than the aggregation of the business strategies. The group might as well be broken up into its constituent parts without the overhead burden of a shared headquarters.

Our antidote: Echo JFK. Stop asking what the businesses can do for you. Ask what you can do for the businesses. Think of them as customers and encourage your colleagues to do the same. Also, give more voice to the businesses. Create opportunities for them to say what they want and do not want. Do a regular survey of their opinion of the usefulness of each corporate function.

Tricky situations

There are some situations where the application of our approach leads to difficult or unpalatable conclusions. Managers are then tempted to compromise on the principles of corporate strategy by looking for other logics that do not require them to face up to the challenge.

Mature or declining heartland

All managers know that the businesses they are in today will mature and may eventually decline. The businesses that represent the heartland today may not provide long-term growth and prosperity. If this situation is imminent, the corporate management team faces some difficult decisions. Should managers accept the decline and use share buy-backs to enhance returns for shareholders? Or should the company launch out into new business areas that have better growth prospects?

Inevitably, the growth option appears much preferable, especially for managers who are concerned about their own careers. Typically, it leads to speculative investments in new growth areas irrespective of business logic, value added logic or capital markets logic. Often companies overpay or overinvest. Frequently, the new activities are well away from the current heartland, and there is little prospect of the company developing the new parenting skills that are needed. Not surprisingly, the failure rate is high.

While the search for new growth is an essential corporate activity, it needs to be overseen by people with a commitment to the three logics. The harsh reality is that most companies, and most corporate strategies, do not survive for 50 or 100 years, and it is unrealistic to expect them to do so. The three logics can lead to the conclusion that a company should shrink rather than grow. They can even guide a company to break itself up or to sell itself to another owner. Managers need to be willing to face these realities when the analysis is pointing in that direction.

Bad parents of attractive businesses

In Chapter 6, we discussed situations when the three logics lead to different conclusions. A particular problem arises when a company owns an attractive business, but is not a good parent for it. The business is probably worth more to another owner. But, by retaining the business, managers are more easily able to deliver growth and margin targets. The plan to sell the business, give the cash back to shareholders and reset the targets seems much less attractive than the plan to hold on.

In these circumstances, it is easy for managers to fool themselves about their ability to be a good parent or to assume that subtracted value is minimal. Clearly, it takes brave and disciplined managers to see their own skills clearly and to listen to the often muted thoughts of managers lower down. But, if the business will be more successful with a different owner, both sets of managers gain from making the change.

Multilevel parents

In large companies, there is often more than one organisation level above the operating units. There may be groups, divisions or regions sitting between headquarters and the operating units. The parenting role and the task of adding value to the operating units is then shared between these levels. Clarifying the role of each layer and what to centralise and decentralise can represent a particularly tricky challenge.

In our experience, clarity is rare. Often, headquarters treats the intermediate parent levels as big businesses and does not recognise that they are in fact playing a parenting role. And the intermediate levels assume that they should discharge all the important parent responsibilities, leaving nothing for the corporate parent to do except duplicate what has already been done by lower levels. Ambiguity about who is doing what is common, and typically results in redundant reviews at multiple levels.

It may well be necessary and desirable to have multilevel parents. But, when they occur, too few companies do the careful analysis needed to lay out the added value, the risks of subtracted value and the complementary roles for each level.

Parents that do not add major value

We have worked with many corporate leaders who wanted to add more value. Typically, they were concerned that their headquarters was not adding enough value. They were sensitive to the need to add value, and aware of the costs of headquarters. Many even understood the ever-present potential for subtracted value. So they asked for help in finding new and major sources of added value.

Our experience is that this quest for major new sources of added value is often fruitless. The desire to find new ways to add value is laudable, but is dependent on the skills of headquarters managers. Some are able to change their skills. Some are willing to bring in new talent. But, more normally, the same team tries to graft on new behaviours, without the insights, experience and drive needed for success. If the "cupboard is bare", it is usually because there are not many opportunities-to-add-value or because this particular headquarters team does not have appropriate skills, or both.

Such a conclusion is not an easy one for managers to accept. It implies that they should break up or sell the company, or resign from their jobs. As a result, the tendency is to plump for dubious or minor sources of added value as the basis for the corporate strategy. Our observation is that this "sticking plaster" solution rarely solves the problem for long. A hostile takeover, a mutiny from below or a restless board normally puts the management team out of its misery. Far better, in our opinion, to take the medicine and be seen to do the right thing.

Simple tips

This book has provided many frameworks and tools already – enough to satisfy the appetite of most corporate strategists. But we end with a few simple tips that will help managers to put into practice the ideas we have put forward.

Set up a corporate-level strategy process

In too many companies, there is no distinctive and separate corporate-level process. Instead, the businesses go through an extensive planning process and the corporate level aggregates the plans of the businesses, with some challenge to business strategies and some attempt to stretch objectives or identify gaps between corporate aspirations and what the businesses think they can deliver. This is not a satisfactory way to develop corporate-level strategy.

The whole thrust of this book has been to argue that corporate-level strategy needs to be seen as a separate topic from business strategy. It needs distinctive analyses and thought processes, and leads to distinctively corporate conclusions about the make-up of the portfolio and the way in which the businesses are parented. As such, it is essential that companies should establish a corporate-level process, which provides a periodic focus on corporate-level strategy, and which builds on but is distinct from the business strategy process. The lack of this separate process is one reason why corporate strategies are often inadequate.

Make corporate functions develop strategic plans

Corporate functions are both the handmaidens of the chief executive in helping to add value and the dragons of bureaucracy and subtracted value. For many managers in business divisions, the dragons are more visible than the handmaidens, and often the subtracted value is greater than the added value.

One way of helping to correct the balance is to treat corporate functions in the same way that businesses are treated. They need a strategy. They need a budget. They need performance reviews. They need structured challenge. So ask corporate functions to produce strategies just as businesses are asked to do. These can then be reviewed and challenged by the businesses as well as by the chief executive. Often the planning diary is already too crowded with reviews of business strategies, so functional strategies can be addressed at a different time of year.

Agree the strategic logic before doing the cash flows

Corporate strategy moves are normally justified by a business case, which includes detailed cash flow projections. A proposed acquisition is pursued because a business case with a 22% internal rate of return has been put together. A reorganisation from independent country businesses into global product lines is justified on a mix of cost reductions and sales increases. But all too often the business case is weak: the detailed numbers have been manufactured to support what key executives want to do anyway. The subsequent performance falls well short of planned projections.

Of course, there is a need for cash flow projections to support corporate strategy initiatives. But the driver of corporate strategy initiatives should be the strategic logic not the financial logic. If the move does not fit with one of the three logics, it should be rejected, irrespective of the cash flow analysis. The cash flows and the detailed business case should only come into play once the underlying logic has been agreed. Their function is to make sure that detailed plans to implement the strategy in a profitable way can be drawn up, not as the primary justification of the move.

Do rival parent analysis

It is now almost a truism to suggest that business managers give too little attention to their competitors when developing their strategies. We have found that this truism is equally if not more valid for corporate strategies.

Analysis of actual or potential rival parent companies – possible alternative owners of your businesses – is necessary to test the corporate strategy you are considering and is often a source of new ideas and learning about how strategies can be improved. If you have a strategy that adds value, but your rivals have strategies that will add much more value, you need to think again. Your strategy will not achieve "parenting advantage", and, at least in principle, everyone would be better off if the rival parents took ownership of your businesses.

More constructively, you may be able to pick up ideas about how to add more value by studying and understanding how your rivals go about it. What do they do that we do not do? Could we add more value by emulating them? What would it take for us to do so, in terms of skills, people, processes and resources? In what respects are we different from rivals, and how can we exploit these differences to add more value? As with best practice analysis, we need to be very careful not to assume that the same approaches will work for us as for others. However, an understanding of what close rivals are doing can lead to new insights.

Be more willing to sell businesses

We have found that corporate managers are usually reluctant to sell businesses. They prefer to believe that they can turn around failing businesses, add more value to businesses outside the current heartland, and achieve a higher NPV by holding on than selling. They also dislike the idea of shrinking the company. So the sale option is often dismissed too readily, even for poorly performing businesses that do not fit in the company's corporate strategy. The result is that they sell only in a crisis or under threat of a hostile takeover, often at a time when they will get less for the business than they should.

In our experience, good corporate strategists see a decision to sell a business as a positive move. First, they can expect to get a premium because the business is likely to be worth more to rival parents. Second, they can often take advantage of capital market conditions that favour sellers over buyers. Third, they are able to get rid of a distraction, which may be preventing them from adding value to other businesses in the portfolio. Fourth, the disposal typically makes it easier to communicate the corporate strategy both to investors and employees. Selling businesses may go against the grain, but is very often a wise step in clarifying and improving the corporate strategy.

Be more willing to change people

Corporate strategy work is often done in the context of the existing corporate team. The question being addressed is really "what strategy should this team pursue?" It is harder, but in our experience more rewarding, to step to one side and ask "what is the best strategy for this company?"

The ability to separate the company from the existing team is particularly important for corporate-level strategy. Corporate headquarters is usually a fairly small entity, in which only a handful of people are capable of moving the needle. It also creates value mainly by influencing others rather than by making products or developing technologies. People and their skills are vital. And we know that developing new skills is hard for senior managers at a relatively late stage in their careers. Hence, any new corporate strategy will likely require new people in the corporate centre and the departure of some existing managers. If the new strategy is implemented by the existing team, the chances of success are low: you will be trying to play tennis with a team of golfers.

Following acquisition or some other crisis that brings in new management, companies are suddenly able to transform in ways that were not possible with previous managers. So a willingness to make some difficult people decisions is probably a precondition of meaningful corporate strategy change.

Summary

It is easy to be distracted from the principles of corporate strategy that we have advocated. Other ideas can get in their way and temptations can arise that lead down a different path. Our approach is simple and logical, so should provide an antidote to these distractions. But it needs commitment and discipline to avoid being blown off course.

Corporate processes that ensure the three logics are kept in centre stage are helpful. But the key is a willingness to follow through on the implications for both businesses and people. Our experience suggests that this is easier said than done. Many highly capable leaders have been distracted or found it difficult to face up to the implications of the analysis. Those who remain steadfast, therefore, are more likely to emerge as the ultimate winners.

THE LINKS BETWEEN INTERNATIONAL STRATEGY AND CORPORATE-LEVEL STRATEGY

"International Strategy" or "Global Strategy" is often seen as a specialist topic within the broader strategy field.[1] Most general strategy textbooks devote one or more chapters to this topic, and it is typically treated separately from "Corporate Strategy and Diversification".[2] However, most International Strategy is really a subset of Corporate-level Strategy: the challenge is about operating in multiple territories rather than multiple products or value chains. Even a company selling a single product line, such as edible oil, with subsidiaries in a number of different countries, will face the two main corporate strategy issues described in this book: which countries to invest in and how to manage multiple operating units from corporate head-quarters? If the subsidiaries are little more than sales offices, the company is highly integrated like those described in Chapter 12; if the subsidiaries are fairly autonomous with control over most of their value chain, the company is a group, maybe even a "*geographic* conglomerate", but in a focused product area.

It is therefore interesting to explore briefly some of the main thinking about International Strategy as a topic in its own right to see if it is consistent with Corporate-level Strategy as described in this book. Does it focus on different concepts and issues? Does it provide specialist insights? Does it cover areas that may become more central to Corporate-level Strategy in the future? On the other side, would International Strategy benefit from using ideas developed for Corporate-level Strategy problems? In this appendix we briefly explore the links between International Strategy and the rest of the book.

International strategy and corporate-level strategy

International Strategy is not entirely a subset of Corporate-level Strategy. It concerns decisions about which countries to operate in and how to organise across country boundaries. These decisions can be as relevant to a simple business unit with a single, unified value chain as to more complex organisations with multiple value chains. For example, a simple business that sells shoes in Ireland may decide to set up a sourcing office in Hong Kong or Portugal in order to access lower cost or more specialised raw materials and components. This is part of its International Strategy, but it does not need a Corporate-level Strategy. Similarly, a small Swedish-based online retailer selling traditional local crafts may decide to target the Midwest of America as its prime market, and may sell the vast majority of its products overseas even if they are all produced in Sweden and simply shipped to the USA when ordered online. Again, the company has an International Strategy but, because it is a company with only one value chain, it is not the type of organisation on which this book is primarily focused.

Conversely, not all Corporate-level Strategy involves any International Strategy. A chicken farming business in Saudi Arabia may decide to integrate forwards into branded prepared foods in the same country. This is a Corporate-level Strategy decision about entering a new business, but does not involve International Strategy.

In some situations, therefore, these two types of strategy are separate, but in practice, they overlap to a great extent. For example, most of the companies described earlier in this book have a presence in multiple countries as well as multiple businesses. Their corporate strategies therefore involve many international strategy issues. The running case of Molsand/CIW/ Carlsen illustrates this point well, as do Procter & Gamble, LVMH, Walmart, GlaxoSmithKline, Hamworthy, Sonae, Metro, General Electric and a host of others. In summary then, Corporate-level Strategy and International Strategy overlap heavily: both are usually concerned with decisions about the portfolio of operating units and the way this portfolio is managed from headquarters.

Six issues in international strategy

The literature on International Strategy covers many interesting topics, but much of the attention relates to six broadly defined issues:

- The first of these concerns the nature, extent and growth in international activity and geographic connectedness at a fairly macro level.
- The second concerns the causes of differences in internationalisation across different industries.
- The third concerns the selection of country markets which a company chooses to serve.
- The fourth concerns the choice of countries in which a company locates its activities.
- The fifth concerns the most suitable type of ownership structure to employ for different international operations.

• The sixth concerns the structures and mechanisms used by headquarters to manage activities and sales in different countries.

In the following sections, we will briefly examine each of these issues and consider how they relate to other parts of this book.

Drivers of international business activity

The importance of International Strategy has grown very significantly since the middle of the twentieth century in line with the scale of international business activity. Reduced costs of trade, including transportation and tariffs; reduction of regulatory barriers; growth of digital products and services; harmonisation of certain standards across countries; and homogenisation of certain customer and consumer preferences have all greatly increased the level of international business activity.

As a result, international trade has grown much faster than overall global output in this period. For example, world production grew eight-fold between 1970 and 2007, but world merchandise trade grew 28-fold.[3] Similarly, within OECD countries, total trade grew from 11% of GDP in 1960 to 52% in 2007.[4]

But growth in foreign investment has been even greater than in trade. By 2009, for example, the stock of direct investment by OECD countries in others was $13 trillion, a full 34% of OECD GDP[5]; and while world output grew by 40% between 1992 and 2007, and world trade grew by 145%, foreign direct investment grew by about 500%.[6]

This increase in international activity and cross-border ownership has created new opportunities for most businesses, but also new threats and surprises. It has not only led to the expansion of most large companies beyond their home markets, but has created a global network that is much more interdependent than in the past, with knock-on effects even for those who do not see themselves as "international players".

For example, it has been noted that one of the early casualties of the US subprime mortgage crisis in 2007 was a regional bank in the UK called Northern Rock.[7] This bank required intervention by the Bank of England and later the government to avoid total collapse, but at first sight it seemed completely separated from the US mortgage market. Based in Newcastle in the North East of England, it had no physical presence in America and only 0.24% of its assets in US collateralised debt obligations or US home equity mortgage-backed securities. Customers (and even staff) of the bank may have felt that they were sheltered from exotic financial instruments in distant lands. But the liquidity of the bank depended on the capital markets, which in turn were affected by non-domestic events. As a result, Northern Rock was unable to refinance its short-term needs, and fell prey to a classic "run on the bank".

It is therefore increasingly important to understand the international strategies of other players and the domestic impact of events in international markets. Corporate-level Strategies, even if focused on one geography, need to take account of potential rival parents from other geographies.

The drivers of globalisation are a particular focus of economists, interested in currency movements, changing flows of trade and investment, and the impact of legislation; but are also relevant to all strategists. Just as strategists need to understand the implications of local market economics and legislation, they increasingly need to adopt a much broader geographical perspective. Paradoxically, these trends towards globalisation have typically reduced the importance and scope of the Diplomatic Service or Foreign Office in many countries, not because the issues are *less* significant but because they are so pervasive in their influence on other departments that they cannot be delegated to a "specialist" international team. Similarly, dividing out International Strategy from Corporate-level Strategy may no longer be viable in most situations, or may even cause unhelpful complacency: "I don't operate internationally, so why do I need to worry about international issues?"

There are some parallels and some differences between the approach to this issue in International Strategy and the discussion of Corporate-level Strategy evolution in Chapter 2. The former has been particularly interested in regulatory changes and general changes in the social and technological environment that have affected the *background conditions* for International Strategy. The discussion in Chapter 2 is more focused on the attitudes and assumptions of key managers and strategists in shaping the development of specific corporate strategies of different sorts over time. While some Corporate-level Strategy writers have examined the shift in overall "corporate activity", such as through the relative size of the largest players versus the smallest, the relative size of corporate headquarters in different countries or the average level of diversity in corporate portfolios over time,[8] there has been less explicit focus on the social, regulatory and technological drivers of Corporate-level Strategy.

And yet, these factors are sometimes important shapers of Corporate-level Strategy. In certain cases the impact is obvious, such as when the Glass-Steagall Act in the USA forced the separation of different types of banking businesses in a way that directly shaped corporate portfolio decisions in the banking industry. Similar regulatory involvement has been considered in many countries since the banking crisis of 2008. This could have a profound impact on the portfolio and parenting strategies of financial services companies, removing some previously important opportunities-to-add-value.

But sometimes the impact is more complex even if highly relevant. For example, the development of information and communication technology has provided fertile ground for much larger and "offshored" shared services. This has led to a significant increase in such central resources even in groups that had previously decentralised many activities back to local operations. Other examples would be the development of new types of utilities and energy groups following the deregulation of these industries in many countries, leading to a major wave of cross-border acquisitions and changes of parenting approach.[9]

More generally, the local existence (or absence) of main-stream institutions and markets, such as employment markets, financial markets and enforceable legal contracts, has a big impact on opportunities-to-add-value across a broader range of businesses. This has led to the growth and survival of highly diversified groups in developing countries with "institutional voids" even as diversity has declined in more developed ones.[10] Interestingly, research on this topic has come more from the International Strategy side (through academics such as Khanna and Palepu) rather than from the Corporate-level Strategy side. Perhaps the latter has something to learn here. Background conditions can change within the same country over time, just as they are different across different countries at any given time.

The background conditions for Corporate-level Strategy and International Strategy activity are therefore subject to similar shaping, but the "macro" drivers are seldom so clearly in centre stage for Corporate-level Strategy. This could lead to dangerous hidden assumptions in rules of thumb, either across different contexts or for corporates as a whole. For example, some authors such as Richard Koch[11] have questioned whether traditional corporations will survive at all in a world with increasing transparency and market-based relationships, but this is an unusual perspective for Corporate-level Strategy.

Drivers of internationalisation in specific industries

Whatever the macro trends in international activity, the degree of internationalisation varies significantly depending on the industry in question. Funeral parlours, fresh milk distributors and hairdressers are much more locally "sheltered" than producers of consumer electronics, jet engines or operating software.[12] Local customer preferences are much more diverse in mid-market shoes and washing machines than in upmarket shoes and credit cards. It is therefore just as dangerous to overestimate the impact of international competition, homogenisation of tastes and transferability of business models as it is to ignore completely what is going on in other countries. This has led to another focal point of International Strategy writing, namely, the drivers of *different* levels of international impact in different industries and business types.

Various frameworks have been developed to help the strategist think through this issue, for example by George Yip, a strategy professor with a particular interest in globalisation and international management. Yip's framework[13] focuses on four types of driver: market drivers (such as similarity of customer needs); cost drivers (such as the importance of global economies of scale); government drivers (such as ownership restrictions and property protection); and competitor drivers (such as the presence of global players in the same industry).[14] While there may be a general move towards standardisation of tastes, for example, some markets remain stubbornly regional or local. While there may be important global scale economies in certain types of software, there are far fewer in manicure salons.

The value of such frameworks is to help strategists recognise that there is different potential for advantageous international expansion depending on the nature of the industry.[15] This is similar to the idea that there are different opportunities-to-add-value, as described in Chapter 10, in different situations. Yip's framework can be seen as a tool for identifying opportunities-to-add-value. It is biased towards opportunities-to-add-value across countries. For example, if consumer tastes are standardising across countries, there may be future opportunities-to-add-value by exporting or internationalising products. If governments are harmonising legislation with other countries, there may be more opportunities for geographic centralisation.

Such frameworks can also help to highlight the dangers of subtracted value described in Chapter 9. They can help explain why ways of working derived from one country or industry will not be suitable for other, different countries or industries. For example, it is tempting for managers in products where customer requirements are similar across countries, such as certain toiletries, to assume that things will be the same in other product categories, such as foods or even other types of toiletries. Testing such assumptions explicitly is an important part of Corporate-level Strategy, but has particular relevance in International Strategy because differences between countries can be less obvious.

Frameworks, such as Yip's tool, could also be used as an aid to Corporate-level Strategy. With small adjustments the tool could assess opportunities across product types within one country to help spot opportunities-to-add-value and risks of subtracting value. Interestingly, Corporate-level Strategy tools in this area are less well developed, possibly because of the availability of SIC coding as a short cut for academics.

Choice of suitable international locations: markets

International Strategy is concerned with which geographical markets to address. Geographical *market selection* is parallel to Corporate Strategy's "business selection". This topic was the primary focus of International Strategy some years ago, though the focus has shifted somewhat, as we will see in the next section.

Looking at geographical market selection, how do the three "logics" of corporate portfolio strategy apply? *Business logic* involves selecting, and investing in, "good" businesses (see Chapter 3). In International Strategy, there has been similar emphasis on selecting "good" countries, but often defining good in different ways. Market size and growth are typically the headlines in International Strategy. Although managers have realised that naïve assessment on these grounds alone is likely to be dangerous.

The opening of China as a new but potentially huge and growing market tempted many Western companies to enter rapidly, just as many European and Asian players had previously entered the United States in search of large, growth markets. In both cases, many entries were costly failures. Just as high growth industries are not necessarily the most profitable, high growth countries are not necessarily "good". Here, International Strategy probably has important lessons to learn from Corporate-level Strategy.

International Strategy also has to deal with the issue of market definition. While the USA is, at least for certain products, a nuanced but meaningfully integrated market, regions of Africa, Europe or large countries like China show significant fragmentation. Definition of relevant geographic market boundaries is therefore an important first step. Frameworks such as "PEST" and "PESTEL", covering local political, economic, social, technological, environmental and legal drivers, can provide insights that help understand market boundaries, just as Five Forces analysis provides insights about business boundaries between different industries. While corporate-level strategists are comfortable using PEST analysis, international strategists are less familiar with using Five Forces analysis to help them understand market boundaries.

Chinese retail provides an interesting illustration of both points.[16] For instance, because there is colder weather and more limited access to hot water in the northern region than in other parts, consumers wash their hair less, preferring smaller sachets of shampoo to complete bottles, eat more red meat and wear more layers of clothing, requiring wider supermarket aisles. Depending on what you are selling and the economics of your business model, such differences can quickly turn an apparently large, single, "good" market into a collection of smaller and potentially less interesting markets.

These attempts to identify "good" markets are very parallel to the *business logic* explored in Chapter 3, but particularly relate to the vertical axis of the GE/McKinsey matrix described there. The horizontal axis – about competitive advantage – gets less attention in International Strategy. However, some writers have stressed the importance of incumbent competitors and their possible reaction to new entrants. MacMillan, van Putter and McGrath suggest an array that measures market attractiveness to the entrant on the vertical axis, and expected "reactiveness" of local defenders on the horizontal axis.[17] If incumbents are likely to be reactive and have significant clout (represented by the size of bubble on the chart) a country should be de-emphasised.[18] Similarly, other academics have explicitly altered the two axes from "Market Attractiveness" to "Country Attractiveness" and from "Competitive Advantage" to "Compatibility with country and competitive strength".[19] Here again, International Strategy probably has lessons to learn from Corporate-level Strategy. The ability to gain and defend local competitive advantage is not given the same prominence in International Strategy.

Added value logic is another important consideration in portfolio decisions. In International Strategy, this idea is also widely recognised. For example, the logic for much international growth is to spread the fixed costs of product development or manufacturing. This allows a competitor with a strong position in some countries to enter a new country without the need to develop products or set up manufacturing just for the latter. The unit in the new country benefits, and the other countries also benefit from spreading fixed costs. This was a major driver of US corporate expansion after the Second World War. Interestingly, the new country does not need to be "good" in the sense of large or fast growing for this added value logic to make sense.

This idea of added value from a global *network* has a central place in International Strategy. The so-called "Transnational"[20] or even "Metanational"[21] adds value from spreading innovations generated in one country around the network of other countries. For example, IKEA was initially renowned for "exporting" Swedish design to other regions. As the company developed, it learnt to adjust to local demands. It then used these local innovations to stimulate learning across the network. Its response to the fanatical quality consciousness of Japanese customers, for example, enabled the company to raise standards in other countries.[22]

Added value logic depends on discovering opportunities-to-add-value. But managers with international strategies can misjudge these opportunities in the same way that happens for managers with multi-business strategies. In concrete roof tiles, for example, Redland's belief that it could add value in markets such as Japan by introducing European product technology and design proved largely illusory due to differences in building traditions and distribution structure.

Possibly, opportunities-to-add-value are even harder to judge in International Strategy. For example, many Europeans visited Disney's theme parks in the USA, and the characters and films embodied in the rides had widespread international success. However, the company's original attempt to replicate its US model close to Paris failed. This was not because of any rejection of Mickey Mouse, but, once the park was much closer to home, many French and other Europeans visited for shorter periods, brought their own food and failed to spend as much on merchandise. As a result, the business model had to be adjusted significantly in order to make money.[23]

In International Strategy, added value logic is as important an idea as in Corporate-level Strategy. Possibly, Corporate-level Strategy has something to learn on this topic from International Strategy. For example, International Strategy has a better developed tradition of trying to spot situations where subtracted value is likely. International Strategy has a variety of tools that attempt to measure compatibility across countries.[24] For example, Pankaj Ghemawat's CAGE framework[25] measures the "distance" between two countries in terms of four dimensions: *Cultural* distance covers aspects such as language, ethnicity, religion and social norms; *Administrative* and political distance deals with political hostility, shared or separate monetary association and similarity of legal and financial institutions; *Geographical* distance covers spatial separation, and issues such as waterway access, transportation, communication infrastructure and remoteness; and *Economic* distance covers differences in consumer incomes, costs and quality of inputs and different levels of information and knowledge.

Interestingly, Corporate-level Strategy has no such well-established framework for identifying distance between product markets. Chris Zook and James Allen's adjacencies framework[26] provides one tool for assessing "steps away from the core": a form of distance measure. The other measure, used by many academics, is SIC code proximity. Neither is as helpful or comprehensive as the CAGE model.

The third consideration for portfolio strategy is *capital markets logic*. While this is less written about in International Strategy, it is certainly a driver of many specific decisions. In particular, companies with good local knowledge are often able to buy or create businesses in markets that have been overly discounted by others. Local experts can often acquire assets at knock-down prices or establish positions in markets that have no serious competition. For example, Savola, a successful foods group in Saudi Arabia, bought out its Irish partner in a highly attractive dairy business during the first Gulf War. After the visiting Irish managers had reportedly witnessed an armed missile pass close by their plane, they were keen to sell. Similarly, Aliko Dangote, a billionaire entrepreneur in Nigeria, saw the potential to establish a local cement plant even though there was limited infrastructure for water and transportation. Remarkably, his investment of several billion dollars had a payback of only two years. International competitors had considered the market too unattractive. While Corporate-level Strategy has a more formalised approach to *capital markets logic*, the ideas are the same in International Strategy.

In summary, many of the frameworks used in International Strategy to address geographic portfolio decisions fit well with broader Corporate-level Strategy frameworks and vice versa. However, there are lessons to be learnt from one to the other. There is still an opportunity to develop a full synthesis.

Choice of suitable international locations: internal activities

Whatever markets you choose to serve, you also have to decide where to carry out the activities required to serve them. This topic concerning the geographic location of *internal activities*, as opposed to the choice of *external markets*, has become more and more important in International Strategy.

Addressing international markets may or may not require much physical presence in those markets. For example, the small Swedish online retailer mentioned earlier does not need a physical presence anywhere outside its home country even though its markets are far-flung and almost all sales are international. This approach to international business was typical of much of the expansion by large Japanese companies in the 1960s and 1970s. By carrying out as much of the value chain as possible in one country, economies of scale, learning effects and managerial control can all be maximised. But there are many good reasons to move activities to other countries, whether you are serving them locally or just seeking a better position in your home market. For example, GE and IBM have tens of thousands of staff in India, mostly serving their customers in other countries.

The original thinking about this topic focused on factor costs and scarce resources. For example, if there is a plentiful supply of cheap, unskilled labour in a country, it makes sense to carry out unskilled activities there; if there is cheap energy, it makes sense to carry out energy-intensive activities there; if there is abundant land for grazing or growing crops, it makes sense to grow food there.

But if you need to integrate all these activities into a single value chain, you must also consider the costs and time of transportation, the complexities of coordinating across countries, the risks of exchange rate fluctuations, regulatory or tariff changes, political risks and so on. This makes the decision about where to locate activities much more complex than just looking for the "cheapest inputs".[27] For example, many clothing or fashion houses in Europe now divide their manufacturing into two types carried out in different places: longer-run, more predictable items are typically made in Asia, where costs are low but lead times long; shorter-run more fashion-based items are typically produced closer to home, for example in Portugal or Turkey, even though costs are higher, because lead times are much shorter.

If trade is free, it makes sense for countries to specialise. This idea was suggested by Adam Smith and explored by David Ricardo back in 1817 under the label of *comparative advantage*.[28] While it seems obvious that simple manufacturing will be cheaper in countries with low factor costs, the impact of reciprocity and "trade", whether internal or external, means that specialisation decisions are complex. Specialisation leads to interconnectedness. For example, as China has specialised in carrying out many types of basic manufacturing and serves a high proportion of these needs for America, a downturn in the US economy immediately creates problems in the Far East.

Also, the economics of specialisation can change over time, sometimes abruptly. In a world with relatively low shipping costs and high energy costs, it makes sense to ship bauxite from mines in the southern hemisphere up to Iceland, where it can be smelted into aluminium using low cost thermal energy, then shipped back down to markets in Europe and America. If cheaper energy sources are discovered, or shipping costs rise dramatically, this arrangement would become unsuitable.

This concept of comparative advantage has also been researched and developed by strategists such as Michael Porter who looked at the "competitive advantage" of nations.[29] For example, Porter's Diamond framework (Figure A1.1) links four elements in determining national (or regional) advantages.

Figure A1.1: Michael Porter's National Diamond framework

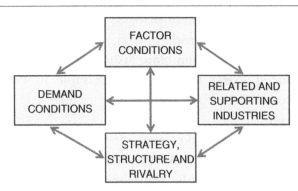

- *Factor conditions* are perhaps the most obvious, covering the availability and cost of "factors of production" such as cheap energy, abundant skilled labour, raw materials or even linguistic ability.
- *Demand conditions* concern the sophistication and requirements of local customers. Regions with more demanding customers in a given industry typically develop advantages in dealing with those demands, such as Japanese demands in electronic products or fashion demands in France and Italy.
- *Firm strategy, structure and rivalry* concerns local competitive behaviour and structure; fierce competition between a small number of local firms seems to lead to much stronger global positions than the creation of a "national champion".
- *Related and supporting industries* addresses the importance of local ecosystems that can foster global excellence, such as the technology and venture capital cluster in Silicon Valley, the finance and legal cluster in the City of London or the ceramics and design cluster in Northern Italy.

How does this critical topic in International Strategy – where to carry out different activities in the value chain – relate to our general discussion of Corporate-level Strategy?

In one sense, it is a specialist decision operating at a more detailed level than the choice of what businesses to be in and how to parent them. But in another sense, it touches on both. First, headquarters activities are often located in different geographies. One company based in Dubai had its group finance function in Switzerland and its group IT function in England. International strategy tools can help with these decisions. Also, in deciding where to locate different but linked activities, managers need to think carefully about how to set up the required coordination across specific countries. If one of the countries involved is very different from the home country of key managers, there is even a risk of subtracted value.

Similarly, in selecting the specific location of each activity, the three logics of *business, added value* and *capital markets* can be used to help:

- *Business logic* focuses on identifying and investing in structurally attractive markets where a business has competitive advantage. The parallel here is in looking for structurally attractive geographical *input* markets, as identified through factor costs and Porter's competitive advantage of nations framework. The value chain is built with an understanding of the best countries for different activities. For example, if you want to develop software you may be better off going to Silicon Valley than Accra; if you want to build TVs you may be better off going to Korea than the Netherlands; if you want to do pharmaceutical research you may be better off going to Switzerland than New Zealand.
- *Added value logic* suggests another basis for choice of geographical location: is the company better at adding value and avoiding subtracted value in some countries rather than others? Factors may include local political influence, knowledge of or relationships with supplier networks or the language skills of managers. For example, while India is a "good" location for shared services for many companies (*business logic*), groups such as Tata can add significant value through their specific reputation in the local labour markets. This added value may justify Tata taking on some of these activities as outsourced contracts. Similarly, many local family-owned groups in the Middle East add value through their networks of social and political contacts. These are hard for outsiders to access.
- *Capital markets logic* concerns the mispricing of debt or equity. The parallel in this context might be the mispricing

of currencies (usually due to political decisions) or mispricing of assets in specific countries. As explained in Chapter 5, it is critical to understand why you may have better judgement than the market. Clearly, in some situations, inside knowledge will be better. For example, you may know more about likely regulatory changes or evolving local factor costs. This could allow you to enter a country at a "discount", or might encourage you to move your activities elsewhere before a major problem occurs.

International Strategy is asking some more focused and detailed questions about the location of value chain activities than Corporate-level Strategy. Yet some of the frameworks of Corporate-level Strategy are still relevant.

Choice of suitable ownership structures

Another major issue in International Strategy concerns the ownership structure of foreign operations. In particular, four main options are usually considered when entering a new geography[30]:

• Exporting
• Licensing (including franchising)
• Joint venturing
• Full ownership

Frameworks have been developed to help select the most suitable vehicle. For example, one framework compares the level of "Tradability" (based on ease of transport and quality of local legal protection) and "Breadth of Competitive Advantages" (measuring how much a company can rely on its own capabilities, or will need to work with a local partner).[31] If there is high tradability and sufficient capability, exporting makes sense; but if capabilities are limited, licensing to a local partner is more appropriate. If tradability is low and capability limited, setting up a joint venture is best. If capability is sufficient, a wholly owned subsidiary is likely to be the best strategy.

This issue of ownership structure has been prominent in International Strategy partly because of regulatory requirements and concerns about intellectual property "leakage",[32] partly because companies need to make an explicit choice when entering foreign markets, and partly because the mode of entry has a significant implication for risk, investment, control and rewards.

Interestingly, the issue of appropriate ownership structure is less mainstream in Corporate-level Strategy, and is not addressed directly in this book or most others on the same subject. So far, it has been seen more as a "specialist topic", often connected to M&A, or covered in relation to outsourcing and corporate alliances. But it is becoming more and more mainstream, driven by the recognition that full ownership rights are expensive and carry obligations, so it is not always worth acquiring them; contracting for more *specific* rights, developing trustful relationships or using power to influence others may be more effective ways of creating and capturing value.[33]

Overall management of international operations

The topic in this area of International Strategy is the "Global versus Local" dilemma. It directly mirrors broader Corporate-level Strategy questions about centralisation and decentralisation and is at the heart of the management or parenting strategy.

Frameworks typically either describe different approaches to this dilemma or define the conditions that favour one approach over another. The most popular version is probably Chris Bartlett and Sumantra Ghoshal's "Transnational" framework.[34] This describes four approaches to international parenting, built on previous research by C.K. Prahalad and Yves Doz.[35]

The four approaches are responses to two external factors: the strength of forces for global integration and coordination, and the strength of forces for national responsiveness and differentiation.

International (low pressure for integration – low pressure for differentiation)

This approach is based on home country expertise, but with sufficient protection to avoid heavy cost pressures. Product development functions such as R&D are usually retained at home, but manufacturing and marketing functions are typically established in each major country or region, with differing levels of autonomy. The development of knowledge and innovation will flow from the home organisation to the subsidiaries. For example, Xerox adopted this approach in the 1960s in exploiting internationally its heavily patented position in photocopiers. Other US companies, such as Coca-Cola, Ford and Procter & Gamble, leveraged their strong home market positions similarly in the early post-Second World War period.

Multidomestic (low pressure for integration – high pressure for differentiation)

This approach is based on responsiveness to local market demands. The company will be a portfolio of rather autonomous national subsidiaries containing their entire value chain. The innovation and knowledge developed at these national subsidiaries will most likely stay there rather than be dispersed to other countries. Many European companies, such as Unilever, Philips, ICI and Shell, adopted this approach in the early twentieth century, often seeking growth beyond a small home market.

Global (high pressure for integration – low pressure for differentiation)

This approach is built around scale economies. The subsidiaries are rather weak and a full value chain will only exist in the company's home market. The subsidiaries are tightly coupled to the home organisation, and are heavily dependent on home-based resources and know-how. Innovation and development are created at home, and later diffused to international subsidiaries. Relevant conditions for this approach prevail in many industrial goods industries, such as semiconductors. Many Japanese corporations, such as Toyota, Matsushita, NEC and Honda, expanded internationally in this way in the 1970s and 1980s.

Transnational (high pressure for integration – high pressure for differentiation)

This approach tries to maximise both local responsiveness and global integration. Knowledge and innovation are sought, developed and dispersed across the world. The company is a network, and each subsidiary is given responsibility linked to its capabilities and strategic mission. The movement of people within the company facilitates the mutual development and dispersion of innovation and knowledge. At the time they wrote, the authors considered ABB under Percy Barnevik as an example of a transnational. Many other companies, such as Unilever, were moving towards the transnational approach.

These four International Strategy approaches have parallels in Corporate-level Strategy: they show the link between portfolio decisions and parenting decisions. For example, early European companies, such as Philips, based their international expansion mainly on *business logic*, selecting good new markets to enter and creating a strong local position before others did. This required a relatively hands-off parenting style and a focus on corporate development. In contrast, the Japanese companies' "global" approach was built on strong *added value logic*, using consolidated manufacturing to maximise economies of scale and learning effects, requiring a more integrated parenting style.

Many commentators at the time believed that Japanese companies also took advantage of currency mispricing (a form of *capital markets logic*) by using the export benefits of a yen that was considered artificially undervalued. This also required a much more integrated and dominant home base. However, as the value of the yen rose, and as many market countries increased trade protection in response to supposed "dumping", Japanese international strategies had to change and the location of their operations became much more dispersed, demanding a change in parenting style.

One parallel contribution of the Bartlett and Ghoshal work was an observation that the parenting styles of international companies were much more rigid than might be expected; the "administrative heritage" from early years cast a long shadow over subsequent development. For example, when European companies came under greater pressure for global standardisation to reduce costs, they found it hard to integrate their previously autonomous subsidiaries. This point supports the issues covered in Chapter 14 in particular, but also throughout this book, about the difficulty of changing parenting skills and approaches.

Another parallel contribution involves the centralisation/decentralisation dilemma. Leaders of international companies struggle to set the right amount of autonomy for their country-based subsidiaries in the same way that leaders of multi-business companies often struggle to find the right balance between centralisation and decentralisation between headquarters and business divisions.[36] In fact the issue of the design of headquarters is central to both International Strategy and Corporate-level Strategy.

However, despite parallels, the broad-brush categories of International Strategy's parenting choices seem relatively generic compared with the more detailed focus of Corporate-level Strategy on *specific* opportunities-to-add-value and *specific* mechanisms to achieve this, linked to the parent's characteristics and the culture and history of the firm. Rather like the broad Corporate-level Strategy types described in *Strategies and Styles*,[37] the categories in International Strategy are helpful in showing conceptual extremes, but as the world converges more and more on strategies that combine conflicting drivers, it becomes critical to focus on *exactly* what is to be influenced by the parent and *exactly* how.

If the drivers of globalisation are squeezing most companies into a tighter space, it is all the more important to focus on differentiated positions within that space. Similarly, few Corporate-level Strategies are now based on extreme centralisation or extreme decentralisation, but instead involve different mixes of high centralisation of certain, very carefully chosen factors and high decentralisation of most others. It is the detailed choices and insights that matter more than the generic blend.

Summary

In this Appendix we have briefly reviewed the topic of International Strategy and explored its links with Corporate-level Strategy. Let us now return to the questions raised in the introduction.

Does International Strategy focus on very different concepts and issues? As we have seen, the main issues addressed in International Strategy are somewhat different, but generally map quite readily onto the issues of Corporate-level Strategy. The language used is often rather different; but the basic concepts are largely compatible. Importantly, there do not seem to be any major areas of *conflict*, rather differences in emphasis and focus.

Does International Strategy provide specialist insights?
International Strategy seems to offer certain insights at
both the macro and the micro ends of the spectrum.
Macro insights about the broader global environment
and the role of technology, regulation and societal
change in shaping the *background conditions* for strategy might be usefully integrated into Corporate-level
Strategy. How will these drivers shape the *types* of corporation that flourish or decline in future, and how
will they impact portfolio and parenting choices in
general? At the micro level, International Strategy has a
number of tools and frameworks, like the CAGE model,
that could provide insights for Corporate-level Strategy.
It also has a focus on *where* to do things, rather than
what to do.

**Does International Strategy cover areas that may become
more central to Corporate-level Strategy?** As described
above, the growth of interconnectedness around the
world is making it increasingly difficult to conceive of
Corporate-level Strategy without an international dimension. Even many relatively small companies serving a
single home market now need to consider appropriate
location for at least parts of their value network. Similarly,
the development of markets and companies in other
countries is increasingly likely to have an impact on local
conditions in all but the most sheltered industries.

The other main area of increasing interest and importance concerns ownership structures. Decisions about
what rights and influence are needed or appropriate are
as relevant in a domestic context as in an international
one. This topic once gained popularity under the banner
of "the virtual corporation", and is resurfacing through
consideration of social and other non-contractually based

networks, but has yet to be fully integrated into main-stream Corporate-level Strategy.[38]

Can International Strategy benefit from being seen less as a separate topic, and more as a part of Corporate-level Strategy? As international issues become more and more important in Corporate-level Strategy, there is a danger that treating them as "specialist" topics for experts will underplay their role. On the other hand, issues such as political risk, currency movements and hedging and the detailed implications of local legal systems clearly require specialist attention. The parallel with areas of functional expertise such as finance or IT suggests that there will continue to be a valid role for experts or specialist advisers on International Strategy.

What would a more rigorous application of Corporate-level Strategy thinking bring to International Strategy? All of the parenting issues discussed in Part IV of this book are highly relevant to International Strategy. The focus on added value and specific corporate insights and capabilities takes the more generic discussion of the "Global versus Local" dilemma to a more detailed and actionable level.

In a similar way, the "three logics" of portfolio strategy can be usefully applied to help with locational decisions, especially in choosing which international markets to serve. Recognising that a "focused" company with subsidiaries in different markets is fundamentally no different from a "diverse" company in a single market could help managers see the true diversity of many international groups.

In summary, there is much to learn from bringing together more closely the thinking about International Strategy and Corporate-level Strategy.

Notes

[1] There are therefore many books focusing solely on this particular aspect of strategy, for example: S. Segal-Horn and D. Faulkner, *Understanding Global Strategy* (South-Western Cengage Learning, 2010).

[2] An interesting exception is G. Johnson, K. Scholes and R. Whittington, "Corporate-Level and International Strategy", Chapter 6 in *Exploring Corporate Strategy*, seventh edition (Pearson Education Limited, 2005).

[3] World Trade Organization, *International Trade Trends and Statistics 2006* (Geneva, WTO, 2007).

[4] *OECD in Figures 2008* (Organization for Economic Cooperation and Development, 2008).

[5] Ibid.

[6] World Trade Organization, *International Trade Trends and Statistics 2008* (Geneva, WTO, 2008) and United Nations, *World Investment Report*, 2008.

[7] Robert M. Grant, *Contemporary Strategy Analysis*, seventh edition (John Wiley & Sons Ltd, 2010), 370.

[8] See, for example: D. Young and Kay Dirk Ullmann, "Benchmarking Corporate Headquarters Staff", Ashridge Business School Report, 1998; D. Young, M. Goold et al., *Corporate Headquarters: An International Analysis of Their Roles and Staffing* (FT Pearson, 2000); L.E. Palich, L.B. Cardinal and C. Miller, "Curvilinearity in the Diversification-Performance Linkage: An Examination of Over Three Decades of Research", *Strategic Management Journal*, Vol. 21, 2000, 155–174; Constantinos C. Markides, "To Diversify or not to Diversify?" *Harvard Business Review*, November 1997.

[9] For a discussion of the problems caused by this stimulus, and others, for groups of companies to change their Corporate-level Strategies see: M. Alexander and H. Korine, "When You Shouldn't Go Global", *Harvard Business Review*, December 2008.

[10] See, for example: T. Khanna and K. Palepu, *Winning in Emerging Markets: A Roadmap for Strategy and Execution* (Harvard Business School Press, Boston, Mass, 2010); T. Khanna and K. Palepu, "Why Focused Strategies may be Wrong for Emerging Markets", *Harvard Business Review*, July–August 1997; T. Khanna and K. Palepu, "The

Future of Business Groups in Emerging Markets: Long-run Evidence from Chile", *Academy of Management Journal*, Vol. 43, No. 3, 2000, 268–285.

[11] R. Koch and I. Godden, *Managing without Management: A Post-Management Manifesto for Business Simplicity* (Nicholas Brearley, 1996).

[12] For a description of "sheltered" industries contrasted with others, see Robert M. Grant, op. cit., 372–373.

[13] G. Yip, *Total Global Strategy II* (Prentice Hall, 2003), Chapter 2.

[14] The impact of the presence of global players in an industry is also well described in G. Hamel and C.K. Prahalad, "Do You Really Have a Global Strategy?" *Harvard Business Review*, Vol. 63, No. 4, 1985.

[15] After initial enthusiasm at the general growth in opportunities-to-add-value due to "globalisation" (see, for example, T. Levitt, "The Globalization of Markets", *Harvard Business Review*, 1983, 92–102), academics and practitioners realised that there were significant differences in opportunities based on the drivers in a given context. See, for example, C. Baden-Fuller and J. Stopford, "Globalization Frustrated", *Strategic Management Journal* Vol. 12, 1991, 493–507.

[16] For more detail, see G. Johnson, R. Whittington and K. Scholes, *Fundamentals of Strategy*, second edition (Pearson Education Limited, 2012), 162.

[17] I. MacMillan, S. van Putter and R.J. McGrath, "Global Gamesmanship", *Harvard Business Review*, May 2003, 62–71.

[18] For example, it has been noted that Walmart's international expansion has been much more successful in developing markets that lacked strong local competitors than in more competitive developed markets with strong incumbents; see G.R. Jones and C.W.L. Hill, *Strategic Management Essentials*, International Edition (South-Western, Cengage Learning, 2012), 150–151.

[19] G.D. Harrel and R.D. Kiefer, "Multinational Market Portfolio in Global Strategy Development", *International Marketing Review*, Vol. 10, No. 1, 1993; C. Phillips, I. Duole and R. Lowe, *International Marketing Strategy* (Routledge, 1994), 137–138.

[20] C.A. Bartlett and S. Ghoshal, *Managing across Borders: The Transnational Solution* (Harvard Business School Press, Boston, Mass, 1989) (second edition 1998).

[21] Y. Doz, J. Santos and P.J. Williamson, *From Global to Metanational: How Companies Win in the Global Knowledge Economy* (Harvard Business School Press, Boston, Mass, 2001).

[22] For more detail, see G.R. Jones and C.W.L. Hill, op. cit., 169 and Robert M. Grant, op. cit., 387.

[23] For more detail, see M. Alexander, "Global Parenting", Chapter 5 in *Globalization: The External Pressures*, ed. P. Kirkbride (John Wiley & Sons, 2001).

[24] These are typically related to national cultural differences and the impact this has on managerial challenges. See, for example: K.L. Newman and S.D. Nollen, "Culture and Congruence: The Fit between Management Practices and National Culture", *Journal of International Business Studies*, Vol. 27, No. 4, 1996, 753–779; J.W. Lu and P.W. Beamish, "Internationalisation and Performance of SMEs", *Strategic Management Journal*, Vol. 22, 2001, 565–586. More generally, the work of Geert Hofstede and Fons Trompenaas, among others, has examined cultural differences on various dimensions, and illustrated how these create potential "misfits" between management practices and approaches in different countries. See, for example: G. Hofstede, *Culture's Consequences: International Differences in Work-Related Values, second edition* (SAGE Publications, 1984); G. Hofstede, *Culture's Consequences: Comparing Values, Behaviors, Institutions, and Organizations Across Nations*, second edition (SAGE Publications, 2001); F. Trompenaas and C. Hampden-Turner, *Riding the Waves of Culture: Understanding Diversity in Global Business* (McGraw-Hill Professional, 1998).

[25] P. Ghemawat, "Distance Still Matters", *Harvard Business Review*, September 2001, 137–147; P. Ghemawat, *Redefining Global Strategy: Crossing Borders in a World Where Differences Still Matter* (Harvard Business School Press, Boston, Mass, 2007).

[26] C. Zook and J. Allen, *Profit from the Core: Growth Strategy in an Era of Turbulence* (Harvard Business School Press, Boston, Mass, 2001). See also C. Zook and J. Allen, *Profit from the Core: A Return*

to Growth in Turbulent Times (Harvard Business School Press, Boston, Mass, 2010).

[27] See, for example, B. Kogut, "Designing Global Strategies: Comparative and Competitive Value-added Chains", *Sloan Management Review*, Vol. 27, 1985, 15–28.

[28] D. Ricardo, *On the Principles of Political Economy and Taxation* (London: John Murray, 1817).

[29] M.E. Porter, *The Competitive Advantage of Nations* (Free Press, New York, 1990).

[30] For comparisons of the main pros and cons of each option, see G.R. Jones and C.W.L. Hill, op. cit., 161–168; and G. Johnson, K. Scholes and R. Whittington, *Exploring Corporate Strategy*, seventh edition (Pearson Education Limited, 2005), 295–297. "Staged international expansion" takes a more dynamic view of the most suitable mode over time. Companies often enter a new market in a way that allows them to maximise learning and local understanding while minimising their economic exposure, and then to change modes if appropriate. See, for example: M.F. Guillén, "Experience, Imitation, and the Sequence of Foreign Entry: Wholly Owned and Joint-venture Manufacturing by South Korean Firms and Business Groups in China, 1987–1995", *Journal of International Business Studies*, Vol. 83, 2003, 185–198; and M.K. Erramilli, "The Experience Factor in Foreign Market Entry Modes by Service Firms", *Journal of International Business Studies*, Vol. 22, No. 3, 1991, 479–501.

[31] G. Johnson, R. Whittington and K. Scholes, op. cit., 178–180.

[32] See, for example, R. Reich and E. Mankin, "Joint Ventures with Japan Give Away Our Future", *Harvard Business Review*, March–April, 1986.

[33] See, for example: J. Hagel III, J. Seely Brown and L. Davison, "Shaping Strategy in a World of Constant Disruption", *Harvard Business Review*, October 2008; M. Alexander, "Managing the Boundaries of the Organisation", *Long Range Planning*, Vol. 30, No. 5, 1997; M. Alexander, "Getting to Grips with the Virtual Organisation", *Long Range Planning*, Vol. 30, No. 1, 1997. A book based on a series of working papers from the Ashridge Strategic Management Centre by Felix Barber and Michael Goold addressing these topics is due to be published in 2014.

[34] C.A. Bartlett and S. Ghoshal, op. cit.

[35] C.K. Prahalad and Y.L. Doz, *The Multinational Mission: Balancing Local Demands and Global Vision* (Free Press, New York, 1987). Many others have used variants of this "Integration-Responsiveness" framework. See, for example: M.E. Porter, "Changing Patterns of International Competition", *California Management Review*, Vol. 28, No. 2, 1987; J. Birkinshaw, A. Morrison and J. Hulland, "Structural and Competitive Determinants of a Global Integration Strategy", *Strategic Management Journal*, Vol. 16, 1995, 637–655.

[36] C. Bartlett, "Building and Managing the Transnational: The New Organizational Challenge", in *Competition in Global Industries*, ed. M.E. Porter (Harvard Business School Press, Boston, Mass, 1986).

[37] M. Goold and C. Campbell, *Strategies and Styles: The Role of the Corporate Centre in Managing Diversified Corporations* (Blackwell Publishers, 1987).

[38] See, for example, R. Koch and G. Lockwood, *Superconnect: Harnessing the Power of Networks and the Strength of Weak Links* (W.W. Norton and Company, 2010).

Index

Printed and bound by CPI Group (UK) Ltd, Croydon, CR0 4YY

16/04/2025

14658820-0002

.